The Legislative Legacy of Congressional Campaigns

Do members of Congress follow through on the appeals they make in campaigns? The answer to this question lies at the heart of assessments of democratic legitimacy. This study demonstrates that, contrary to the conventional wisdom that candidates' appeals are just "cheap talk," campaigns actually have a lasting legacy in the content of representatives' and senators' behavior in office. Legislators face clear incentives to offer sincere claims in their campaigns, so their appeals often serve as good signals about the issues they will pursue in Congress. Levels of promise keeping vary in a systematic fashion across legislators, across types of activity, across time, and across chamber. Moreover, legislators' responsiveness to their appeals shapes their future electoral fortunes and career choices, and their activity on their campaign themes leaves a tangible trace in public policy outputs. Understanding the dynamics of promise keeping thus has important implications for our evaluations of the quality of campaigns and the strength of representation in the United States.

Tracy Sulkin is Associate Professor in the Department of Political Science at the University of Illinois, Urbana-Champaign. She is the author of *Issue Politics in Congress*, which won the American Political Science Association's Fenno Prize for the best book in legislative studies. Her work has appeared in leading journals such as the *American Political Science Review*, *Journal of Politics*, and *Legislative Studies Quarterly*.

The Legislative Legacy of Congressional Campaigns

TRACY SULKIN
University of Illinois, Urbana-Champaign

CAMBRIDGE UNIVERSITY PRESS
Cambridge, New York, Melbourne, Madrid, Cape Town,
Singapore, São Paulo, Delhi, Tokyo, Mexico City

Cambridge University Press
32 Avenue of the Americas, New York, NY 10013-2473, USA

www.cambridge.org
Information on this title: www.cambridge.org/9780521730488

First published 2011

Printed in the United States of America

A catalog record for this publication is available from the British Library.

Library of Congress Cataloging in Publication data
Sulkin, Tracy.
The legislative legacy of congressional campaigns / Tracy Sulkin.
p. cm.
Includes bibliographical references and index.
ISBN 978-0-521-51449-1 (hardback) – ISBN 978-0-521-73048-8 (paperback)
1. Legislators – Professional relationships – United States. 2. Political campaigns – United States. 3. Political planning – United States. 4. Representative government and representation – United States. I. Title.
JK1118.S85 2011
328.73–dc22

2010040153

ISBN 978-0-521-51449-1 Hardback
ISBN 978-0-521-73048-8 Paperback

Contents

Figures

Tables

Acknowledgments

During the writing of this book, I benefited greatly from the assistance and support of a number of individuals and institutions, and it is a pleasure to have this opportunity to thank them.

I am grateful to the many colleagues and friends who provided feedback on early versions of the argument and whose comments improved the book immeasurably. For help along the way, I thank John Aldrich, Larry Dodd, John Geer, Rick Hall, Frances Lee, Bruce Oppenheimer, Kathryn Pearson, Wendy Schiller, John Sides, Sean Theriault, Rick Vallely, and John Wilkerson. Special thanks are due to Bryan Jones, who read the manuscript in its entirety and provided his usual insightful critiques and helpful suggestions. Closer to home, at the University of Illinois, I thank Scott Althaus, Xinyuan Dai, Jim Kuklinski, Kris Miler, Gisela Sin, and, especially, Bill Bernhard. Despite being subjected to repeated discussions of the project over the past few years, they have always responded with their customary support and thoughtful advice.

I was fortunate to have the opportunity to present portions of the book at seminars at Georgetown University, the Harris School at the University of Chicago, Pennsylvania State University, Texas A&M, the University of Michigan, the University of Minnesota, the University of North Carolina, the University of Rochester, the University of Washington, and the University of Wisconsin. I greatly appreciate the lively discussions and the useful insights that emerged from them.

The project would not have been possible without the assistance of a number of scholars and organizations that graciously shared their data. I owe a debt of gratitude to Scott Adler and John Wilkerson and the Congressional Bills Project, Kenneth Goldstein and his colleagues with the Wisconsin Advertising Project, and Project Vote Smart, as well as Brian Gaines, Jeff Mondak, Daron Shaw, Craig Volden, and Alan Wiseman. In particular, I thank John Wilkerson, who first introduced me to the study of Congress and legislative behavior, and who has been a model of generosity with his time, his expertise, and his data ever since.

I benefited from expert research assistance from a large cadre of undergraduate and graduate students at the University of Illinois, including Neil Baer, Jason Coronel, Jillian Evans, Katie Graham, Jeff Harden, David Hendry, Chera LaForge, Beth Popp, Carly Schmitt, Katie Slaughter, Nathaniel Swigger, Sergio Wals, and Meredith Wieck. The Campus Research Board generously supported the data collection efforts for this project.

It was a pleasure to work once again with Cambridge University Press, and I thank Lew Bateman, Anne Lovering Rounds, Andy Saff, and the production team.

Most of all, I thank my family and friends. I count myself lucky to have family who are also friends, and friends who are like family.

I

Promises to Keep?

Do members of Congress follow through on the appeals they make in campaigns? In other words, do they keep their promises? These questions may be simple, but their answers lie at the heart of assessments of democratic legitimacy. In representative democracies, election campaigns are intended to serve as the central linchpin, providing a venue for debate about issues, educating citizens about the activities of their elected representatives, and informing legislators about the interests of their constituents. Campaigns are, as Riker (1996) argued, "a main point – perhaps *the* main point – of contact between officials and the populace over matters of public policy" (3). The existence of strong links between elections and governing is therefore one of the most fundamental prerequisites for accountability. In short, in healthy democracies, candidates in campaigns should provide voters with information about the issues and policies they will pursue in Congress, and, once in office, should follow through on these appeals.

The prevailing view among the public and many pundits, though, is that politics in the United States falls far short of this ideal. Instead, many believe that campaigns have little issue content and have devolved into nothing more than opportunities for candidates to launch personal attacks at one another. Moreover, the advantages of incumbency seem to free legislators from any pressures to be accountable for their past records or sincere about their future plans. Candidates' campaign appeals are therefore often accused of being just "cheap talk," designed to sway voters and maximize vote shares on Election Day, but with little connection to what the candidates actually plan to do once in office. For instance, in the 2004 National Annenberg Election Study, only one-third of respondents said they thought candidates even *try* to keep their promises "always" or "most of the time," and only about one in six respondents to the 2006 Congressional Elections Study reported that they felt that their member of Congress had done "very well" in keeping his or her campaign promises.[1]

To the extent that these accusations are true, they raise serious questions about the legitimacy of the American democratic process. It comes as somewhat of a surprise, then, that there has been very little scholarly attention to the linkages between legislators' behavior as candidates in campaigns and their activities as policy makers in office. Although evaluations of the quality of campaigns and the nature and strength of representation are central to research on American politics, the study of promise keeping has been largely peripheral to work in these fields. As such, while scholars are typically more sanguine than the public and punditry about the prospect that campaigns can successfully fulfill their role as a linking mechanism between elected officials and the public, we simply do not have answers to a number of crucial questions about promise keeping, including the frequency with which campaign promises are kept, the relationship between the rhetoric that candidates use and the sincerity of their claims, the characteristics of those legislators who follow through most faithfully on their appeals, and the factors that encourage such responsiveness. Even more fundamentally, we lack agreement on a meaningful and workable definition of what it means for a candidate to make a promise and a legislator to keep one. The result is a large gap in our understanding of one of the most important mechanisms underlying representative democracy.

This book is intended to fill this gap. I explore the dynamics of promise making and promise keeping for a large sample of representatives and senators elected or reelected in the 1998, 2000, and 2002 elections, analyzing both their campaign appeals and the content of their subsequent legislative activity. I define promise keeping as occurring when legislators are active in Congress on the issues they prioritized in their campaigns. In this agenda-based conception, responsive legislators are those whose campaign appeals serve as strong and accurate signals about the issues they will pursue in office, through their introduction and cosponsorship of

[1] These findings are line with earlier polls as well. In a 1999 survey by the Project on Campaign Conduct, nearly three-fourths of respondents reported that they were "very" concerned about candidates saying one thing and doing another once elected (Spiliotes and Vavreck 2002), and, in a 1988 ABC/*Washington Post* poll, 71 percent agreed that "most members of Congress make campaign promises that they have no intention of fulfilling" (Ringquist and Dasse 2004), down from 81 percent who agreed with a similar statement in a 1971 Harris Survey.

legislation. My findings reveal that campaign appeals are indeed meaningful, although not always in the manner predicted by the conventional wisdom; that promise keeping varies in a systematic fashion across legislators, across types of legislative activities, across time, and, perhaps most notably, across chambers of Congress; that it is affected by legislators' relative vulnerability and in turn shapes their future electoral fortunes; and that legislators' follow-through on their appeals leaves a tangible trace in public policy.

The systematic study of promise keeping thus has the potential to make a number of contributions to our understanding of the dynamics of representation and the electoral connection. At the aggregate level, promise keeping serves as an important indicator of collective responsiveness in Congress – the extent to which the issues and concerns raised in elections are reflected in the legislative policy-making process. At the level of individual legislators, it provides new insight into dyadic representation (i.e., between each legislator and his or her district or state), as well as how representatives and senators negotiate the dual demands of campaigning and lawmaking. Most generally, a focus on the linkages between campaign and legislative agendas yields a more nuanced view of responsiveness and the role of campaigns in promoting it.

An interest in the relationships between elected officials' campaign behavior and their governing behavior may seem natural and intuitive. As Fenno notes, election campaigns are the place where representation begins and where it is sustained (1996, 9), and classic "mandate" models of democracy depend upon elections as the mechanism that links the governed with their representatives and ensures accountability. Mansbridge (2003), for example, identifies *promissory representation*, focused on "the idea that during campaigns representatives made promises to constituents, which they then kept or failed to keep" as the "traditional" model of representation (515).

However, empirical research on legislative representation and responsiveness, at least in the American context, has only rarely given a central place to campaigns (but see Sulkin 2005). Instead, virtually all of the extensive literature on the topic has revolved around Miller and Stokes' (1963) concept of "policy congruence" – the correlation between the issue positions of legislators (as expressed through their roll call votes) and those of their constituents (as expressed in opinion polls). My conception of promise keeping departs from this traditional approach in two ways. First, by targeting the relationship between the content of campaign appeals and the content of legislative action, it offers a new locus for representation.

Second, and equally important, it shifts the focus from a sole focus on candidates' and legislators' issue *positions* to include their issue *priorities*. In so doing, it also highlights the process of responsiveness, as legislators raise issues in their campaigns and address them in office. Thus, this conception of representation is less about the alignment of positions between representatives and the represented and more about the transmission of information between different stages of the political process. Representation "works" when candidates' campaigns serve as accurate predictors of how they will behave as policy makers.

Assessing the linkages between the electoral and legislative arenas also enables me to put critiques about campaign discourse into context. The frequent laments in both scholarly and journalistic circles about the vague and general nature of candidates' appeals are rooted in the assumption that such appeals are uninformative and insincere. Similarly, a common argument in the debates about negativity in campaigns is that time candidates spend attacking their opponents is time taken away from serious attention to policy problems (but see Geer 2006). Importantly, though, these intuitions have never actually been tested, so we do not know whether certain types of appeals serve as stronger signals about legislators' intentions than others. A rigorous investigation may provide empirical support for the conventional wisdom, but it may also call into question some of the criticisms commonly leveled at candidates and at the broader electoral system.

WHY SO LITTLE ATTENTION TO PROMISE KEEPING?

The connections between campaigns and governing thus have clear normative, theoretical, and practical implications for a variety of audiences, including political scientists interested in explaining the dynamics of representation; citizens, interest groups, and policy specialists seeking to predict how vigorously a candidate will advocate for a particular issue once in Congress; and reformers wishing to promote higher-quality campaigns. Why, then, have scholars of electoral politics and Congress devoted so little attention to them? A variety of methodological and conceptual constraints, discussed in more detail in this section, have contributed to the relative neglect. However, I attribute it mostly to the fact that promise keeping falls between or outside the traditional lines of inquiry in research on American politics. The increasing specialization of the field along a variety of dimensions (the study of institutions versus behavior, elites versus masses, elections versus policy making) has brought about many benefits, most obviously the development of theoretically rich and empirically nuanced literatures on a number of important questions. The major disadvantage, though, is that it discourages attention to phenomena that sit astride the lines that separate the subfields and even to those that differentiate research areas within a single subfield.

For example, work on legislative studies has long been marked by a division of labor between scholars of congressional campaigns and elections and those of legislative behavior and organization. In fact, it would not be much of an exaggeration to say that the "Two Congresses" distinction – that legislators "spend their time moving between two contexts, Washington and home, and between two activities, governing and campaigning" (Fenno 1989, 19) – has been felt more acutely by *scholars* of Congress than by *members* of Congress. While there is considerable evidence that representatives and senators see these two contexts as tightly intertwined, the literatures on legislators' behavior in Washington, D.C., and their activities at home on the campaign trail have developed along largely separate lines.[2]

The depth of this division might not be immediately obvious to a casual observer. After all, following on Mayhew (1974), the idea of the "electoral connection" has been central to theorizing about congressional behavior. However, most research conceives of this connection in a fairly narrow way, as synonymous with the "reelection imperative" – that, as Mayhew described it, members of Congress "think they can affect their own percentages, that in fact they can affect their own percentages, and furthermore that there is reason for them to try to do so" (33). Indeed, in the thirty-five years since Mayhew wrote these words, nearly all work on the topic has focused on testing these three assertions, either by exploring the relationship between electoral vulnerability and legislative behavior or by estimating the effects of legislators' activity in office on their future electoral fortunes.

More often than not, then, the "electoral" component of the electoral connection has been reduced to vote shares, either past or future. This approach has yielded a great deal of leverage into a variety of phenomena of interest to legislative scholars, including committee requests and participation (Fowler, Douglass, and Clark 1980; Frisch and Kelly 2006; Hall

[2] This division is manifested in the content of most "state of the field" review articles, which have focused on one dimension or the other (see, for example, Polsby and Schickler 2002; Squire 1995). Along the same lines, the Midwest Political Science Association maintains two separate divisions for work on Congress: "Legislative Politics: Institutions" and "Legislative Politics: Campaigns and Elections."

1996); introduction and cosponsorship of legislation (Harward and Moffett 2010; Kessler and Krehbiel 1996; Koger 2003; Ragsdale and Cook 1987; Schiller 1995; Wawro 2000); casework and constituency service (Bond 1985; Cain, Ferejohn, and Fiorina 1987; Johannes 1984; Parker 1980); and, perhaps most prominently, roll call voting patterns (Ansolabehere, Snyder, and Stewart 2001; Bovitz and Carson 2006; Canes-Wrone, Brady, and Cogan 2002; Erikson 1971; Fiorina 1974; Kuklinski 1977).

At the same time, though, it is clear that electoral margins are not the whole of the story. In fact, evidence of a relationship between legislative behavior and vote shares (and vice versa) is mixed at best. Some work finds that more vulnerable legislators are more active and responsive, some finds that the safest are, and some finds no relationship at all. Of course, the lack of consistent correlations between vulnerability and behavior does not mean that legislators do not take electoral considerations into account. As Arnold (1990) points out, perhaps the best explanation for this result is that legislators are so concerned about reelection that they become adept at anticipating constituency concerns and avoiding behavior that would provoke a reaction (see also Erikson, MacKuen, and Stimson 2002). What these findings do mean, though, is that if we want to gain insight into the ways in which particular electoral experiences are related to legislative activity, we are more likely to do so by targeting other dimensions of the electoral connection.

These other dimensions become clearer when we shift the focus slightly to think not only of an electoral connection, but also of a "campaign connection." In short, legislators' behavior in office is likely shaped not only by how well they performed in the previous election, but also by what actually transpired during that campaign. The process of campaigning teaches candidates about the interests of their districts or states, about the issues that resonate with their supporters (as well as those that do not), and about their perceived strengths and weaknesses. If legislators are indeed reelection-oriented, these lessons should affect their subsequent behavior. Accordingly, Fenno argues that "it is through the interpretation of a campaign that the winning candidate derives some of the impulses, interests, and instructions that shape his or her legislative behavior" (1996, 75; see also Hershey 1984 and Kingdon 1968).

Just what might these "impulses, interests, and instructions" be? In previous work, I demonstrated one way in which campaigns shape legislators' governing activity: "issue uptake," wherein winning legislators take up and pursue in office the issue themes highlighted by their challengers

(Sulkin 2005). Legislators are motivated to engage in this behavior for electoral reasons; because challengers tend to focus their campaigns on their opponents' weaknesses (Arnold 1990, 2004; Bailey 2001), savvy winners should act in office to remedy these weaknesses and shore up their records before the next campaign. Thus, in the process of looking out for their own electoral interests, legislators also demonstrate responsiveness to the issues on which they are critiqued, and this shift in their agendas leaves a legacy in congressional politics and public policy.

In studying promise keeping, the focus is on legislators' own campaign themes rather than those of their challengers. Since they select these themselves, it is less likely that their campaigns will exert an independent effect on their activity in office. However, the content and circumstances of their campaigns should be manifested in observable ways in their subsequent governing behavior. For example, if candidates use voters' reactions to their campaigns as indicators of their level of interest in and concern about particular issues, this feedback should help them decide whether and how to pursue that issue in Congress. More generally, as I discuss in the next chapter, electoral and policy considerations should lead to linkages between the content of representatives' and senators' campaign and legislative agendas, and the strength of these linkages should vary with features of the legislator, his or her campaign, and the institutional context.

Thus, I argue that there are clear advantages to bridging the gap between the "Two Congresses" and extending work on the electoral connection to include the relationship between the content of campaign and legislative behavior. We gain similar leverage by crossing traditional boundaries in the literature on electoral politics. A longstanding division in this subfield has been between research on the behavior of candidates and research on the behavior of voters, with much more attention to the latter. Indeed, the vast majority of the literature on electoral politics has been devoted to explaining voting decisions and election outcomes. As a result, a number of scholars have noted that, while we know a great deal about *elections*, we know comparatively little about *campaigns* (Fenno 1996; Franklin 1991; Riker 1996). Riker (1996) argued that this lack of attention to candidates and their appeals was particularly problematic because it rendered us unable to answer one of the most fundamental questions about representation: how policies are "presented, discussed, and decided upon" in a democracy (4).

Over the past ten to fifteen years, much has been done to fill this gap, with the development of a growing research agenda on candidates' issue selection strategies (see, for example, Ansolabehere and Iyengar 1994;

Boatright 2004; Brasher 2003; Druckman, Kifer, and Parkin 2009; Holian 2004; Kahn and Kenney 1999; Petrocik 1996; Sellers 1998; Sides 2006, 2007; Simon 2002; Spiliotes and Vavreck 2002). Importantly, though, given the divisions of labor in political science research, much of this work has been undertaken by specialists in campaigns and political communication, who have focused primarily on explaining the dynamics of campaigns themselves. This orientation is entirely understandable, and has yielded substantial new insight into campaign messages. From the perspective of promise keeping, though, it has two shortcomings. First, it means that the search for how campaigns matter typically ends when campaigns end – on Election Day. The large literature on campaign effects thus focuses almost entirely on the ways in which campaigns do (or do not) affect voters, which leaves out a number of other ways in which campaigns might be important.

Second, the focus on Election Day as the end game leads to potentially incomplete theories of candidate behavior. As I discuss in more detail in Chapter 2, most models of how candidates select campaign issues seek to identify strategies that will maximize vote shares. When candidates deviate from the patterns predicted by these strategies (i.e., if a Democrat highlights a "Republican" issue), there is no clear explanation that can be offered for this behavior. One possibility, of course, is that candidates' agendas are driven by their policy intentions. However, explanations of campaign behavior that do not consider legislative politics will not be able to capture these dynamics.

In sum, then, the primary obstacle to the development of an empirical literature on congressional promise keeping has been the prevalence of approaches to the analysis of campaigns and legislative behavior that treat the two as separate. Election Day is seen as the dividing line, and, depending on what side of the line they are on, scholars offer nuanced explanations of one or the other, but not both. Phenomena such as promise keeping thus often fail to receive attention, not because they are uninteresting or unimportant, but because they do not fit easily into existing lines of research.

CAMPAIGNS AND POLICY MAKING

This is not to say that no efforts have been made to link campaigns and policy making. In fact, several studies of presidential promise keeping undertaken in the 1980s found fairly high levels of responsiveness (Fishel 1985; Krukones 1984; see also Jamieson 2000). This finding is echoed in a number of investigations of more aggregate-level phenomena such as the ability of parties to implement their platforms (Aldrich 1995; Budge and Hofferbert 1990; King and Laver 1993; Pomper 1968); presidential and congressional responses to perceived mandates (Conley 2001; Grossback, Peterson, and Stimson 2006); and the role of electoral realignments in producing policy change (Brady 1988; Sinclair 1977).

However, two important constraints have limited the applicability of these approaches to modeling and measuring promise keeping by individual members of Congress. The first is the disjuncture that exists between most normative and formal theories of the elections–policy linkage and the realities of contemporary congressional politics. The second is the predominant focus on issue *positions* in the literatures on candidate strategy and legislative representation and responsiveness, which results in an overly restrictive definition of what it means for a candidate to make a promise and a legislator to keep one.

Theories of the role of campaigns in the policy-making process generally rely on some variant of textbook "responsible party government" models of representative democracy, presuming that during campaigns, parties make promises about what policies they will enact if voted into office; on Election Day, voters select candidates from the party whose policy positions and priorities most closely approximate their own; in office, winners do or do not implement their promises; and, in the next election, voters decide whether or not to reelect them (Harrington 1993; Schattschneider 1942; Schedler 1998).

This perspective may provide a fairly accurate depiction of parliamentary systems where parties are the central focus (see, for example, Klingemann, Hofferbert, and Budge 1994), but it captures less adequately the dynamics of most U.S. congressional elections. Because policy making in Congress is necessarily a collective enterprise and because few, if any, individual members can speak authoritatively for their parties, no single representative or senator can meaningfully promise to bring about a specific outcome, nor is it reasonable to blame a legislator if his or her preferred policies fail to become law. As such, congressional candidates make explicit promises more rarely than one might expect, and models of promise keeping based on policy outcomes make little sense at the individual level.

The response to this situation among students of legislative behavior has been to retain traditional conceptions of promise keeping, but to shift the focus from policy outcomes to issue positions. In particular, scholars have adapted Miller and Stokes' (1963) policy congruence criterion to ask whether the positions legislators take on issues in office align with their stated positions from the campaign (Ringquist and Dasse 2004). By this definition, a candidate who declared her support for "No Child Left Behind" in the 2002 election would be credited for keeping this promise if she voted in favor of it in the 108th Congress.

This conceptualization undoubtedly provides a meaningful and useful way of thinking about promise keeping. If candidates tell us they will vote a particular way on an issue, then whether or not they actually do so is clearly relevant for understanding responsiveness. The problem, however, is that this standard can be applied in only a very narrowly circumscribed set of situations. One important limitation is that we can only determine whether a promise on an issue is kept if that issue comes up for a roll call vote in the next Congress (and, equally important, if the framing of the choice in the roll call corresponds to the framing of the choice from the campaign). However, whether or not this occurs is largely outside of the control of individual legislators. This is unlikely to pose a problem for salient issues, but it is quite possible that candidates at least occasionally take positions on more obscure issues that never make it to the floor of the House or Senate.

More consequential, though, is the second constraint presented by position-based conceptions of promise keeping: they require that candidates actually stake out clear positions on a variety of issues in their campaigns. In reality, relatively few candidates make statements of the type that would enable us to connect a campaign appeal to a later roll call vote, and those who do so are not necessarily representative of the population of candidates as a whole. When discussing an issue like education, rather than offering a position on a policy like No Child Left Behind, many candidates make valence claims along the lines that they are "champions for education" or "want to improve our schools" (Sides 2006; Stokes 1992; Sulkin, Moriarty, and Hefner 2007; Vavreck 2001). Because there can be considerable disagreement about what types of policies would best support these general goals (i.e., both a yea vote or a nay vote on No Child Left Behind could be framed as pro-education), it becomes difficult, if not impossible, to assess meaningfully legislators' responsiveness to their vague appeals by examining their roll call voting decisions.

Scholars have attempted to get around this problem by using surveys of candidates taken before the election or during the campaign itself as the source of information about their positions (see, for example, Ringquist and Dasse 2004; Sullivan and O'Connor 1972; Wright and Berkman 1986). An obvious concern about this solution, and one that is acknowledged by the authors themselves, is that survey responses are not campaign appeals. There is potentially a big difference between a candidate who is opposed to a policy and makes that opposition a feature of his or her campaign and one who is opposed but chooses not to talk about the issue. Survey results do not allow one to differentiate these types of candidates.

Most generally, a solely position-based approach to assessing promise keeping takes what is an atypical, and perhaps even strategically unwise, behavior on the part of candidates (i.e., staking out specific positions on issues) and makes it the central target of responsiveness. Shepsle (1972), for example, argues that under certain circumstances, there are clear electoral incentives for candidates to be ambiguous about their positions (see also Page 1976). Recent experimental work by Tomz and Van Houweling (2009) provides empirical support for this claim, finding that ambiguity often increases support for a candidate. Thus, savvy candidates may choose to avoid staking out positions, but may indicate their policy intentions in other ways.

REASSESSING PROMISE MAKING AND KEEPING

A complete understanding of promise keeping thus requires that we adopt a broader approach, taking into account the realities of politics in both the electoral and legislative arenas and recognizing that there are a number of ways, beyond explicit position taking, that candidates can signal their policy priorities, and a number of avenues, other than roll call voting, through which legislators can demonstrate their attentiveness to these priorities. A useful starting point in developing such an approach is to ask why we restrict our study of campaign appeals to promises and positions in the first place. Is it reasonable to assume that only those claims that use explicit promise-making language or offer a particular position carry policy information? Consider the following campaign advertisement, "Leadership," aired by incumbent Representative Ernie Fletcher (R-KY) in 2002:[3]

[Announcer]: A leader should be someone we can believe in. Someone who's gained the respect of Democrats and Republicans for his ideas, his expertise, his character.

[3] All advertisements were obtained from the Wisconsin Advertising Projects archives of storyboards for the 1998, 2000, and 2002 elections (Goldstein 2000; Goldstein, Franz, and Ridout 2002; and Goldstein and Rivlin 2005).

Someone we look to for leadership on the big issues like health care, education, jobs. Someone who's never satisfied with the way things are and knows we can always do better. That someone is Congressman Ernie Fletcher. Leadership, vision, results.

As I demonstrate in later chapters, this ad is fairly typical of those run by House candidates. It neither makes a promise nor articulates a position. However, it would seem shortsighted to argue that it has conveyed no potentially useful information to voters, or that it has failed to offer any claims that Fletcher might reasonably be held accountable for down the line. Of all the things he could have talked about in the ad, he chose to discuss health care, education, and jobs.[4] Given the language he uses, it would be fair for a citizen to infer that he views these issues as priorities and will pursue them in office. As such, a logical measure of promise keeping is the extent to which this inference is correct. In other words, is Fletcher actually active on health care, education, and jobs in his next term? If so, we can judge him to have followed through on his appeals. If not, he has failed to keep his campaign promises.

Is this expanded definition of promise making and promise keeping justifiable? From a normative perspective, the answer is clearly yes. Presumably, what candidates say about policy issues in campaigns is important not because their views or attitudes are themselves inherently interesting, but because they are assumed to have some connection to the actions they will take.[5] As Mansbridge argues, "Promissory representation works normatively through the explicit *and* implicit promises that the elected representative makes to the electorate" (2003, 516, italics added). Thus, privileging explicit promises is an overly restrictive approach to capturing the signals that candidates send to their potential constituents. Instead, we should aim to capture any language that implies that a legislator views an issue as a priority.

Considering the entirety of candidates' appeals rather than just any positions candidates may take also opens up the possibility of studying how *variation* in the rhetoric they use in their claims is connected, or not, to subsequent follow-through. As I show in Chapter 3, among the group of

[4] In all, Fletcher produced four ads, which aired a total of 1,059 times. The other issues mentioned in those ads included Medicare, Social Security, and taxes. About 27 percent of his advertising time was devoted to health care; 18 percent each to education, jobs, and Medicare; and 9 percent each to Social Security and taxes.

[5] For this reason, using candidates' survey responses as a measure of campaign promises is potentially problematic – having actually expressed the opinion in some way during the campaign seems an important prerequisite for defining a claim as a promise.

candidates who discuss a given issue, some make it a centerpiece of their campaigns, while others mention it only in passing. Some offer specific appeals, while others are vague. Some discuss only their own interests in the issue, while others criticize their opponents on it. Some talk about their future plans, others discuss their past accomplishments, and still others do both. Instead of assuming a priori that some types of appeals are more meaningful than others, my approach allows me to treat this as an empirical question for investigation. For example, do candidates who advocate specific solutions to policy problems pursue those issues more intently than those who talk about them in a general fashion? Do positive appeals about an issue serve as better or worse predictors of legislators' later activity than negative appeals? Do candidates who talk about their future plans on an issue demonstrate more follow-through than those who talk about only their present interests or past actions?

Because my conception of promise *making* is rooted in the content of candidates' campaign agendas, my answers to these questions and my measure of promise *keeping* are rooted in the content of legislators' policy agendas in office. In particular, I target their introduction and cosponsorship of legislation. A focus on activities other than roll call voting reflects a substantial departure from the traditional way of thinking about representation in general and promise keeping in particular. However, while voting on legislation is clearly a very important component of legislative behavior, it is certainly not the only activity representatives and senators engage in, or even the most time-consuming one. As Bauer, Pool, and Dexter (1963) noted, "A congressman must decide what to make of his job. The decisions most constantly on his mind are not how to vote, but what to do with his time, how to allocate his resources, and where to put his energy" (405). A complete understanding of legislative responsiveness therefore requires that we consider legislators' allocation of effort on issues, not just their positions on votes (see also Burden 2007; Hall 1996; Schiller 1995, 2000; Sulkin 2005).

This agenda-based approach offers several distinct advantages. First, it enables me to assess legislators' responsiveness to those campaign appeals that cannot be connected to a roll call vote. This can occur either because there is no clear position taken on an issue (as was the case with Fletcher's appeals about health care, education, and jobs) or because a campaign theme never comes up for a vote. Imagine, for example, that during a campaign, a candidate says that he wants to increase protections for privacy on the Internet and, once in Congress, introduces a bill on this issue. That bill subsequently dies in committee and never reaches the floor of the House or Senate.[6] Should that legislator be credited for keeping his campaign promise? The introduction of legislation on Internet privacy seems to indicate responsiveness, but by the traditional, position-based definition of promise keeping, this behavior would be invisible.

A focus on agendas also allows for more variation in responsiveness than dichotomous yea/nay choices and thus offers insight into the intensity of legislators' commitments to an issue. If two candidates both say that children's health care is a priority, then how they vote on the State Children's Health Insurance Program (SCHIP) is clearly important. However, if one limited her participation to that vote, and the other was active in proposing the legislation and cosponsoring a variety of other measures dealing with children's health care, then rating them as equally responsive misses this important difference.

Finally, there are strong normative arguments for including agendas as a dimension of representation. Position-based approaches focus on the very end of the legislative process, after the various alternatives have been debated and a single proposal has been selected for a vote. As Schattschneider famously argued, control over earlier stages of the lawmaking process, where agendas are set, is "the supreme instrument of power .... He who determines what politics is about runs the country because the definition of the alternatives is the choice of conflicts and the choice of conflicts allocates power" (1960, 66). Neglecting to consider these stages thus results in a narrow view of what constitutes democratic responsiveness. Put another way, representatives and senators could vote in line with their constituents on every bill that comes before them, but if none of those bills deal with issues that were salient and important to those constituents, then we might reasonably question the quality of representation (Bachrach and Baratz 1962; Dahl 1989; Jones, Larsen-Price, and Wilkerson 2009).

EVALUATING CAMPAIGNS

Although my primary focus will be on promise keeping as an indicator of legislative responsiveness, my findings also have important bearing on evaluations of campaign discourse, as well as the perennial question of whether or not campaigns "matter." Extant work on campaign quality

[6] This is the fate of the vast majority of introduced measures – in recent years, only about 10 percent have been formally reported out of committee (although this varies considerably across committees).

typically invokes one of two basic standards: the degree to which candidates' discourse approximates normative ideals about elections as a locus of deliberation and debate (Kelley 1960), and the extent to which exposure to campaign messages has positive versus negative effects on voters' knowledge and attitudes. Research on the first standard has asked whether candidates devote more time to discussion of substantive issues or character traits (Kahn and Kenney 1999; Sides 2006); whether they offer specifics about their issue priorities or limit themselves to vague valence claims (Geer 2006; Sides 2006); whether competing candidates engage in a back-and-forth dialogue on issues or "talk past one another" (Kaplan, Park and Ridout 2006; Sigelman and Buell 2004; Simon 2002); and whether critiques of opponents are fair and factually accurate or unfounded and misleading (Geer 2006). Research on the second has explored the influence of media coverage and candidate advertising on citizens' knowledge about politics, evaluations of candidates, turnout decisions, and attitudes toward government. Most notably, work has focused on the impact of negative ads, investigating whether negativity makes voters informed and interested or cynical and disengaged (see, for example, Ansolabehere and Iyengar 1995; Brooks 2006; Brooks and Geer 2007; Goldstein and Freedman 2002; Lau and Pomper 2004; Wattenberg and Brians 1999).

Left out of these discussions is a third, equally important question: whether campaigns serve as accurate predictors of what winners will do once in office. The answer to this question is crucial because it offers context for assessing the others. From the standpoint of normative democratic theory, a detailed claim may be normatively superior to a vague one, but if they serve as equally strong signals about what the winner will do, we should be less concerned about the tendency of candidates to offer vague appeals. Similarly, negative appeals may have the potential to make voters cynical, but if they carry more information about what legislators will do as policy makers, the good effects may counteract or even outweigh the bad (Geer 2006).

In evaluating campaigns from this perspective, there are at least three related but distinct standards one could offer. The first is that campaigns should serve as *signals* about legislators' priorities, so that observing candidates' campaign issues and rhetorical choices enables voters to make reliable predictions about how the candidate will behave once in office. In other words, is there "truth in advertising," with high correspondence between legislators' campaign and governing priorities? It is often noted that most voters do not pay much attention to what their legislators do in office, and political scientists have devoted considerable effort to determining whether or not they are able to make good choices in the absence of this information. However, if legislators' appeals in campaigns are sincere, reflecting their longstanding interests and priorities, even those citizens who are normally inattentive to politics can learn about these priorities from campaigns and make accurate inferences about what a winner will do in Congress. Campaigns thus "matter" because they provide information, serving as potentially useful heuristics to votes.

The second standard takes signaling a step further, viewing campaigns as important to the extent that they serve as *independent* predictors of legislative activity, above and beyond what one could expect based on other factors (e.g., the legislator's party affiliation or past record or characteristics of the constituency). From this point of view, campaigns matter when they serve as a unique source of information about the content of legislators' behavior in office. This standard is most likely to apply to newly elected legislators, for whom campaigns often provide one of the only avenues for learning of their likely priorities, but it could also hold true for incumbents. For instance, among the group of candidates whose background *should* lead them to raise an issue, the decisions of some to highlight it and some to avoid it could offer insight into their likelihood of continuing to pursue it.

The third standard reflects an even stronger statement: that campaigns themselves should be *consequential*, having a direct causal effect on the content of legislative behavior and the aggregate congressional agenda. Issue uptake reflects such a campaign effect, and one could also occur if having raised an issue in the campaign somehow commits a legislator to following through on it. From this view, campaigns matter only when they change the shape of legislative politics. Stated as a counterfactual, this standard requires that a legislator would have behaved differently in office had his or her campaign not occurred, or had it unfolded with different content.

It might be tempting to conclude from this discussion that these standards for evaluating when and how campaigns matter can be equated with the strength of promise keeping – that it is somehow stronger or more meaningful if candidates' campaigns serve as independent predictors of their subsequent activity or if they drive that activity. This is a temptation that should be avoided. In reality, there is often a clear tension between the criteria for good representation and those for strong campaign effects.

Imagine, for example, a legislator who represents a district with a large population of senior citizens. Accordingly, he has been active in policy making on Medicare and Social Security and focuses his next campaign on these accomplishments. By viewing his campaign ads, constituents learn about his past activity and infer that he will continue to pursue these policies in his next term. When he returns to office, this inference proves true, and he is again very active in working on senior issues. As such, the legislator clearly followed through on his campaign appeals, providing good representation to his constituents. However, we would be hard pressed to argue that the campaign itself was consequential, or even that it offered any new information. An attentive voter who had carefully followed the legislator's behavior in office would probably not learn anything new about his policy priorities by observing his campaign for reelection.

Now imagine a second legislator from an identical district with an identical past record. She decides, though, that she is no longer interested in Medicare and Social Security and uses her campaign to unveil her new priority: early childhood education. In this case, the campaign certainly serves as an independent source of information about her intentions; without having been exposed to it, there would be no way for constituents to have guessed that their representative had changed her priorities. Does this mean that she is a "better" representative than the first legislator? Probably not, as most would argue that quality representation means focusing on issues that the constituency cares about. In addition, by shifting the focus away from her previous areas of expertise, she may be moving into issues where she is less likely to be influential and hence less likely to be able to deliver on her promises.

The main point, then, is that it would be a mistake to confound the strength of campaign effects with the strength of representational linkages. Indeed, the independent effects of campaigns would be strongest if candidates randomly selected issues at the beginning of their races and then followed through on them in the next Congress. Almost no one, though, would claim that this is a superior form of representation. As such, from the perspective of normative democratic theory, independent or consequential campaigns are not a necessity for promise keeping. Correspondence between what candidates say they will do and what legislators actually do is sufficient for responsiveness. Whether promise keeping occurs at high rates and whether campaigns have an independent effect on legislative behavior are ultimately separate questions.

The same logic applies to other models of legislative representation. For example, if voters choose to reelect an incumbent whose issue positions align with their own, then policy congruence is high. We would not accuse that legislator of failing to represent his district's interests because he did not *change* his own policy views to bring this alignment into being. As Burden (2007) points out, arguments for descriptive representation revolve around the value of this "coincidental" correspondence in the views of representatives and constituents. More fundamentally, these points bear on debates about whether the principal–agent relationship between legislators and constituents should more accurately be thought of as one characterized by *selection* or by *sanctions* (see Fearon 1999; Mansbridge 2009), an argument I return to in some depth in the concluding chapter.

For present purposes, these distinctions have implications not only for normative assessments of promise keeping, but also for how it should be studied. To assess the extent to which campaigns serve as signals about winners' later activity calls for very minimalist models, including few controls. Once other characteristics that may explain legislators' relative activity on a given issue (e.g., their party affiliations or past activity levels or committee assignments) are included in the models, we move from a test of the first standard to a test of the second. As I discuss in the next chapter, I anticipate that campaigns will often serve as strong signals about the content of legislators' governing agendas, but will more rarely serve as independent predictors of those agendas.

PLAN OF THE BOOK

In what follows, I explore in detail the linkages between campaign appeals and legislative action. Chapter 2 develops the theoretical foundations for my arguments about these links and presents hypotheses about variation in promise keeping across legislators and across institutional contexts, as well as expectations about its effects on legislators' electoral fortunes. In Chapter 3, I describe my strategy for measuring the content of agendas in campaigns and legislative activity and demonstrate the linkages between appeals and activity on an issue-by-issue basis, highlighting variation in the signaling power of different types of appeals (e.g., positive versus negative, specific versus vague, prospective versus retrospective) and differences in the dynamics of these relationships in the House and Senate. In Chapter 4, I investigate why these differences across chambers and types of rhetoric emerge, arguing that they are rooted in factors that explain candidates' issue selection strategies and their choices to discuss issues in the manner that they do. Chapter 5 explores in more depth promise making and promise keeping on two issues: defense and foreign policy and the environment. By opting for more detailed case studies, I am able to ask questions that are not feasible to address for the full sample. My examination of legislators' appeals and activity on these issues also provides further confidence that legislators do indeed follow through on their appeals in a genuine and meaningful way.

In Chapter 6, I shift my analytical focus away from campaign and legislative activity on particular issues to examine the promise-keeping behavior of individual representatives and senators across all of the issues in their agendas. For instance, what explains why some devote more attention to their campaign appeals than others? How do levels of promise keeping vary across activities and time within the term? Chapter 7 focuses on the electoral impacts of promise keeping. I demonstrate that legislators' follow-through on their previous promises affects the quality of competition they face in their next election and their ultimate electoral fates. I also show how levels of promise keeping are related to legislators' career decisions (i.e., to retire or to run for higher office). In Chapter 8, I examine the policy effects of promise-keeping behavior, demonstrating that legislators' attentiveness to their campaign themes leaves a tangible legacy in public policy outputs. Finally, in Chapter 9, I conclude by discussing the implications of my findings for broader debates about the nature of representation and accountability.

2

Campaigns as Signals

For promise keeping to occur at high rates, candidates must have the incentive to make sincere appeals in their campaigns and winning legislators must have the motivation and the opportunity to follow through on these appeals once in office. For it to be meaningful, the actions legislators take on their campaign promises must not be solely symbolic. This chapter addresses both of these issues. I first establish in more detail legislators' reasons for engaging in promise keeping and discuss why the content of their governing agendas serves as a useful target for measuring this responsiveness. I then develop hypotheses about variation in this behavior at the individual and aggregate levels. I anticipate that promise keeping will be widespread, but that levels will vary in a predictable fashion across types of appeals, across legislators, across activities, across chambers, and across time.

As is conventional in work on legislative behavior, I begin with the assumption that reelection is legislators' most proximate goal (Mayhew 1974). As such, I expect that legislators will not knowingly endanger their electoral prospects and will devote time and effort to actions that promote them. To the extent that promise keeping helps them to accomplish this goal, we should observe them engaging in it at high rates. At the same time, though, I also assume that reelection is not legislators' sole goal, that there is not a single route to achieving it, that it is interconnected with legislators' other goals, and that there is at least some path dependency at work. In particular, legislators also have policy interests and governing histories, and these should shape their choices, both as campaigners and as lawmakers. To understand why legislators make and keep the particular promises that they do, we must also take these factors into account.

CONVENTIONAL WISDOM ABOUT PROMISE KEEPING

My assertion that legislators will regularly follow through on their campaign appeals is in sharp contrast to the view held by many pundits and most citizens, who believe that promise keeping is quite rare. Instead, they argue that candidates typically say what it takes to win, but then follow their own interests and preferences (or perhaps those of their contributors) once in office (see Hibbing and Theiss-Morse 1995; Ladd 1990; Spiliotes and Vavreck 2002). Individuals' opinions about whether levels of promise keeping are high or low have been shown to be more a function of general factors like their trust in and knowledge about government than the particular policy actions of their elected representatives (Craig, Niemi, and Silver 1990). For instance, as illustrated in Figure 2.1, among the respondents to the 2006 Congressional Elections Study, the most recent academic survey to ask about promise keeping, those who reported that they felt it was "very important" to follow what goes on in Congress or to keep track of how members of Congress vote were also more likely to report that their representative did "very well" in following through on his

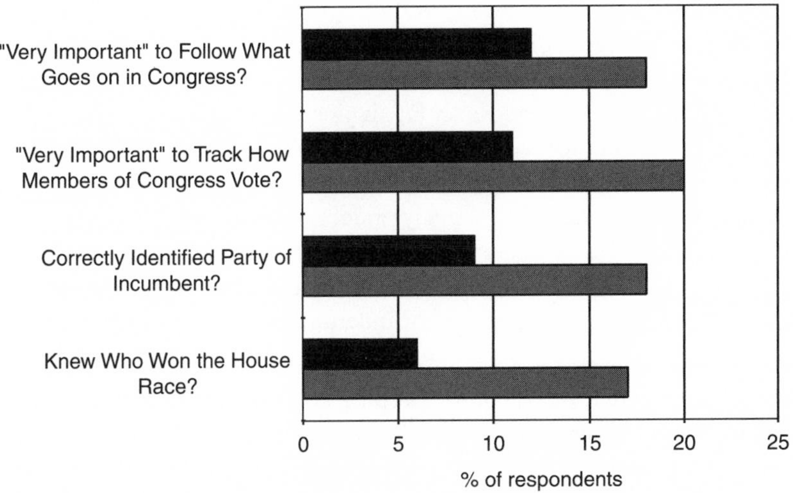

FIGURE 2.1 Constituents' Perceptions of Incumbent Promise Keeping
Note: The bars reflect the percentage of 2006 Congressional Elections Study respondents who reported that their incumbent member of Congress had done "very well" in keeping his or her campaign promises. Gray bars represent the group of respondents who answered yes to the survey question or display the feature of interest; black bars represent the group who responded no or who do not display the feature of interest

or her promises. Even more tellingly, those respondents who were able to identify correctly the party of their current representative (pre-election) and who were aware enough about politics to know who had won the contest in their district (post-election) offered more positive assessments of levels of promise keeping than those who incorrectly guessed the party of their incumbent or admitted that they did not know who had won the election (see Sulkin 2009a, 121).

Thus, it appears that the most knowledgeable and engaged citizens, those who are the best equipped to assess meaningfully whether their representatives follow through on their appeals, are also the most likely to think that they are doing so. As a result, we should avoid taking laments about the lack of promise keeping at face value. Nonetheless, two observations about the nature of modern politics might reasonably lead one to conclude that politicians will rarely keep their campaign promises. The first is that it appears easy and low cost for a candidate to claim interest in an issue, particularly in a vague way. The second is that most voters pay little attention to what their elected representatives do in office and so are unlikely to punish them for failing to follow through on their campaign promises. Together, these would seem to give legislators both the incentive to make insincere appeals and the freedom to ignore them.

Political scientists have been less directly critical of legislators, but, as discussed in Chapter 1, divisions of labor in the study of American politics have meant that research on representation and responsiveness seldom focuses on the linkages between campaigning and governing. Indeed, this separation of the electoral and legislative arenas often leads to the implicit conclusion that representatives' and senators' campaign and legislative priorities and strategies are largely independent of one another. For example, most models of how candidates select campaign issues focus not on their post-election policy goals, but on the more immediate aim of winning the election. In the classic formulation, Downs (1957) asserts that candidates

> ... never seek office as a means of carrying out particular policies; their only goal is to reap the rewards of holding office *per se* .... Upon this reasoning rests the fundamental hypothesis of our model: parties formulate policies in order to win elections, rather than win elections in order to formulate policies. (28)

Building on this foundation, scholars have argued that rational candidates should focus their campaigns on those issues that will maximize their vote shares. Thus, campaigns can be thought of as heresthetical battles, where competing candidates maneuver to set the agenda in a way that benefits them (Hammond and Humes 1993; Riker 1986, 1996). One strategy they might adopt to do so is to "ride the wave" by highlighting those issues that are most salient in news coverage and, hence, in the minds of the public at the time of the election (Ansolabehere and Iyengar 1994; Sides 2007). A second option is to discuss only those themes for which they hold some sort of advantage over their opponents. Sometimes this advantage is theorized to stem from a legislator's own record (Sellers 1998; Sides 2006), but more often it is thought to relate to general factors such as ideology or party. Spatial models suggest that a candidate should highlight an issue if his or her position on it is closer than the opponent's to that of the median voter (Downs 1957; Simon 2002) and issue ownership models suggest that candidates should highlight those issues that their party is thought most competent to handle (Abbe, Goodliffe, Herrnson, and Patterson 2003; Ansolabehere and Iyengar 1994; Brasher 2003; Kaufmann 2004; Petrocik 1996; Spiliotes and Vavreck 2002).

While none of these strategies is necessarily inconsistent with linkages between campaign appeals and policy activity, neither do they imply that campaign and legislative priorities will be strongly interrelated. For example, if crime is high on the public agenda, then a riding the wave strategy should lead all candidates to highlight that issue, regardless of whether it is a priority for them. Similarly, a pure issue ownership strategy would suggest that Democrats should talk about issues like the environment, even if they are not particularly interested in or active on environmental policy, and, conversely, that Republicans should avoid trespassing on this issue, even if they have records on it and view it as a priority. If this is the case, then observing a candidate's choice to discuss crime or the environment will not permit us to predict how active he or she will be on those issues in Congress.[1]

INCENTIVES FOR PROMISE KEEPING

Why, then, do I expect that linkages between campaign appeals and legislative priorities will be relatively widespread? Despite the fact that the literature has been largely silent about the signaling potential of campaigns, I argue that legislators actually face clear incentives to make sincere

[1] Interestingly, the evidence that congressional candidates actually use these strategies and that they pay off electorally is mixed at best. For example, recent studies show that contrary to expectations, candidates regularly discuss the same issues as their opponents, highlight relatively obscure issues, and trespass on the other party's themes, all without appearing to harm themselves at the polls (Kaplan, Park, and Ridout 2006; Sides 2007).

appeals and to follow through on them once in office.[2] Perhaps most importantly, because legislators' electoral and policy goals are often intertwined with one another, they should reap a number of benefits from focusing their campaigns on their governing priorities. On the policy side, many representatives and senators have strong interests in particular issues and, when given the opportunity, should pursue them. Thus, at the very least, their personal priorities should be an important criterion in selecting among the broader set of issues for which they enjoy some advantage. As Fenno (2007) argues, a consistent focus on these issues at home in their districts, on the campaign trail, and in Washington, D.C., contributes to the aura of authenticity for which successful legislators strive.

Moreover, there is concrete evidence that by pursuing their policy goals, legislators can also promote their electoral goals. Research shows that candidates do better at the polls when they highlight issues for which they have a background, and claiming to care about an issue without a record of action to back up such an assertion can even hurt them (Sellers 1998). More generally, constituents may value having a representative who has a reputation for expertise and influence (Fenno 1973; Price 1989; but see Wawro 2000). Thus, a legislator may initially choose to be active on an issue because of his or her own background or personal interests, but once having built up a record on it, there are electoral payoffs to continuing to highlight accomplishments on this issue in his or her reelection campaigns. From the perspective of legislators, then, the distinction between campaign behavior and governing behavior may be largely artificial.

Finally, after having raised an issue in the campaign, regardless of the reason for doing so, the candidate should also enjoy future electoral payoffs for actually following through on it in office (and/or pay future electoral costs for failing to do so). Some voters may directly reward promise keeping, but even if citizens rarely monitor their elected representatives' behavior in office, critics of the incumbent, particularly potential challengers, are always on the lookout for weaknesses they can exploit (Arnold 1990, 2004; Bailey 2001; Jacobson 2001; Sulkin 2005). Evidence of forgotten promises makes an especially compelling narrative for challengers, particularly given the proportion of voters who believe that failure

[2] One possibility, of course, is that at least some legislators view campaign appeals as implicit promises and so feel that their job as representatives compels them to follow through on them, but even barring this, there are also more direct motivations.

to keep promises is a big issue, so savvy incumbents should seek to avoid such critiques. Even if in reality there was no retribution for failing to follow through on appeals, we know that legislators are particularly risk averse about their reelection prospects and so may behave *as though* it matters.

As such, there are both pre- and post-election factors that should encourage strong linkages between the content of winning legislators' campaign appeals and their activity in office. Candidates stand to gain from talking about issues that they plan to pursue in Congress and, once having highlighted them, there are potential downstream payoffs to following through. As discussed in Chapter 1, this is the reason that legislators' campaigns should more often serve as signals about the content of their subsequent legislative agendas than as independent predictors of these agendas. In short, to the extent that legislators' campaign appeals are sincere, a reflection of their preexisting interests and priorities, it is likely that they will also be manifested in their future activities. However, because the same set of factors explains both the choice to raise an issue in a particular campaign and the choice to be active on it in the subsequent Congress, appeals themselves will not necessarily provide new information about legislators' priorities.

Put another way, my argument is that campaign appeals will be largely *endogenously* determined. Occasionally events will occur that elicit responses from previously inattentive legislators (e.g., following the terrorist attacks of September 11, 2001, or Hurricane Katrina in 2005), but most of the time, legislators' agendas will shift slowly from campaign to campaign or congress to congress. Although endogeneity is often framed as a "problem" to be solved statistically, here it is really a central part of the theoretical story. My argument is that promise keeping should occur at high rates precisely because candidates are sincere in their campaigns, drawing on their individual interests and priorities when choosing their themes.[3] Thus, from a normative perspective, predictable (and hence endogenous) campaign appeals are a good thing because their presence means that candidates' priorities are not just pulled out of thin air or selected purely because of their vote-maximizing potential.

This logic leads to two expectations: first, that promise keeping should be common; and, second, that it should vary systematically, both with

[3] In Chapter 4, I test this assertion directly, investigating the relationship between candidates' past records and their decisions to raise a given issue, as well as their decisions about *how* to discuss it.

characteristics of legislators and their appeals and with contextual variables related to activity type and chamber. Certain types of rhetoric may reflect more of a commitment to act, some groups of legislators may be more likely to follow through on their appeals than others, differences in the incentives presented by introductions and cosponsorships may lead promise keeping to be more prevalent on one activity than the other, and institutional variation between the chambers of Congress may result in different dynamics for representatives and senators. Later in this chapter, I take up these possibilities and develop hypotheses about where and when levels of promise keeping should be the highest. However, before doing so, it is necessary to discuss in more detail the nature of legislators' activity in office and their options for demonstrating responsiveness to their campaign appeals.

AGENDAS AND PROMISE KEEPING

In the agenda-based approach to promise keeping that I propose, legislators follow through on their campaign appeals by actively pursuing those issues in their next terms, through their introduction and cosponsorship of legislation. This view of responsiveness is rooted in legislators' participation in the policy-making process, or, more precisely, in their allocation of attention to issues. The idea that attention is a crucial element of governance has an early provenance (Bauer, Pool, and Dexter 1963; Schattschneider 1960) and is central to the public policy literature on agenda setting (see, for example, Baumgartner and Jones 2009; Cobb and Elder 1983; Downs 1972; Jones and Baumgartner 2005; Kingdon 1984). Until recently, though, few congressional scholars studied this facet of legislative activity. Instead, the vast majority of the literature on legislative behavior and representation has focused solely on representatives' and senators' issue positions or ideological preferences, usually as expressed through their roll call votes.

By highlighting the implications of this oversight, Hall's (1996) work on House members' participation marked a major advance. In *Participation in Congress*, he explored when and why legislators choose to be active in committee and subcommittee deliberations, arguing that for every policy issue, members of Congress face the same two decisions: "what position to take and how active to be" (1). His results demonstrate convincingly that the latter offers insight into the dynamics of policy making and the nature and extent of representation that the former does not and cannot provide. Most importantly, participation in activities other than voting is *selective*.

Although most legislators vote on nearly every measure that comes before them,[4] they focus their active participation on a much smaller set of issues.

As such, while voting is essentially reactive, activities such as introductions and cosponsorships are proactive (Burden 2007, 9). To engage in these activities, legislators must initiate action or seek them out, making a conscious decision to participate. The choice to be active at all on an issue should therefore reveal something about legislators' interests, and relative differences in attention to issues across legislators or within individual legislators' agendas offer further signals about how important that issue is to them. This ability to discern differences in the intensity of interest is critical. No matter how much legislators care about an issue, they can vote only once on each roll call. In contrast, they face few formal limitations on how active they can be in pursuing that issue at earlier stages of the policymaking process.

It is important to note, though, that the lack of formal institutional constraints does not mean that proactive participation is effortless or unlimited. Instead, informal constraints, most notably time and resources, lead most legislators to undertake a fairly small number of activities. For instance, representatives in my sample introduced an average of 11 to 12 bills and resolutions[5] per two-year congress, and senators introduced about 34. Both groups cosponsored more, averaging about 220 measures for representatives and 167 for senators. To put this in context, approximately 5,500 bills and resolutions were introduced in the House and 3,500 in the Senate during each of the congresses I study. Legislators' participation, even on the activity engaged in most frequently, reflects action on only a very small percentage (about 4–5 percent) of the total number of bills. Therefore, it does not seem likely that they treat these activities lightly or haphazardly, and instead we should expect them to make careful choices about which issues to pursue. To assume otherwise is to suggest, as Hall

[4] Of course, abstention on a vote is always an option, but it is one that often has costs. Interest groups that issue voting scorecards typically treat an abstention the same as a vote against a policy and challengers often critique incumbents for missed votes.

[5] I limit my analysis of introductions and cosponsorships to bills and joint resolutions because "no practical difference exists between a bill and a joint resolution" (Oleszek 2004, 333). In contrast, other types of resolutions (i.e., concurrent and simple) are not sent to the president for approval and so do not have the force of law if passed. Although studies of introductions and cosponsorships often focus only on bills, an important reason to include joint resolutions is that measures on defense and foreign policy often take that form. Thus, as Mayhew (2005) notes, a failure to include joint resolutions may result in an incomplete understanding of lawmaking on these issues (203). In this and future chapters, my references to "introductions" or "bills" include both bills and joint resolutions.

put it, that "reasonably rational legislators, who already suffer from serious time constraints, will spend nontrivial amounts of time on trivial pursuits" (1996, 26).

The implication is that the content of legislators' activity should be predictable. Studies of legislators' proactive participation confirm this, demonstrating that their agendas are a function of factors such as constituency concerns (Hall 1996; Harward and Moffett 2010; Hayes, Hibbing, and Sulkin 2010; Schiller 2000; Woon 2009), personal policy interests (Burden 2007), and critiques from challengers (Sulkin 2005). More generally, it is through these types of activities that legislators go about the important tasks of specialization and reputation building, which have the potential to increase both their legislative and electoral success (Fenno 1996, 2007; Rocca and Gordon 2010; Schiller 1995; Sellers 1998; Wawro 2000). As a Senate staffer interviewed by Schiller (1995) explained, "it is very important what they do legislatively. Bills generate themes of the senator's overall services .... [L]egislation defines the senator" (187). The same should hold true for House members, and perhaps even more so since they are less active overall and are less able than their Senate colleagues to present themselves credibly as generalists (Baker 2008).

The question of interest for understanding promise keeping is to establish why legislators should be motivated to devote their scarce activities to the set of issues they highlighted in their campaign appeals. From a policy perspective, the answer is simple: they should do so because they are interested in these issues, which is why they raised them in the campaign in the first place. From an electoral perspective, the potential payoffs come from being able to demonstrate action on those issues they proclaimed to be their priorities. Thus, I argue that this behavior falls under the more general reelection-oriented strategy of credit claiming. As Mayhew described it, legislators benefit from the perception that they can deliver good outcomes to their constituents, and so "it becomes necessary for each congressman to try to peel off pieces of governmental accomplishment for which he can believably generate a sense of responsibility" (1974, 53).

The introduction and cosponsorship of bills and resolutions provide a clear vehicle for engaging in credit claiming because they enable legislators to point to concrete, traceable evidence of their attention to an issue (Arnold 1990). This is important because claims of credit are not easy or costless; in order to make a believable claim, legislators must have an established record of activity to back it up (Hall 1996). As a legislative staff member put it, "You can't go out and say that you are doing something without physical evidence" (Schiller 2000, 93). In the absence of such evidence, efforts at credit claiming will not be credible and, as Sellers (1998) demonstrates, may even backfire. In particular, they may open the door for challengers eager to point out how the incumbent has failed to keep his or her promises.

Of course, sponsoring or cosponsoring legislation is not the only option at legislators' disposal for demonstrating attentiveness to their constituents' interests and follow-through on their campaign appeals; they can also use their roll call votes in this manner. However, proactive activities have the potential to offer a greater payoff. While voting is a collective enterprise, introducing or cosponsoring legislation can more clearly be argued to be an individual contribution (Schiller 1995; Wilson and Young 1997). One of the House staffers Koger (2003) interviewed for his study of cosponsorship explained it this way:

> Cosponsorship means you recognized early on that the bill is good public policy and that it has merit and should be acted on. If a member cosponsors, that implies he or she contributed to its success; the member's cosponsorship may have made the difference. If you just vote yes, you had no role in bringing the bill to the floor. There's more credit in cosponsoring a bill and then voting for it. (231)

It is also the case that, as discussed in the previous chapter, these activities permit legislators to pursue issues of interest to them and their constituents that may not regularly make it to the floor of Congress. This should be particularly true for members of the minority party. A Democratic representative serving in Congress in the late 1990s argued that:

> When you're in the minority, the bills that you introduce and cosponsor define your philosophy. A lot of the votes and legislation that come up don't address the problems that are important to you; it is not the stuff that you really want to push. If you want to show your constituents who you are and what you really want to do to move the country forward, you've got to cosponsor bills. (Koger 2003, 232)

Engaging in activities such as introductions and cosponsorships thus allows legislators to attempt to shape the agenda. Even if the bills they support in this manner are ultimately unsuccessful, they still can point to evidence that they have actively pursued their campaign promises, and, as discussed in more detail later in this book, their efforts may have important indirect or downstream effects on policy.

Finally, proactive behaviors are particularly well suited for demonstrating follow-through on campaign appeals because the language that candidates use in these appeals often suggests that they will be leaders in solving particular problems, not just (or even usually) that they will support a specific preexisting solution to those problems. For example, a candidate such as Ernie Fletcher, who promises to provide "leadership on the big issues like health care, education, [and] jobs," would be hard pressed to argue that he has done so if all he has done is cast roll call votes on bills formulated and introduced by other members. However, if he has been active in setting the agenda on these issues, shaping legislation and doing his best to promote it in Congress, he will be better able to make a credible claim of leadership and influence.

THE MEANING OF INTRODUCTIONS AND COSPONSORSHIPS

My assumption, then, is that introductions and cosponsorships are meaningful, both for representation and for lawmaking. It is through these activities that legislators respond to the interests of their constituents, follow through on their campaign appeals, and pursue their policy goals. These proactive behaviors also serve as proxies for other, less readily observable actions such as efforts at coalition building, participation in committees, approaching colleagues to ask them to cosponsor, and so on (Burden 2007; Hall 1996; Wawro 2000). And of course, all laws passed by Congress originate as bills and resolutions introduced by individual members.

It is important to note, though, that a common undercurrent in the literature is that these activities should be viewed as mostly symbolic and inconsequential rather than substantive and meaningful (Hall 1996). This claim is typically based on the (correct) observation that most introduced measures do not progress very far in the legislative process and hence have little direct effect on policy outputs. Thus, the argument goes, it seems plausible that legislators undertake them not out of the sincere desire to affect policy, but simply to reap the electoral benefits of position taking (i.e., by publicly expressing positions that please the constituency, but without any responsibility for or interest in actually producing any effects). In his discussion of reelection-oriented behaviors, Mayhew himself struggled with how to classify the sorts of activities I study here, concluding as follows: "A difficult borderline question here is whether introduction of bills in Congress should be counted under position taking or credit claiming. On balance probably under the former" (1974, 63).

This is a critique to be reckoned with. If introducing and cosponsoring legislation is symbolic and insincere (especially if it is more symbolic and less sincere than other activities), then we should rightly question the value of an agenda-based approach to promise keeping. However, rather than immediately accepting this claim, it is useful to think about it more critically. The first issue to consider is whether the view that bills matter only if they become law accords with what we know about how the policy-making process works. While this is clearly the most direct effect an introduced measure might have, scholars have pointed to a number of other ways in which bills may influence policy. Most notably, Kingdon (1984) argues that the agenda-setting process often takes place over an extended period of time, with support for a policy alternative "built gradually through a process of constant discussion, speeches, hearings, and bill introductions" (18). A particular introduction may be crucial to this "softening up" process, but it could be almost impossible to link it directly to a downstream policy outcome. Along the same lines, Koger (2003) contends that legislative success should be defined broadly because measures that fail to become law may still fulfill their sponsor's and cosponsors' goals in a variety of other ways. For example, the measures may "[be] incorporated into subsequent legislative proposals[,] ... stop another bill or class of bills[,] ... [or] send a signal of congressional interest to the executive branch on some regulatory issue" (230). Under all of these scenarios, a legislator's behavior can leave a legacy in policy that could not be predicted by simply tracking the fates of his or her introductions or cosponsorships.[6]

As an illustration, consider the activity of Representative Bob Goodlatte (R-VA), a member of my sample for the 1998 election/106th Congress. Goodlatte had long been interested in reducing limitations on the export of encryption software and introduced a measure in the 106th Congress on this matter. That bill, HR 850 (one of only twelve he introduced during that congress), received 258 cosponsors and was reported out of committee, but did not reach the floor and thus was not the subject of a vote. However, according to Koger, "the real effect of this bill, its cosponsors, and its committee action was to push the Clinton Administration to relax its encryption export policy, which the Commerce Department did in a series of steps from 1996 to 2000" (2003, 230).

It would therefore seem shortsighted to argue that HR 850 was inconsequential simply because it did not pass. In fact, it likely had much more of

[6] Although the magnitude of any individual contribution is smaller for cosponsorships than for introductions, cosponsorships can still be meaningful legislatively because they serve as an early signal about the level of support for a proposal and hence may influence policy outcomes (Kessler and Krehbiel 1996; Koger 2003; Wilson and Young 1997).

a policy impact than many of the bills that did become law during that congress, which, as always, were comprised mostly of small matters and routine business.[7] From the perspective of promise keeping, it is important to note that trade was one of the issues Goodlatte raised in his campaign ads in 1998. Is it reasonable to accuse him of failing to deliver on his appeals about this issue because his introduction did not pass? I would argue, as Goodlatte himself did, that the answer is no. In fact, he highlighted his accomplishments on the policy during his next campaign, issuing a press release in the fall of 2000 taking credit for the Commerce Department's updates to guidelines on exports of encryption software (Koger 2003, 243).

In short, that a given measure fails to progress to the end of the legislative process does not enable us to draw firm conclusions about its policy impact. Nor, as the preceding discussion suggests, is it sufficient to make reliable inferences about a sponsor's or cosponsor's intentions or sincerity. After all, bills die for a variety of reasons,[8] and, among the group of legislators who take action on any particular measure, there may be a number of different motivations at work. This raises a related point, which is the necessity of differentiating *activities* from *strategies*. Legislators may indeed benefit from position taking and may wish to engage in it, but there is a difference between the argument that activities such as introductions and cosponsorships can be used for position taking and the argument that introductions and cosponsorships *are* position taking. Since we cannot get inside the heads of legislators, we cannot and should not infer the strategy from the activity (Hall 1996).[9]

This confounding of activities and strategies has actually presented a fairly large stumbling block in the development of theories linking representation and lawmaking. Put simply, if activities such as introductions and cosponsorships are not substantively meaningful, then what is? If we also rule out roll call voting, which Mayhew explicitly called out as position taking (1974, 61), there is not much left. One possibility might be committee participation, but there is little evidence that legislators focus

[7] Some scholars offer a harsher interpretation of the importance of most statutory output. As Cameron (2000) puts it, "There is a little secret about Congress that is never discussed in the legions of textbooks on American government; the vast bulk of legislation produced by that august body is stunningly banal . . ." (37).

[8] In addition, a particular bill dying does not mean that policy does not proceed, as a related or even virtually identical measure may be chosen as the legislative vehicle.

[9] What can be done, and is the approach I take in Chapter 8, is to try to determine whether legislators pursue their promise-keeping bills less intently than their other introductions.

their introductions and cosponsorships on a different set of issues than those they pursue in committees, and, in fact, more often the opposite is true (Hall 1996; Schiller 2000). So, unless we are prepared to say that every legislative activity is symbolic, or that legislators simply do not care about policy,[10] categorizing whole classes of activities as symbolic offers us little analytical leverage. In a twenty-fifth anniversary retrospective on *Congress: The Electoral Connection*, Hurley (2001) summarized the dilemma this way:

> By emphasizing position taking, Mayhew may have led congressional scholars to discount the value of studies of policy representation. Mayhew's conceptualization of position taking suggests that nearly every policy-related activity a member undertakes can be interpreted as symbolic. Analysts have used such disparate activities as members' passage of measures by wide margins and their proposal of measures with full knowledge that they would fail as indicators of symbolic behavior. If no actions fail to qualify as position taking, no hypothesis generated by the theory is falsifiable and any study of members' attempts to represent constituency policy preferences can be dismissed. Under such a theory of legislative behavior, policy representation assumes the character of a pseudoevent. (259)

How, then, can we reconcile these competing views? The solution I advocate is to think about proactive behaviors not from an aggregate legislative success/productivity perspective, but from the point of view of individual legislators seeking to achieve their policy and electoral goals. Policy making is a complicated enterprise involving a large number of actors and institutional constraints, and there is little most representatives and senators can do to ensure that their preferred policies become law. Their only option is to pursue their priorities through active participation in the legislative process, and, as such, their choices about how to allocate their attention to issues in their introductions and cosponsorships are important. This is not to say that every activity has an impact on policy, or that legislators always undertake them sincerely. However, they are what legislators "do," so analyses of congressional behavior should take them seriously.

It is important to note too that constituents care about the issues their legislators pursue, so the content of their agendas also matters for assessments of representation. Although most work on the topic focuses on legislators' issue positions or roll call votes, the view that these are of primary concern to citizens is called into question by research on people's

[10] The assertion that legislators are indifferent about policy outcomes, even if true at some point in the past, is much less likely to be so now in an era of increasing partisan polarization (Sinclair 2006).

knowledge about and attitudes toward their elected officials. Instead, it may be just as accurate to say that the public most often cares about solving problems, and is willing to grant substantial leeway to its representatives to pursue these problems as they see fit (Arnold 1990; Bianco 1994). From this standpoint, responsiveness occurs when legislators are active in office in addressing the policy problems that are important to their constituents. Applied to promise keeping, this means pursuing those issues they prioritized in their campaigns.[11]

EXPLAINING VARIATION IN PROMISE KEEPING

My basic expectations, then, are that promise keeping should be relatively widespread, but that rates should vary in a systematic fashion with features of legislators, their appeals, and the institutional setting. Thus, there are three levels of analysis that are of interest. The first is the signaling power of campaign appeals themselves. This bears on the most basic question about promise keeping: Do candidates' decisions to talk about an issue (or not) in their campaigns reveal anything about their likelihood of acting on that issue in Congress? Furthermore, are certain types of language indicative of more follow-through? For instance, is there a difference between legislators who had made positive versus negative appeals, or vague versus specific appeals, or prospective versus retrospective claims?

The second and third levels focus on variation in legislators' promise keeping across the issues that comprise their campaign agendas (rather than issue by issue). More precisely, among individual legislators, what are the characteristics of those who follow through the most and least on their campaign appeals? Also, when we aggregate across legislators, do we see patterns that suggest that promise keeping is influenced by institutional factors? Is it more evident for introductions or cosponsorships? Do legislators' levels of attentiveness to their past campaign themes change as their terms progress? Are there differences in representatives' and senators' propensity to follow through on their campaign appeals? The remainder of the chapter is devoted to developing hypotheses about each of these levels.

[11] One concern, of course, would be if legislators actively pursued issues their constituents cared about but took positions that went against their interests. However, there is little reason that reelection-oriented legislators would engage in such behavior. Moreover, as I have shown in previous work, legislators' volume of activity on an issue is correlated with their interest group voting scores on that issue (Sulkin and Swigger 2008). As such, it seems likely that the same set of factors influences both types of activity (see also Aleman et al. 2009; Burden 2007; Krehbiel 1995). I explore this issue in more depth in Chapter 5.

Rhetoric and Follow-through

In the next chapter, I first test the hypothesis that campaign appeals serve as signals – that legislators who had discussed a particular issue are more active on it in office than those who had not. However, there may also be important variation in levels of follow-through *within* the group of candidates who discussed any given issue. For instance, recall the claim Ernie Fletcher (R-KY) made about education in his 2002 election campaign:

[Announcer]: A leader should be someone we can believe in. Someone who's gained the respect of Democrats and Republicans for his ideas, his expertise, his character. Someone we look to for leadership on the big issues like health care, education, jobs. Someone who's never satisfied with the way things are and knows we can always do better. That someone is Congressman Ernie Fletcher. Leadership, vision, results.

Now compare his appeal to those made by his colleagues Mike Ross (D-AR) and Jim Gerlach (R-PA), who also discussed education in their 2002 campaigns:
Ross, "Different Kind":

[Girl] He is a different kind of congressman. [Announcer] Mike Ross voted against the Congressional pay raise and used the money for a scholarship program to help local high school students pay for college. [Girl 2] "Thanks to Mike Ross I can afford college." [Announcer] The same Mike Ross fighting to modernize public school buildings, reduce class sizes, and put character education back in to schools. [Girl] "Congressman Ross puts families and education first." [Announcer] Mike Ross, making a difference for you.

Gerlach, "Education":

[Announcer]: It doesn't take a genius to know which candidate can do more for education. Since Jim Gerlach has been in office, the funding for schools in the sixth district has gone up $100 million. He won the fight for higher standards, stronger accountability, and more training for teachers. While Dan Wofford was Governor Casey's key education advisor, state funding for basics fell to a twenty-year low.

A number of differences immediately jump out. Most obviously, while Fletcher talked about education in only a vague and passing way, Ross and Gerlach devoted more time to the issue and offered more specifics. Also, compared to both Fletcher and Ross, Gerlach not only discussed his own views on the issue, but also criticized his opponent on it.

Are these rhetorical differences meaningful? Should we expect them to translate to differences in follow-through? In answering this question, the crucial point to consider is whether the choices candidates make about *how* to discuss an issue are reflections of the intensity of their interest in it or whether they are driven by strategic considerations that are unconnected to policy intentions. If the former is true, we should expect variation in language to be linked to variation in follow-through. If the latter is the case, then language differences in discussion of an issue should not be important indicators about the extent of subsequent action on it.

Consider the difference between positive versus negative appeals. Most research on negativity in campaigns points to the conclusion that candidates' appeals about themselves should be better indicators of their interests than their criticisms of their opponents because decisions to "go negative" are largely a function of the closeness of the race (Ansolabehere and Iyengar 1995; Jamieson 1992; Kahn and Kenney 1999; Sigelman and Buell 2003). Relatedly, choices about the content of attacks are usually based on the opposition research that most candidates undertake. If these investigations indicate that attacking the opponent on an issue like the environment will help the candidate, then he or she should do so, regardless of whether the issue is a priority. As such, I expect that positive appeals candidates make about their own interest in an issue will serve as stronger predictors of their subsequent activity than negative appeals that criticize their opponents on the issue.

Expectations about the relationship between the specificity of appeals and later activity are a bit less clear a priori. In general, specific appeals are viewed as normatively superior because they provide more information and are assumed to reflect more commitment to an issue. Offering a specific plan for an issue like education would seem to suggest that the candidate has thought about it in some depth and, because such specificity often takes up more advertising space than the claim that one is "for" education or will provide "leadership" on it, means that he or she is devoting more of a scarce resource to it. Specific appeals may also indicate that the candidate cares enough about the issue that he or she is willing to alienate potential supporters who would disagree with the details of the plan, or that he or she has been active on the issue in the past and so will continue that activity in the future (Kahn and Kenney 1999; Sides 2006).

On the other hand, there are some situations in which ambiguity may be a better strategy (Page 1976; Shepsle 1972; Stokes 1992; Tomz and Van Houweling 2008), so candidates may choose to be vague for electoral reasons that have little to do with their level of commitment to an issue. Moreover, savvy candidates should see that vague appeals offer them more leeway in following through. A candidate who promises to support a particular policy proposal could well find his or her attempts thwarted in the legislative process (e.g., if an unacceptable rider is attached to the bill), but one who promises to be active in solving a problem will be better able to adapt to circumstances outside of his or her control. For instance, having made the claim that he wants to reduce class sizes, Ross opens himself up to criticism if he votes against a bill that includes this policy or if the legislation he pursues on education does not address it. Fletcher, however, can avoid this problem. Thus, the decision to offer specifics or not may not be a function of interest, but of strategy. As a result, and contrary to the conventional wisdom, I do not expect that specific appeals will necessarily serve as stronger signals than vague appeals. In fact, if candidates who lack savvy are both more likely to make specific appeals *and* less likely to recognize the potential advantages of following through on them, it is even possible that there could be a negative relationship between specificity and subsequent activity.

A similar logic applies to expectations about the strength of the relationship between the prominence of an issue in a candidate's appeals and the volume of later activity on it. To the extent that campaign appeals serve as signals, it seems reasonable to assume that featuring an issue in all of one's ads would be a stronger signal than discussing it rarely. However, how much attention any one issue receives is related to the overall size of a candidate's agenda, which, like the propensity to attack, is influenced by the competitiveness of the race (Kahn and Kenney 1999; Sulkin, Moriarty, and Hefner 2007). Thus, while we might expect that candidates who devote a great deal of attention to an issue in their ads will be more attentive to it in office than those who mention it only once and in passing, it is unlikely that there will be consistent linear relationships between the relative prominence of issues in winning candidates' campaign and legislative agendas.

Finally, there is the question of whether candidates' choices to reference the past or the future in their claims about issues are indicative of differences in subsequent promise keeping.[12] Expectations about prospective appeals are the clearest; if these are more than just a rhetorical flourish, it seems reasonable to assume that a candidate who says explicitly that he or she *will* do something on an issue if elected should be more likely to be

[12] It is important to note that, as demonstrated in more detail in the next chapter, most ads do neither, speaking instead in the ambiguous present.

active on it. The situation for retrospective appeals is a bit more complicated. On one hand, they probably indicate that the legislator has actually been active on the issue in the past. On the other, issue priorities can shift, and that a candidate discusses what he or she has done in the past does not necessarily mean that he or she was *more* active than those who talk about the issue, but do not reference their past actions.

Who Keeps Promises?

The preceding discussion suggests that there is much leverage to be gained by an in-depth, issue-by-issue investigation of the linkages between the content and type of campaign appeals and levels of subsequent activity on an issue. However, most candidates talk about multiple issues, so when we think about their follow-through, we also should consider these issues taken together. Thus, in evaluating promise keeping, I am interested not just in whether there are differences among legislators who had and had not talked about an issue, but also in understanding why some legislators are, in general, more attentive to their past campaign themes than others.

As is the case with all potentially reelection-oriented activities, the factor that immediately jumps to mind is electoral vulnerability. The conventional view in the literature on the electoral connection is that vulnerable legislators, who are the most worried about their reelection prospects, should engage in the highest levels of reelection-promoting behavior. For instance, in work on roll call voting, the expectation is that relatively vulnerable legislators should have voting records that approximate closely their constituents' preferences, while safer members will likely diverge more.[13] If this holds for promise keeping, we should observe a negative relationship between legislators' vote shares in the previous election and their levels of follow-through on their campaign issues.

However intuitive this logic may be, it makes an important assumption about legislators' underlying motivations for promise keeping that contradicts the basic tenets of the theory I have outlined. It suggests that, all other things being equal, legislators would rather *not* follow through on their appeals, and it is only fear of electoral reprisal that compels them to do so. But if candidates raise issues out of a sincere interest in them and intent to act, then they should *want* to be active on them. In other words, there is little reason to expect that most safe legislators would simply ignore their promises if given the chance. Of course, it is possible that if events intercede

[13] As indicated earlier, though, there is only mixed evidence that this is the case.

or opportunities arise that pull legislators away from their campaign appeals toward new issues, those with more security should feel more free to take advantage of these. It seems likely, though, that this should matter only at the margins.

More generally, the argument that the electoral connection necessitates a negative correlation between safety and potentially reelection-promoting activities like promise keeping is based on only a snapshot view of legislative behavior. It assumes that legislators with high vote shares in one election can act in an unresponsive manner in the next term and face no repercussions. However, although legislators' vote margins are not entirely within their control, their relative vulnerability or safety is not independent of their activity in office. Instead, as Mayhew explained, "what characterizes 'safe' Congressmen is not that they are beyond electoral reach, but that their efforts are very likely to bring them uninterrupted electoral success" (1974, 37). Thus, if engaging in promise keeping in one term helps them to maintain or improve their vote margins in the next election, this should provide legislators with an incentive to continue it in their next terms. Given what we know about legislators' caution when it comes to their reelection prospects, it seems unlikely that they would abandon behaviors and activities that contributed to their security.

This longer-term view suggests that the causal arrow in the electoral connection may actually go in a direction opposite to that of the conventional wisdom, with responsiveness leading to security (or, at the least, that the relationship is reciprocal). Canes-Wrone, Brady, and Cogan (2002) make a similar argument in their work on roll call voting, finding that "safety itself is a function of members' voting. That is, safe members are 'safe' partially as a consequence of their roll call decisions" (137). This perspective suggests that we will observe a *positive* relationship between vote shares and promise keeping, with relatively secure legislators engaging in the most. This result would be in line with the patterns for issue uptake, where I found that, compared to their vulnerable peers, safer legislators devote a larger portion of their governing agendas to addressing the critiques their challengers made of them (Sulkin 2005).

A similar logic applies to the effects of seniority on promise keeping. If there are electoral advantages to keeping campaign promises, senior members will have had more opportunity to learn this, and so may follow through at higher rates. However, after controlling for the relative electoral security that usually coincides with seniority, we may see less responsiveness among senior members, possibly due to differences in their legislative responsibilities and portfolios (i.e., senior members may be stretched further, making it more difficult for them to focus only on their own priorities). As such, in assessing the differences between junior and senior members' levels of promise keeping, it will be important to control in any analyses for characteristics of their campaign agendas (i.e., size and scope) and their legislative activity levels.

Legislators' party and ideology could also influence their levels of subsequent action on their campaign appeals. If status as a member of the majority party provides members with institutional advantages for follow-through, we could see more promise keeping for legislators from that party.[14] However, any representative or senator can introduce or cosponsor legislation, and, as discussed earlier, these activities may serve as more important venues for minority members to express their interests, since they are less likely to be able to do so in other ways.

Finally, there are competing expectations about the effects that ideological extremity might have on legislators' propensity to keep their promises. One hypothesis is that relatively ideologically extreme legislators care more intensely than moderates about their issue agendas and so will be more likely to follow through on them. But if ideologues are strategic in their campaigns and try to appear more moderate in order to appeal to a broader constituency, they may choose to avoid raising issues for which their relatively extreme positions will be attacked by their opponents, even if those issues are their priorities. As a result, compared to moderates, there could be a weaker correlation between ideologues' "real" interests and the interests they express in their campaigns, resulting in a negative relationship between extremity and levels of promise keeping.

Variation across Activities and Time

In addition to making choices about overall levels of promise keeping, legislators must make decisions about *how* to demonstrate their responsiveness and *when* to do so. Is there reason to expect that we would observe higher levels of promise keeping for one type of legislative activity than the other (i.e., introductions versus cosponsorships) or that it would vary systematically across their terms? Understanding this aggregate variation is important because of the insight that it offers into legislators' decision making, and because it bears on the question of whether promise keeping is

[14] Across the time period I study (the 106th–108th Congresses for the House and the 106th–110th for the Senate), the Republicans were in control of the House of Representatives and there were multiple switches in partisan control of the Senate.

mostly symbolic or whether it is likely to have effects on policy. If legislators engage in it only on low-effort activities, and only as a last-ditch effort to improve their vote margins, promise keeping is likely to have less of an effect on representation and lawmaking than if we observe it occurring at similarly high levels across activities and throughout the term.

In the preceding discussion, I did not draw much distinction between introductions and cosponsorships, and instead highlighted their joint value as indicators of legislators' priorities. However, there is a big trade-off between the two in the effort involved and in their amenability to credit claiming. In short, to sponsor a bill requires more time and resources than simply signing on to an existing measure as a cosponsor. This is the primary reason that the former are undertaken far less frequently than the latter. The clear advantage of introductions, though, is that they enable a legislator to claim sole credit for a measure and should therefore offer stronger evidence that he or she has kept a promise on an issue. As such, there may be more of a payoff (electoral and/or policy) for engaging in promise keeping on introductions, and we should therefore expect legislators to devote relatively high proportions of their introductions to their past campaign themes.

In contrast, with cosponsorships, it is more difficult for a legislator to make a convincing argument that he or she alone is responsible for a bill.[15] Nonetheless, they do provide legislators with a fairly straightforward and tangible method of demonstrating their interest in an issue. Moreover, multiple cosponsorships in a single issue area may provide more ammunition for credit claiming than a single introduction, particularly if some of the measures are highly visible. Representatives and senators should not depend entirely on cosponsorships for promise keeping, but because they help legislators in their quests to claim credit, levels of promise keeping should be relatively high for them as well. And, because overall activity levels on each individual issue tend to be fairly low,[16] it may often make

[15] However, although it is conventional to point out that cosponsorships are less amenable to credit claiming, to my knowledge no one has studied whether constituents actually interpret the claim "I sponsored X . . ." differently from "I cosponsored X . . . ." It is likely, though, that potential challengers and other elites more carefully scrutinize campaign claims.

[16] My coding scheme, introduced in the next chapter, consists of eighteen issues. Because most legislators are active on a number of issues, their 150 to 200 cosponsorships per congress are divided across a variety of categories. Thus, the difference between their volume of activity on introductions versus cosponsorships on an issue is typically not large.

sense to combine introductions and cosponsorships into a single measure of activity.

In making decisions about their promise-keeping activities, legislators also face the choice of *when* to engage in it. Should we expect to see the highest levels immediately following an election, when the past campaign is freshest in their minds, as well as those of constituents, potential future challengers, and other elites? Or might it increase as their terms proceed and the next reelection battle looms nearer? For representatives, there is likely to be little variation, as there is no practical difference between "early" and "late" in a term. As Arnold (2004) explained, "Most representatives start running for reelection within days of their election to Congress. With two-year terms, they have no time to spare. As a consequence, no sharp line exists between periods when representatives are legislating and periods when they are campaigning" (156). It is likely, then, that representatives should engage in similarly high (or low) levels of promise keeping in the first and second years of their terms.

Senators have the luxury of more time. What is not immediately clear is how this should manifest itself in their promise-keeping behavior. One possibility is that they return to office eager to act on their appeals and, after having done so, move on to other activities, leading to less promise keeping as time passes. Another is that they feel little pressure to attend immediately to their campaign claims, but as the next election approaches, they are reminded of the necessity of fulfilling their past promises. If this is the case, we should see an increase in the relative amount of attention they devote to their campaign themes from one congress to the next. This hypothesis is more in line with other work on senators' behavior that demonstrates their tendency to become more reelection-oriented as their terms progress – for example, by moderating the extremity of their roll call voting decisions (see Ahuja 1994; Bernhard and Sala 2006; Bernstein 1988; Wright and Berkman 1986).

Chamber Differences in Promise Keeping

Thus, there is reason to expect that the dynamics of promise keeping may differ across the chambers. Should we also anticipate overall differences in the levels of follow-through for representatives and senators? This question feeds into broader debates about the extent of responsiveness in the House and Senate. The framers intended representatives to be more attentive than senators to their constituents, and even with reforms such as direct election, senators' longer terms and larger (and often more heterogeneous) constituencies may lead them to be less responsive.

Much work on congressional representation focuses on one chamber or the other, rather than both, so there have been few explicit comparisons. The research that has been done, though, calls into question the assertion that the House is always more responsive. Erikson, MacKuen, and Stimson (2002) find, for example, that overall levels of responsiveness to public opinion are similar across the chambers. In the Senate, this appears to be due to electoral replacement of unresponsive members, whereas in the House, members adapt their behavior (321). However, this still means that *individual* senators are, on average, less responsive than individual representatives.

In making specific predictions about the direction of any effect for promise keeping, we need to consider differences both in representatives' and senators' campaigns and in their legislative lives. The biggest difference in campaigns is in the size of agendas: as demonstrated in more detail in the next chapter, Senate candidates typically discuss more issues than do House candidates. Once in office, senators engage in higher volumes of activity (mostly because of their longer terms) and are less constrained in that activity. Given the smaller size of the chamber, they are more likely to be active across a variety of issues, including those that fall outside of the jurisdiction of their committee assignments. Senators often mention this opportunity to influence policy in a variety of areas as one of the advantages of a Senate career over the time in the House many of them had before taking their current seats (Sinclair 1989).

What effects should these differences have on promise keeping? Senators' relatively greater freedom of action might be expected to increase their levels of promise keeping, but this should be mitigated by the fact that candidates select their own campaign issues. Knowing the constraints that they face, House candidates should not choose to raise issues that they do not believe they can pursue credibly. Also, given their smaller campaign agendas, they may be more likely to limit their appeals to only those themes that are truly priorities for them. If this is the case, their campaigns may be better reflections of their interests and intentions, and we should therefore observe higher levels of promise keeping for them.

CONCLUSIONS

Although promise keeping itself is a straightforward concept, it is clear that to fully understand its dynamics and effects requires asking a number of different types of questions and approaching the analysis from a variety of angles. Doing so will provide further insight into legislators' strategies, the linkages between electoral and legislative politics, and the nature and quality of representation. The building blocks for all of these analyses are precise and valid measures of promise making and promise keeping. Developing these measures and providing some basic tests are the tasks of Chapter 3.

3

Campaign Appeals and Legislative Activity

At the heart of my approach to promise making and promise keeping are candidates' and legislators' agendas. Understanding the nature of the linkages between them enables me to address the central questions that motivate my analyses. First, do campaign appeals serve as good signals about the content of legislators' policy activity in office? In other words, by observing the issues that candidates talk about and how they discuss them, can we predict how actively they will pursue them in Congress? Second, what explains why some legislators are more attentive to their campaign appeals than others, devoting a larger portion of their agendas in office to the issues they highlighted in their campaigns? Third, what implications does promise keeping have for legislators' electoral fortunes and for the policy-making process? Does following through on their promises help representatives and senators to achieve their reelection goals, and what sort of legacy does it leave in the congressional agenda and in public policy outputs?

The analyses in this chapter are intended to offer an initial answer to the first of these questions. However, before moving on to investigate the relationships between campaign and legislative priorities, it is first necessary to explore their individual content in more detail. The scope and variation in candidates' and legislators' agendas provide crucial background for putting findings about promise keeping into context. Equally important, my conception of promise keeping relies upon several assumptions about the nature of agendas, so studying them directly allows me to test these assumptions. For instance, in campaigns, I assume that candidates *do* raise substantive issues, that they vary in the issues they highlight and in the language they use when discussing them, and that there are reliable and meaningful ways of measuring this variation. On the governing side of the equation, I expect that all legislators participate in the process of introducing and cosponsoring bills and resolutions (though, of course, the volume of this activity varies across individual members), that they are free to pursue action on issues of their choosing, and that a similar categorization can be used to capture these issue priorities in both the electoral and legislative arenas.

DEFINING ISSUES AND AGENDAS

My definition of an individual's "agenda" is straightforward: it is simply the set of substantive issues a candidate discusses or a legislator pursues. This conceptualization accords well with those developed by public policy scholars who have studied the processes of agenda formation and change at the national level. Cobb and Elder (1983), for example, conceive of the agenda as "a general set of political controversies that will be viewed at any one time as falling within the range of legitimate concerns meriting the attention of the polity" (14),[1] and Kingdon (1984) describes it as "the list of subjects or problems to which governmental officials, and people outside of government closely associated with those officials, are paying some serious attention" (3). Baumgartner and Jones's Policy Agendas Project, a large-scale effort to capture the content of the national agenda across time, is built around this idea, with numerous government activities (hearings, budget authority, executive orders, etc.) and indicators of media attention and public priorities categorized into a set of common issue categories (Baumgartner and Jones 2002, 2009; see also Jones and Baumgartner 2005).

A defining feature shared by all of these conceptualizations is that they clearly distinguish the "issues" that comprise the agenda from various alternatives or solutions that might be available for addressing them. Issues are thought of as broad themes that have multiple dimensions; go beyond particular incidents, events, and policy proposals; and persist across time. Because there are typically differences of opinion about how best to deal with these issues, public and elite debates about them often focus on the advantages and disadvantages of particular solutions, but these alternatives do not themselves constitute issues. For instance, topics such as "Social Security" or "agriculture" count as issues, and policies such as privatization or subsidies are potential alternatives for dealing with

[1] Cobb and Elder also distinguish this broader "systemic" agenda from the more focused institutional agenda, which consists of "specific items scheduled for active and serious consideration" by a policy-making body (1983, 14).

them. Thus, issues and alternatives are analytically separable, and, indeed, as Kingdon (1984) argues, one sign of a successful policy entrepreneur is the ability to attach his or her preferred solution to a particular issue or problem that is currently high on the agenda.

This distinction between issues and solutions has practical importance for the operationalization and measurement of agendas in campaigns and legislative activity. It also forms the crux of the theoretical difference between position-based models of representation and agenda or priority-based conceptions (see also Jones, Larsen-Price, and Wilkerson 2009). In the former, the question of interest is whether government pursues solutions desired by the public or, in the case of promise keeping, whether the alternatives that legislators vote for in Congress align with those that they advocated in their campaigns. In the latter, the question is whether government addresses those problems viewed by the public as priorities or, applied to promise keeping, whether legislators actively pursue in office those issues they raised as priorities during their previous campaigns.

There are a number of existing schemes for coding the issue content of campaign themes and government attention, most of which include about twenty broad categories (see, for example, Baumgartner and Jones 2009; Sides 2006; Simon 2002). I follow suit here, with a scheme of eighteen categories that is designed to be exhaustive and mutually exclusive, such that every issue appeal made by a candidate and every legislative activity undertaken by a representative or senator receives one and only one code.[2] The categories include agriculture, budget, campaign finance and government reform, children's issues (child care, family law, family leave, etc.), civil rights, consumer issues (consumer safety, fraud, credit cards, etc.), corporate regulation, crime, defense and foreign policy, education, environment, health, jobs and infrastructure, Medicare, moral issues, Social Security, taxes, and welfare.

This scheme is based largely on those developed by the Policy Agendas Project and the Wisconsin Advertising Project, but with a few modifications to develop a single set of categories that work across both the electoral and legislative arenas. For instance, defense and foreign policy are fairly distinct topics within legislative activity (i.e., they are typically addressed within different committees and most bills and resolutions are easily grouped into one category or the other), but they are almost always

[2] The one exception to this rule relates to some campaign appeals about taxes that target agriculture and Social Security. For example, a claim that the candidate wanted to eliminate the estate tax to help farmers would be coded under both taxes and agriculture.

rolled together when candidates talk about them in campaigns. As such, in my scheme, they comprise a single category. In addition, my analyses of campaign appeals and legislative activity focus solely on attention to *substantive* issues. In campaigns, this means I seek to identify policy-relevant themes raised by candidates – those that could be the topic of a bill or resolution. Accordingly, themes such as crime or education or taxes count as substantive issues, but references to candidates' backgrounds, attendance records, ideology, or personal traits (e.g., honesty, integrity, etc.) do not. Similarly, in legislative activity, I separate policy-relevant activity from "governmental operations" matters related to the logistics of daily business in the House or Senate, nominations and appointments, general appropriations bills, naming of post offices, use of the Capitol for ceremonial purposes, and the like. As shown later in this chapter, these matters typically comprise about 15 to 20 percent of all introduced measures.

IDENTIFYING CANDIDATES' CAMPAIGN AGENDAS

In contrast to finding data on legislative activity, which is fairly readily available, locating information on candidates' appeals in campaigns presents more of a challenge. Until recently, there have been few systematic efforts to capture campaign communication, particularly in congressional races. Fortunately, beginning with the 1998 elections, the Wisconsin Advertising Project (in conjunction with the Campaign Media Analysis Group) collected and archived all televised campaign advertisements aired in the top seventy-five media markets in the United States, and expanded their efforts beginning in 2002 to include the top one hundred markets. The analyses that follow utilize their archives of ads, focusing on those produced and aired by winning House and Senate candidates in the 1998, 2000, and 2002 elections.

Although there are other potential sources of information about the content of campaigns, candidates' advertisements are particularly well suited to the study of promise making. Their most important strength is that compared to secondary sources such as news coverage, they are unmediated and thus enable me to assess what a candidate said (or, equally important, did not say) about an issue, in his or her own words.[3] Along the

[3] For this reason, my analyses focus solely on ads aired by candidates and do not include any that may have been aired on their behalf by parties or interest groups. The latter are much more common in presidential elections than congressional races, particularly across this time period.

same lines, in contrast to surveys of candidates like those conducted by organizations such as Project Vote Smart, I can be sure that the messages were actually conveyed to voters by the candidate during the course of the campaign, and that the candidate himself or herself chose to raise the issue (i.e., rather than just responding to a survey question).[4]

Candidates' campaign websites, which are also unmediated, offer some of the same strengths (see Druckman, Kifer, and Parkin 2009), but there are still clear advantages to focusing on advertisements. The first of these is that television ads present candidates with a limited amount of time in which to make their appeals, so they force them to make choices, and therefore should serve as good indicators of their priorities (see also Kaplan, Park, and Ridout 2006; Sides 2006). In contrast, on websites, candidates face few formal restrictions on how many issues they can discuss, and, as a result, tend to raise more. In the 2000 elections, for example, House candidates who both aired ads and launched a website talked about twice as many issues on their sites than in their ads (Sulkin, Moriarty, and Hefner 2007). Focusing on advertisements as the source of information about candidates' issue agendas thus provides for fairly conservative estimates of the extent of the linkages between appeals and activity.

More importantly, although the Internet has become increasingly central in campaigns, it is only in the past election or two that congressional candidates' use of websites has become widespread. As recently as the 1998 elections, only 35 percent of major-party House candidates sponsored sites (Kamarck 1999), and through the early 2000s many sites remained quite rudimentary (Druckman, Kifer, and Parkin 2007). Moreover, candidates may now be taking full advantage of technological advances, but citizens still rely far more on more traditional media venues such as television for their information about campaigns. The Pew Center's Internet and American Life Project has followed the role of the Internet in elections from 1996 to the present, and their surveys show that even in the 2008 elections, which represent the high water mark in Internet usage, only about 55 percent of American adults reported using the Internet to get information about politics and the election (Smith 2009).[5] In 2006, which serves as a better indicator of the role of the Internet in congressional elections since it was a midterm year, 31 percent of respondents had

[4] Of course, candidates may choose to raise an issue in response to criticisms from the opponent or other political actors, but the choice to address or ignore it is still theirs.

[5] In 1998, the first election included in my analyses, only 15 percent reported doing so.

gone online for campaign information, and, of those, only one-fifth reported visiting candidates' websites. This means that just 6 percent of potential voters had done so (Rainie and Horrigan 2007). In fact, as many observers have noted, a major segment of the audience for websites is not voters at all, but journalists looking for information for their stories (Bimber and Davis 2003; Herrnson 2008; Semiatin 2005).

For all of these reasons, ads remain the best source for identifying how candidates present themselves and their priorities to their potential constituents, particularly if one wants to examine campaigns across several election cycles extending back into the late 1990s and early 2000s. However, another important issue should be considered: does this approach generate a representative sample of candidates and legislators? In order to appear in my analyses, winning candidates must meet two criteria: they had to have lived in one of the top seventy-five to one hundred media markets, and they must have aired ads. The first criterion does not present as much of an issue for generalizability as it might seem at first glance because the top markets represent all but a handful of the smallest states[6] and comprise the vast majority (more than 80 to 85 percent) of the population of the United States. As a result, my sample of 391 representatives and 84 senators very closely approximates the group of winning candidates who ran ads during these elections.[7]

The second criterion requires a more careful assessment. Do winning candidates who air ads comprise a good representative sample of winning legislators overall? For the Senate, the question is moot, as all of the candidates in the sampled states aired television ads in the elections I study. For the House, the answer is clearly no, and the primary reason for this is simple: while many representatives "run" in races where they face no major party opposition, few of these candidates actively campaign and, as a result, they do not air ads.[8] However, because the goal in studying

[6] The only states for which there are no representatives or senators in the sample are Alaska, Hawaii, Montana, North Dakota, South Dakota, and Wyoming.

[7] A total of 397 winning House candidates ran ads. However, there were 5 candidates for whom no storyboards were archived and one candidate (Newt Gingrich in 1998) who did not take office for a long enough time after the election to accumulate a legislative record. In addition, a number of the House candidates appear in the sample in more than one election year, which is controlled for in the analyses of follow-through. The 391 cases include 250 different representatives. The sample also includes 84 senators, 79 of whom served a full term.

[8] Indeed, between 1998 and 2002, about one-fifth of all House members ran in races where they faced no major party challengers, but only about 3 percent of my sample was unopposed.

TABLE 3.1 *House and Senate Sample Characteristics*

Variable	House	Senate
# of Candidates	391	84
Election Years	1998–2002	1998–2002
Congresses	106th–108th	106th–110th
States Represented	43	42
Mean Seniority in Office (Years)		
Sample	6.2	8.0
All Legislators	8.7	9.8
% of Democrats		
Sample	42	45
All Legislators	48	48
% Unopposed		
Sample	3	4
All Legislators	18	5
Mean Vote Share for Unopposed (%)		
Sample	61	61
All Legislators	66	62

Sources: All data were collected from Barone and Ujifusa (2000), and Barone, Cohen, and Ujifusa (2002, 2004).

promise keeping is to assess whether appeals made in campaigns serve as predictors of subsequent activity, it is clear that the population I really wish to generalize about is *not* all legislators, but is instead the group of legislators who launched a campaign in the previous election.

When we consider this group to be the population, the sample compares much more favorably. Although targeting winners who aired ads does yield a sample that leans a bit more toward competitive races (among winners in contested races, the average vote share for sampled candidates is 61 percent, compared to 66 percent for all winners), *all* sources of data about campaign appeals are skewed in this direction. Competitive races generate much more news coverage (Arnold 2004), and candidates in tight races raise and spend more money on virtually every type of communication with voters, from yard signs to television advertising to websites (Herrnson 2008; Jacobson 2004). Given the relatively greater expense of ads, particularly in some urban markets, the skew is potentially a bit larger in magnitude than for some other sources, but this is a matter of degree rather than a qualitative difference.

As shown in Table 3.1, the sample approximates the group of all legislators on a number of variables of interest, including geography, seniority, and party. There is also considerable range for competitiveness and seniority, with vote shares ranging from 50 to 100 percent for both the House and Senate samples, and years in office ranging from zero to twenty-six for the House and zero to forty-two for the Senate. Accordingly, concerns about generalizability should be minimal.

CODING PROCEDURES FOR ADVERTISEMENTS

To construct my measures of candidates' campaign agendas, I make use of two features of the Campaign Media Analysis Group (CMAG)/Wisconsin Advertising Project data collection efforts: the actual storyboards for each of the advertisements (which include screenshots of the visuals and the text of the audio) and the figures on how often each ad was aired by each candidate. The 391 winning candidates in the House sample ran a total of 1,468 unique ads representing 209,221 ad airings and the 84 in the Senate sample ran 786 ads representing 195,912 airings. The first step of the coding process was to read each of these 2,254 ad storyboards and note all of the substantive issues discussed, using the coding scheme described earlier. Each storyboard was coded by three coders, working independently.[9] In all, the coders identified 4,637 distinct issue appeals in the 2,254 ads.[10] Figure 3.1 presents the percentage of issue appeals devoted to each of the eighteen themes. As shown, the most popular issues in the 1998–2002 elections include education, health, jobs and infrastructure, Medicare, Social Security, and taxes, each of which constitute about 10 to 15 percent of the issue appeals.

Ultimately, though, the unit of interest is the candidate rather than the appeal, so I aggregate these data up to the level of individual candidates. When I do so, two important findings emerge about the scope of candidates' agendas. First, nearly all discuss issues in their ads. Indeed, only 5 of the 391 House winners and 1 of the 84 Senate winners ran advertisements that were completely devoid of substantive content. Second, most candidates have fairly focused agendas. The average House candidate discussed between four and five of the eighteen issues in the scheme (with a range of

[9] Differences between the coders were rare, and most that did exist were the result of one coder missing an issue that the others identified rather than disagreements about the appropriate category for a claim. Findings about the relative prominence of various issues correspond closely to Sides' (2006) results, offering a confirmation of the validity of the coding procedures.

[10] I define an "appeal" as discussion of an issue within an ad. If an ad discussed the same issue at two different points in the text, that counts as a single appeal.

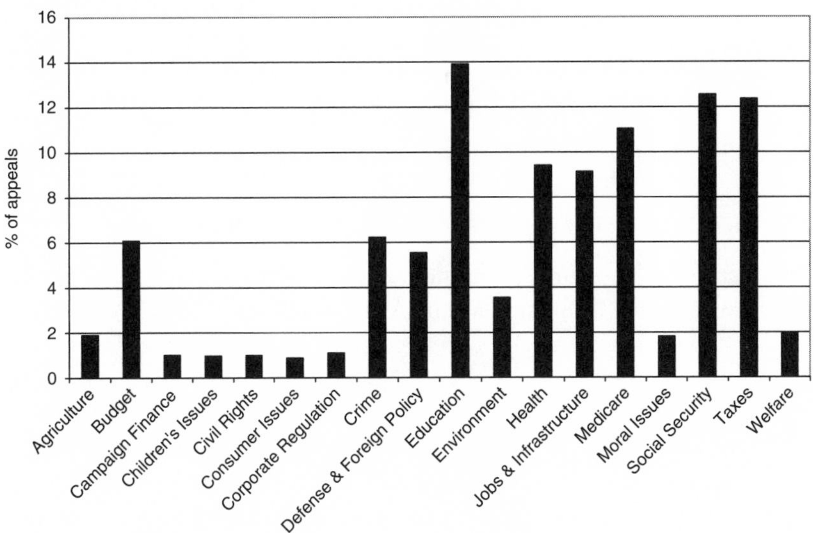

FIGURE 3.1 Percentage of Appeals by Issue
Note: The figure presents the overall proportion of campaign appeals devoted to each of the eighteen issues in the scheme across all election years and by candidates for both chambers.

0–10 issues), and the average Senate candidate discussed between seven and eight (with a range of 0–13 issues).[11]

What, though, of the content of these agendas? Is there a broad distribution of themes, or do candidates coalesce around the same small set of issues? The aggregate results for issue appeals in Figure 3.1 suggest that the answer lies somewhere in the middle, and, as demonstrated in Table 3.2, the same pattern does indeed hold at the level of candidates. This table presents the number of House and Senate winners who raised each of the issues in the scheme, as well as the percentage of Democrats and Republicans who did so. These findings indicate that there is considerable variation in the content of agendas; all eighteen issues are raised by at least

[11] Importantly, there is little evidence that differences in the cost of advertising across media markets lead to sizable differences in the size of candidates' agendas. Data on media market costs in 1998 and 1999 (provided by Daron Shaw) indicate that the average cost per 100 points ranges from about $3,000 to about $90,000 (for New York City, though that is a clear outlier, as the next most expensive market is San Francisco–Oakland–San Jose, at about $55,000). However, when I compare agenda size of candidates in the top and bottom quartiles of media market cost, I find a difference of only about 1 issue; those in the most expensive markets average 3.9 issues, and those in the least expensive average 4.8 (the medians are 4 and 5, respectively), and there is considerable variation within these groups.

TABLE 3.2 *Campaign Attention to Issues*

Issue	# of House Candidates	# of Senate Candidates	% of Democrats	% of Republicans	Partisan Difference?
Agriculture	42	23	12	16	t = −1.21
Budget	134	41	36	40	t = −.73
Campaign Finance	27	6	12	4	t = 2.76***
Children's Issues	16	13	9	5	t = 1.74*
Civil Rights	6	9	5	2	t = 1.34
Consumer Issues	17	10	11	2	t = 3.52***
Corporate Regulation	28	10	10	7	t = .96
Crime	120	41	44	29	t = 3.26***
Defense & Foreign Policy	101	44	24	36	t = −2.93***
Education	254	70	72	67	t = 1.33
Environment	73	33	23	23	t = .17
Health	178	65	68	42	t = 5.66***
Jobs & Infrastructure	185	51	48	53	t = −1.07
Medicare	207	63	59	58	t = .31
Moral Issues	40	17	15	11	t = 1.09
Social Security	237	60	62	66	t = −.80
Taxes	207	64	46	67	t = −4.76***
Welfare	39	26	12	17	t = −1.53

Note: The cells present the number of House and Senate candidates who raised each issue and the percentage of Democrats and Republicans who did so. Differences for the latter were assessed using independent samples t-tests.
*** = p < .01; ** = p < .05; * = p < .10.

a handful of candidates, and no single issue dominates. At the same time, there is a clear difference in the relative popularity of issues, with some mentioned by a majority of candidates and others receiving substantially less attention. In fact, with a couple of exceptions, it is fairly easy to break out the issues into two groups; relatively popular issues that are raised by between one-third and two-thirds of candidates and less popular issues that are mentioned by about one in ten.

Equally important, the results also show that there is substantial variation *within* the agendas of Democrats and Republicans, so it is not the case that the overall pattern of distribution is produced solely by winners from the two parties highlighting different issues. As should be expected, though, there are also some important differences in the content of Democrats' and Republicans' priority themes. Republicans are more likely than Democrats to have highlighted defense and taxes, a finding that is readily explainable since these are both themes that studies of partisan issue ownership (e.g., Petrocik 1996; Sides 2006) have shown to be "owned" by the Republican Party.[12] The pattern for Democrats is a bit more complicated. Their greater tendency to discuss children's issues, consumer issues, and health care is in line with issue ownership expectations. They are also more likely to raise campaign finance and government reform, which is understandable given their status as the minority party in House across all these elections (and the Senate in some of them), since that status may have provided incentives for criticizing the status quo. However, they also talk about crime more frequently do than their Republican counterparts, and this is an issue that historically has been owned by the GOP. Sides (2006) shows, though, that in recent years the Republican advantage on crime has almost disappeared (413–14; see also Holian 2004; Sulkin, Moriarty, and Hefner 2007). Moreover, many of the appeals about crime across these elections focus on school safety and gun control, dimensions of the issue that align more closely with Democrats' priorities.

Finally, as is illustrated in Figure 3.2, which presents the percentage of winning candidates in each of the three election years who raised each issue, campaign agendas are also quite diffuse *across* election years, so the aggregate patterns are not a function of concentrated (but different) agendas in each year. Of course, this diffusion of agendas across elections does not mean that there are no important changes in the relative salience of issues from year to year. For example, it is clear that issues such as the budget and crime waned in importance across this time period, while attention to Medicare (particularly provisions regarding prescription drug coverage) increased.[13] Not surprisingly, the issue with the sharpest change from one election to the next is defense and foreign policy. It was highlighted by 18 percent of candidates in the 1998 and 2000 elections, but in 2002, in response to the terrorist attacks of September 11, 2001, 58 percent of

[12] Issue ownership perceptions are tapped by survey questions that ask respondents to report whether they think one party or the other does a better job at "handling" the issue (Petrocik 1996).

[13] Of course, these changes are not fully independent of one another. Because candidates have fairly focused agendas, a shift in attention toward one issue often means a shift away from another (see Jones 1994; Jones and Baumgartner 2005).

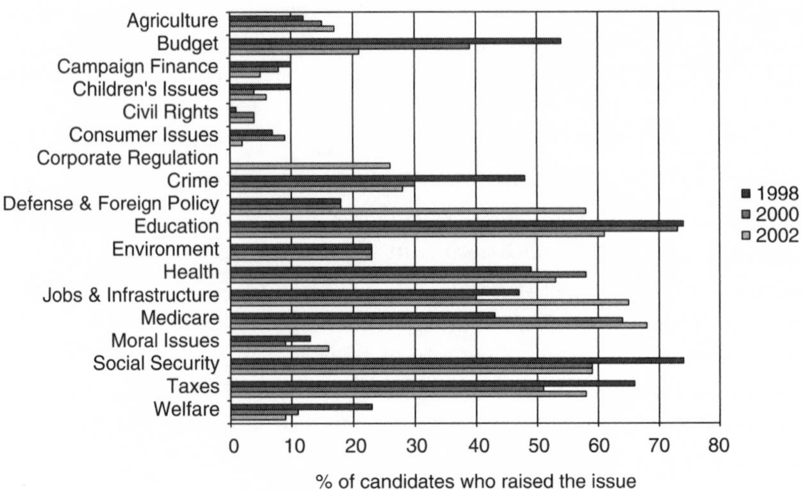

FIGURE 3.2 Relative Attention to Issues across Elections
Note: The figure presents the proportion of candidates in each election year who raised each issue.

candidates discussed it. The 2002 election also saw corporate regulation hit the agenda in response to Enron and other associated scandals. In fact, that issue was so salient in 2002 (one-quarter of candidates raised it, and none had done so in previous years), I decided that it merited its own category. To account for the effects that year-to-year variation in issue salience could have on follow-through (i.e., are candidates who raise an issue when it is less salient more or less likely to pursue it in office than those who jump on the bandwagon to talk about it when it becomes highly salient?), I include controls for election year in all of the analyses.

That candidates regularly raise issues and have focused agendas but talk about different themes provides an important backdrop for understanding promise making and promise keeping. If substantive issues were rarely discussed, it would be difficult to study follow-through, and if all candidates raised all of the issues (or if they all highlighted the same subset), there would be no meaningful variation to explore. Focused agendas may be due in part to the limitations on time and space presented by ads, but there is also evidence that they are a component of a broader communication strategy that candidates pursue in order to connect with voters. As Senator Wyche Fowler (D-GA), whose (ultimately unsuccessful) 1992 reelection campaign Fenno (1996) followed, explained:

One of the things I'm working on now is to take the twelve things I could talk about and reduce them to three things I will talk about (175).... One of the reasons I have the trouble I have is because when I talk I say whatever comes into my head and I end up being all over the ballpark. I know the most successful politicians are those who boil everything down to three things and repeat them over and over again.... Elect me and I'll do them one, two, three.... I've never been able to do that. (177)

In the next chapter, I explore in more detail *how* candidates narrow their choices to select the small set of priorities they will discuss in their campaigns, but for present purposes, the tasks are to establish what those priorities are and to identify the types of language each candidate uses when talking about them. Thus, after having coded all of the substantive issues raised by each winning representative and senator in his or her ads, I conducted a second round of content analysis of how each issue was discussed. In particular, did the candidate mention his or her own views, criticize the opponent, or both? Were the appeals vague or did he or she offer specifics? Was there a reference to past actions or future plans (or both, or neither)?[14]

To identify the tone and referent of appeals, I coded two dummy variables for each issue appeal in an ad: whether or not the candidate referenced himself or herself and whether or not the opponent was mentioned, either by name or by a term such as "my opponent."[15] There is some variation across issue categories, but in all cases, the vast majority of appeals (between ~70–100 percent) mention the sponsoring candidate's views. Discussion of the opponent occurs more rarely, in about 20 to 25 percent of appeals. The clear outlier is moral issues (including topics such as abortion and gay marriage); over half of House and Senate candidates' appeals about this theme criticize their opponents. This is because discussion on this issue, although fairly atypical, actually comes closest to meeting the ideal espoused by those interested in increasing the informational value of campaign discourse: candidates who raise it tend to present their own positions and then contrast them with those of their opponent.[16]

To code the specificity of appeals, I analyze the amount of detail provided in each and categorize all issue claims as either specific or vague. I define vague claims as those that merely state that an issue is

[14] Each of the issue appeals was coded by four coders, with levels of agreement on referent, specificity, and past/future ranging from 80 percent to >90 percent, depending on the issue.

[15] All claims were coded as referring to the candidate unless the only language about the issue was clearly directed solely at the opponent.

[16] For this reason, claims about moral issues also tend to be more specific. Whether or not these depictions of the opponent's positions are accurate is, of course, a separate question.

important or that the candidate cares about it, while specific claims offer more elaboration, often by taking a position, proposing or discussing a plan for dealing with the issue, or highlighting a contribution the candidate has made. For example, in the "health" category in the 2000 House elections, vague claims include those such as "She is a champion for health care" (Corrine Brown, D-FL) or "Fighting for ... healthcare reform" (David Bonior, D-MI). Specific claims include assertions such as the following: "I helped write the Children's Health Program and today 11,000 West Virginia children have healthcare that didn't before. That's a commitment to helping people I'll take to Congress" (Shelley Moore Capito, R-WV); or "Every family should have insurance that will cover serious illness in their family. I strongly favor a PBR [Patients' Bill of Rights] that makes it clear that doctors and patients are going to make the decisions about your healthcare" (Richard Gephardt, D-MO).

These examples are all claims candidates made about themselves, but they highlight that it is also important to think about separating the specificity of a claim from its referent and tone. As Geer's (2006) study of presidential campaign ads showed, negative appeals are more likely to provide specifics because effective criticisms of an opponent must be backed up with hard evidence. Thus, in addition to coding the overall specificity of a candidate's discussion of an issue in a particular ad, I also code the specificity of only those parts of the appeal that reference the candidates themselves.

My results show that the proportion of specific claims for House candidates' appeals ranges from 37 to 86 percent, depending on the issue. Senate appeals fall in a similar range, from 46 to 89 percent. Social Security anchors the low end for both House and Senate candidates, with moral issues on the high end for House candidates and children's issues on the high end for Senate candidates. Because the volume of claims about the sponsor greatly outweigh those about the opponent, the proportions and the relative ranking of issues for the "specific claims about oneself" measure do not change much from those for the overall specificity variable. However, these differences may matter at the individual level, so I use them as the measure of specificity in the analyses that follow.

The final rhetorical feature of interest is whether candidates reference the past or the future when talking about an issue. Coding for this is based solely on the tense of the actual language used and so is straightforward. However, several points are worth noting: these codes focus only on claims candidates make about themselves,[17] claims about the past or future can be either vague or specific (e.g., "I fought/I'll fight to improve education" versus "I voted for/I'll vote for No Child Left Behind"), and it is possible for a single ad appeal to contain both a claim about the past *and* one about the future. Consider, for instance, Senator Jeff Sessions' (R-AL) ad, "Seniors," which aired during his 2002 reelection campaign. About Medicare, he said:

> I'm going to preserve and strengthen Medicare. Medicare is critical for seniors. It's been of eminent importance for my family .... We're going to see an increase, but we are going to develop a prescription drug plan. I voted for a $300 billion plan to fund prescription drugs to drive down the cost for everyone ....

His claims that he is going to preserve Medicare and develop a prescription plan constitute an appeal about the future, and his reference to a previous vote on prescription drugs constitutes an appeal about the past, so this ad would receive a value of 1 for both rhetorical features. More often, though, claims about an issue discuss neither past actions nor future intentions. For House candidates, the proportion of "past" appeals about issues ranges from 0 to 30 percent and future appeals from 0 to 20 percent. For the Senate, the range is similar, from 7 to 24 percent for past appeals and 0 to 26 percent for future appeals.

CHARACTERIZING CAMPAIGN AGENDAS

The discussion thus far has focused on the proportion of appeals that reflect a particular rhetorical feature. Figure 3.3 summarizes these appeals data when they are aggregated up to the level of *candidates*. The typical House winner raises four or five issues, about 40 percent reference their opponents on at least one of the issues they discuss, about 90 percent make a specific appeal about at least one of their issues (though, depending on the issue, between one-fifth and two-thirds make only vague appeals), 44 percent make a reference to past actions, and 34 percent reference the future. Senators have larger campaign agendas (seven to eight issues on average), are somewhat more likely to mention their opponents (about 50

[17] This is because, as with specificity, I am interested in what the nature of candidates' appeals about themselves signal about their future activity. In addition, my initial rounds of coding revealed that very few winners discussed past actions of their opponents on an issue (largely because the vast majority of winners are incumbents) and virtually none talked about what their opponent would do in the future.

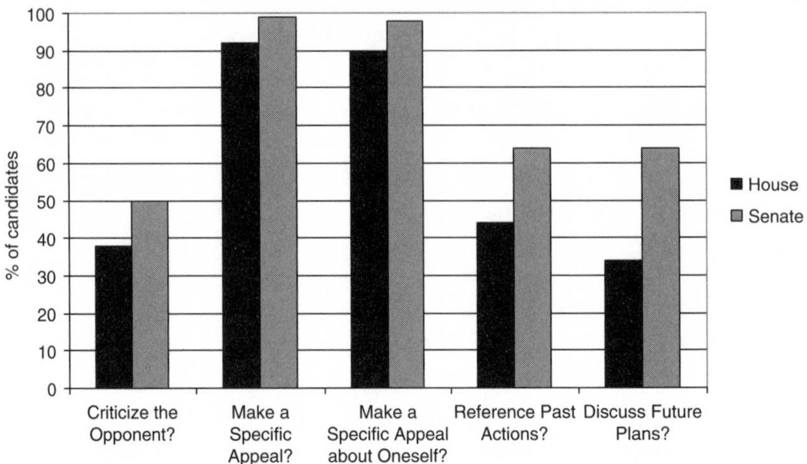

FIGURE 3.3 Rhetorical Features of Candidates' Campaign Appeals
Note: The figure presents the percentage of candidates who criticized their opponents, made a specific appeal, made a specific appeal about themselves, referenced past actions, or discussed future plans on at least one of their campaign issues.

percent do so on at least one of the issues in their agendas), and are considerably more likely to offer specific appeals (rates of specificity by issue range from 67 percent for Social Security to 100 percent for children's issues, though the latter are mentioned by only twelve candidates) and to reference the past and the future (about two-thirds of candidates do so on at least one of their issues).

I first derive the set of dichotomous variables for each candidate for each issue. (That is, did the candidate raise the issue? If so, did he or she mention himself or herself, the opponent, or both? Was there at least one specific appeal made about the issue? Was that appeal in reference to the candidate? Was there at least one claim that discussed the past? The future?) I then calculate the relative amount of candidates' advertising that included each of these features. For the proportion of advertising devoted to an issue, I use two measures. The first is simply the percentage of a candidate's ad airings that mentioned the issue.[18] For instance, in 2002, Representative Adam Smith (D-WA) produced two ads that aired a total of 455 times. His agenda consisted of three issues: defense and foreign policy, health care,

[18] Because there is substantial variation in how often each of the ads a candidate produces is aired, the total number of airings, not the total number of ads, is the appropriate denominator here.

and jobs and infrastructure. Both of his ads discussed jobs and infrastructure, so 100 percent of his ad airings did so. However, he raised health care and defense and foreign policy in only one of the ads, and that ad aired 276 times, so 61 percent (276 of 455) of his airings featured these two issues.

The second measure, what I call "advertising time," adapted from Sides (2006), more directly captures the relative place of each issue within a candidate's agenda. It takes into account both how many times ads that discussed a particular issue ran, as well as how many other issues were discussed in those ads (because an ad that is devoted entirely to a single issue reflects more discussion of that issue than an ad that discusses multiple issues) and sums to 100 for each candidate, allowing for comparisons across candidates and issues. For example, the ad that featured all three of Smith's issues aired 276 times and the ad that discussed only jobs and infrastructure aired 179 times, so the total size of his "agenda space" is 1,007 issue airings (179 + [276 * 3]). His advertising time would be 45 percent for jobs and infrastructure ([276+179]/1,007) and 27 percent for defense and for health (276/1,007).

Finally, the proportions for rhetorical features utilized in discussing an issue are calculated by taking the total number of ad airings about the issue as the denominator and the number of ad airings on the issue that include the feature of interest as the numerator. However, because the number of unique ads produced tends to be quite low, particularly for House candidates,[19] it is common for an issue to be discussed in only a single ad, so these percentages tend to be bimodal, with a high proportion of scores falling at 0 percent and 100 percent. As such, in analyses of the relationship between the rhetorical features of appeals and follow-through, I focus on the dichotomous measures (i.e., whether the feature was present or absent).

CODING LEGISLATIVE AGENDAS

Candidates' appeals form the measure of promise *making*, and the target of promise *keeping* is the content of their agendas in office, so I code legislative activities using the same issue scheme. I began by compiling lists of all of the bills and resolutions introduced and cosponsored by each sampled representative and senator in the term preceding and following

[19] The mean number of ads per candidate is 3.7 for the House and 9.1 for the Senate, with medians of 3 and 8.

the campaign of interest.[20] I obtained lists of bill introductions from the Congressional Bills Project and lists of resolutions and cosponsorships from the Library of Congress's THOMAS site. In all, the representatives in the sample made a total of 4,412 bill and joint resolution introductions and 87,644 cosponsorships, whereas senators introduced 8,294 measures and cosponsored 41,132.

As the first step of the content analysis of these activities, I assigned an issue code to each of the 41,819 bills and joint resolutions introduced in the 105th to 108th Houses and the 105th to 110th Senates.[21] The categories were identical to the eighteen used for campaign appeals, and I added an additional category for "governmental operations" matters that were procedural rather than policy-relevant. After all of the introductions were coded, the issue category for the "parent" introduction was then assigned to the corresponding cosponsorships made by each of the sampled representatives. Finally, I aggregated up to the level of the individual legislator to determine how many activities each undertook on each issue.

The results indicate that the typical representative in the sample introduces about 11 measures per term, 9 of which are policy-relevant (i.e., not related to governmental operations matters), and cosponsors about 221 measures, 203 of which are policy-relevant. Senators are more active, making about 83 policy-relevant introductions and 458 policy-relevant cosponsorships (out of a total of about 101 intros and 501 cosponsorships) across their six-year terms. These activities tend to be spread across a number of issue areas, with the average representative introducing in about five of the eighteen areas (with a range of 0–18) and cosponsoring in seventeen (with a range of 11–18). The average senator introduces in about eleven of the eighteen areas (with a range of 3–18) and cosponsors in seventeen (with a range of 13–18).

The content of legislators' behavior across introductions and cosponsorships is highly related – those who introduce the most measures on an issue also tend to cosponsor the most. Indeed, when I correlate the percentage of their introductions devoted to each issue with the percentage of their cosponsorships on it, I find significant ($p < .05$) relationships for sixteen of the eighteen issues for the House and fourteen of the eighteen

[20] Three hundred and five of the 391 representatives and 54 of the 84 senators in the sample were also in office in the congress preceding the campaign of study. Their previous activity is investigated in the next chapter in the analysis of candidates' rhetorical strategies.

[21] The initial categories provided by the Congressional Bills Project were the starting point for these codes, but all measures were individually recoded into the new scheme.

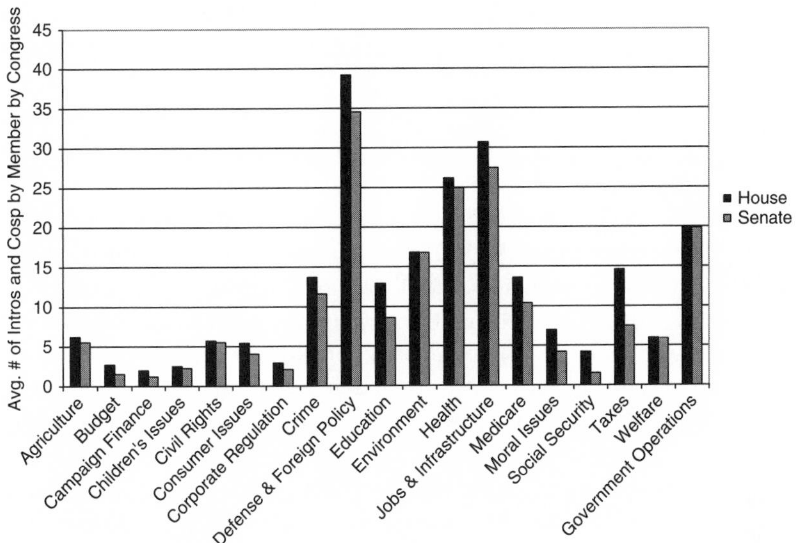

FIGURE 3.4 Legislative Activity by Category
Note: The figure presents the average number of introductions and cosponsorships made by each representative or senator on each issue in every two-year congress.

for the Senate.[22] Thus, combining them into a single measure of activity is justifiable, particularly for the preliminary exploratory analyses.

Figure 3.4 illustrates the average volume of activity on each issue (introductions plus cosponsorships) for the sampled representatives and senators. For the sake of comparability, I have divided the totals for the Senate by three, so that they are by individual sessions of Congress. Thus, although overall volumes of activity are higher for the Senate, it is clear from the figure that during the typical two-year congress, the average representative engages in more activity per issue than the average senator. The results also demonstrate that the overall volume of activity on any given issue tends to be quite low – often between about five and fifteen activities. This will become important as a baseline in evaluating the magnitude of any promise-keeping effects.

[22] The correlations for the House range from .12 and .40 and for the Senate from .12 to .63. The issues for which the relationships are not significant are those such as campaign finance and Social Security, where the overall number of introductions is quite low. The relatively low introduction counts across issues for representatives also explain why the correlations tend to be higher for senators.

ASSESSING THE LINKAGES BETWEEN CAMPAIGN APPEALS AND LEGISLATIVE ACTIVITY

With both pieces of the promise-keeping puzzle collected and coded, I can now assess the relationship between legislators' campaign appeals and their policy activity. My initial investigations focus on whether there are indeed linkages between the two, whether the extent of these linkages differs across the chambers, and whether they vary with the type of language used in the appeal (i.e., positive or negative, specific or vague, etc.).

I begin with some very simple regression analyses, presented in Table 3.3. Each of the eighteen issues is analyzed separately, and the dependent variable in each of the models is the proportion of legislators' agendas (i.e., of their policy-relevant introductions and cosponsorships) devoted to a particular issue. The independent variables include a dummy variable for whether or not the legislator had mentioned the issue in the previous election and controls for election year.[23] Thus, if the dummy variable is positive and significant, it indicates that legislators who had raised the issue in their previous campaigns were more active on it in office than those who did not. (More specifically, the coefficients reflect the difference in the proportion of legislative agendas devoted to an issue for representatives or senators who had raised it in their campaigns versus those who had not.) I intentionally limit my use of controls at this stage because my goal is to approximate the signal the typical voter receives from a campaign.[24] In other words, by observing what candidates say in their ads and considering little else about their predispositions, can we predict their relative activity on issues in office?

The results reveal that the answer to that question depends upon the chamber one is considering. For the House, evidence of linkages between campaign and legislative agendas is quite obvious. For fifteen of the eighteen issues, those who raised the issue in their previous campaigns

[23] Because many members of the House of Representatives appear in the sample in multiple election years, in those models, I cluster the standard errors on the legislator. For the Senate, I limit the analyses to the seventy-nine in the sample who served a full term. For both, the analyses for corporate regulation are limited to the 2002 election sample (since that is the first year in which the issue was raised in campaigns).

[24] This choice also means that it is unlikely that these models will explain all or most of the variation in legislative attention to an issue, since they purposefully omit other factors that could influence this attention. Thus, the relatively low adjusted R^2 values are not surprising. In the next chapter, I move beyond testing for signaling to assess the independent effect of campaigns on activity.

TABLE 3.3 *Linkages between Campaign Appeals and Legislative Action*

	Mention Issue?	2000 Election	2002 Election	Constant
House				
Agriculture (N = 371; Adj. R^2 = .09)	1.89***	−1.10***	−1.05***	3.72
	(.46)	(.29)	(.31)	(.29)
Budget (N = 376; Adj. R^2 = .03)	.47***	−.21	.13	1.35
	(.18)	(.15)	(.17)	(.17)
Campaign Finance (N = 370; Adj. R^2 = .21)	.03	−.04	−.99***	1.35
	(.15)	(.12)	(.09)	(.08)
Children's Issues (N = 368; Adj. R^2 = .10)	.68**	−.44***	−.27***	1.30
	(.27)	(.08)	(.10)	(.07)
Civil Rights (N = 368; Adj. R^2 = .05)	2.68***	−.60***	.15	2.51
	(.85)	(.16)	(.23)	(.18)
Consumer Issues (N = 368; Adj. R^2 = .06)	.80*	−.62***	−.83***	2.93
	(.41)	(.18)	(.21)	(.17)
Corporate Regulation (N = 121; Adj. R^2 = .02)	.39	–	–	1.61
	(.25)			(.12)
Crime (N = 373; Adj. R^2 = .15)	.76***	1.21***	2.52***	5.04
	(.28)	(.27)	(.29)	(.21)
Defense & Foreign Policy (N = 371 Adj. R^2 = .09)	1.49*	2.45***	3.18***	15.44
	(.82)	(.51)	(.73)	(.46)
Education (N = 384; Adj. R^2 = .02)	.77**	.28	−.15	−.15
	(.32)	(.29)	(.32)	(.32)
Environment (N = 374; Adj. R^2 = .18)	3.24***	−1.18***	−2.88***	8.59
	(.68)	(.43)	(.42)	(.31)
Health (N = 374; Adj. R^2 = .07)	2.24***	−.69	−.88	10.82
	(.47)	(.44)	(.54)	(.42)
Jobs & Infrastructure (N = 382; Adj. R^2 = .14)	.93**	−2.54***	−3.70***	6.12
	(.42)	(.44)	(.49)	(.28)
Medicare (N = 380; Adj. R^2 = .04)	.72**	−.06	−1.14***	6.12
	(.33)	(.29)	(.35)	(.28)
Moral Issues (N = 371; Adj. R^2 = .15)	1.59*	1.47***	3.69***	2.26
	(.88)	(.27)	(.45)	(.23)
Social Security (N = 381; Adj. R^2 = .06)	.19*	.07	−.46***	2.03
	(.11)	(.12)	(.12)	(.12)
Taxes (N = 381; Adj. R^2 = .10)	2.90***	1.99	1.89	5.17
	(.50)	(.47)	(.47)	(.45)
Welfare (N = 371; Adj. R^2 = .02)	−.07	−.39***	−.33**	2.91
	(.18)	(.13)	(.16)	(.10)

TABLE 3.3 (*cont.*)

	Mention Issue?	2000 Election	2002 Election	Constant
Senate				
Agriculture	1.26**	−1.44**	−1.61**	3.88
(N = 74; Adj. R^2 = .12)	(.62)	(.72)	(.71)	(.54)
Budget	.28	−.14	.48*	.76
(N = 76; Adj. R^2 = .08)	(.22)	(.26)	(.27)	(.24)
Campaign Finance	.01	−.015	−.05	.70
(N = 74; Adj. R^2 = −.04)	(.26)	(.17)	(.18)	(.13)
Children's Issues	.76***	−.44*	.14	1.14
(N = 73; Adj. R^2 = .14)	(.27)	(.25)	(.25)	(.19)
Civil Rights	−.40	−.26	−.38	3.08
(N = 72; Adj. R^2 = −.02)	(.59)	(.46)	(.46)	(.33)
Consumer Issues	1.49***	−.16	−.65*	2.27
(N = 74; Adj. R^2 = .18)	(.41)	(.34)	(.34)	(.25)
Corporate Regulation	−.48*	–	–	1.29
(N = 26; Adj. R^2 = .09)	(.26)			(.16)
Crime	−.10	.75	.11	6.62
(N = 77; Adj. R^2 = −.03)	(.73)	(.88)	(.88)	(.79)
Defense & Foreign Policy	1.61	2.06	2.57*	17.55
(N = 77; Adj. R^2 = .05)	(1.12)	(1.33)	(1.34)	(1.08)
Education	.59	.41	.64	3.81
(N = 79; Adj. R^2 = −.02)	(.67)	(.59)	(.61)	(.72)
Environment	1.84*	−.55	−.73	9.29
(N = 77; Adj. R^2 = .01)	(1.02)	(1.22)	(1.21)	(.96)
Health	1.01	1.93	1.89	11.10
(N = 78; Adj. R^2 = .02)	(1.19)	(1.18)	(1.17)	(1.23)
Jobs & Infrastructure	1.23	−.32	−1.36	15.79
(N = 76; Adj. R^2 = .00)	(1.00)	(1.18)	(1.17)	(1.07)
Medicare	1.22*	.29	−.24	4.57
(N = 78; Adj. R^2 = .01)	(.68)	(.70)	(.72)	(.65)
Moral Issues	−.56	−.69	−.04	3.42
(N = 74; Adj. R^2 = −.02)	(.81)	(.81)	(.81)	(.60)
Social Security	.05	−.56***	−.46***	1.21
(N = .76; Adj. R^2 = .12)	(.15)	(.17)	(.17)	(.16)
Taxes	1.17*	−1.11	−.27	4.29
(N = 78; Adj. R^2 = .05)	(.66)	(.70)	(.68)	(.74)
Welfare	.54	−.16	.30	3.06
(N = 73; Adj. R^2 = .09)	(.40)	(.44)	(.45)	(.37)

Note: Cell entries are ordinary least squares (OLS) regression coefficients with standard errors in parentheses. Separate models were estimated for each issue. The dependent variable in each is the percentage of each legislator's agenda devoted to that issue.
*** = $p < .01$; ** = $p < .05$; * = $p < .10$.

devoted significantly more attention to it in Congress than those who did not.[25] For only three issues (campaign finance, corporate regulation, and welfare) is campaign discussion *not* associated with higher subsequent activity. For all others, including some that were very popular and salient (e.g., education, Social Security, Medicare, health) and some that were mentioned only rarely (e.g., children's issues, civil rights, consumer issues), those who discussed the issue were significantly more active on it.

For the Senate, though, the situation is different, with much less clear linkages between appeals and activity. Although most of the coefficients are positive, for only six of the eighteen issues (agriculture, children's issues, consumer issues, environment, Medicare, and taxes) does having mentioned an issue serve as a significant predictor of subsequent activity. For a seventh issue, corporate regulation, those who had raised the issue were actually *less* active on it than those who did not.

Given that we are examining results for eighteen issues across two chambers, the table of regression results is somewhat unwieldy. The patterns are clearer when the results are summarized in graph form, as they are in Figure 3.5. This figure shows the coefficient on mentioning each issue (represented by the dots) and the 90 percent confidence interval (presented by the lines). Thus, if the full interval falls above zero, the coefficient is positive and significant, and if it falls below zero, it is negative and significant. (If it crosses the zero line, the relationship for that issue is not statistically significant.) This enables us to compare at a glance the differences for the House and Senate. We see that the effects that do exist are of similar magnitude across the chambers, but that the relationship between appeals and activity is more systematic in the House.

Four things should be noted about these findings. First, the patterns are quite robust. They hold with a number of other operationalizations of the dependent variable (i.e., raw counts of activity, proportions of total activity rather than just policy-relevant activity) and a variety of different

[25] The *N*s vary across the models because of the availability of only partial advertising data for some candidates (i.e., those who aired advertisements, but had one or more storyboards missing from the Wisconsin Advertising Project Archives). For the House, I have full advertising data for 365 candidates and partial advertising data for 26, and for the Senate, I have full data for 77 and partial data for 7. Those for whom I have only partial data are included in the analyses when appropriate. For example, if a candidate produced two ads and I have the storyboard for one where he or she discussed agriculture and budget, I can confidently say that the candidate raised those issues. However, I cannot say anything about discussion of other issues because I do not know the content of the missing storyboard. As such, that candidate would be included in analyses of agriculture and the budget, but excluded in analyses of other issues.

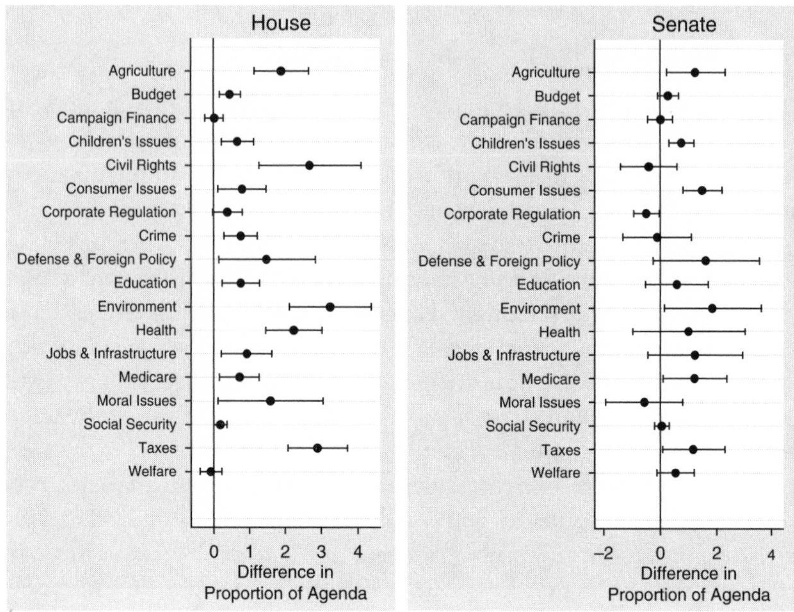

FIGURE 3.5 Comparing the Appeals–Activity Linkage in the House and Senate
Note: The figure summarizes the results from Table 3.3. The dots represent the coefficients on having mentioned an issue and the lines represent the 90 % confidence interval around those estimates.

specifications (controlling for party, for the total number of issues raised by the candidate, for the number of ads aired, etc.). Second, the links between appeals and activity that emerge are not just statistical regularities, but are also substantively meaningful in magnitude. At first glance, the percentage differences may seem small, but a one-point increase in the coefficient on having mentioned an issue amounts to about two additional activities on it for representatives and five for senators. Since the level of activity on any particular issue tends to be low, small shifts reflect a meaningful difference. Thus, for example, across a six-year term, the typical senator introduces or cosponsors about twelve measures on consumer issues, but those who had discussed consumer issues in their campaigns engage in about eight more activities on it than those who did not. Similarly, on average, representatives undertake about seventeen activities on the environment and twenty-six on health care, but those who mentioned these issues as candidates undertook about seven more activities on the environment and five on health.

Third, it is also important to underscore that the difference in the extent of the appeals–activity linkages between the House and Senate is not just a function of differences in the length of terms. For instance, one could argue that senators might start out their terms following through on their appeals at high rates, but over time events intercede and new issues arise, so they move on to other priorities. Thus, if we looked only at the first congress following an election, we might see similarly high levels of responsiveness for representatives and senators. However, this possibility is fairly easily dispatched with. Indeed, it turns out that the relationships between the content of appeals and the content of activity are more evident *later* in their terms. When I replicate the basic analysis in Table 3.3 broken out by congress, I find that in the first congress following the sampled senators' election or reelection, there are only two issues (children's issues and defense and foreign policy) for which legislators who had mentioned the issue were more active than those who had not. In the later two congresses, there are links for six issues (agriculture, children's issues, consumer issues, environment, Medicare, and taxes). Thus, the aggregate findings for the Senate are driven by late-term promise keeping, and at no time does the number of links for that chamber approximate that for the House. These results suggest that the differences in responsiveness between the chambers are "real" and not a function of formal institutional differences.

Fourth, although cosponsorships are undertaken far more frequently than introductions, the patterns are evident across both types of activities. When introductions and cosponsorships are analyzed separately, in total I find significant ($p < .10$) linkages for fifteen of the eighteen issues in the House and ten of the eighteen issues in the Senate. For the House, seven of the relationships between campaign discussion and subsequent activity (agriculture, crime, education, environment, Medicare, moral issues, and taxes) hold for both introductions and cosponsorships, with the remainder holding for cosponsorships only.[26] In the Senate, for two issues (consumer issues and children's issues), there are linkages for both introductions and cosponsorships; for four (agriculture, education, health, and Medicare), there are linkages for introductions but not cosponsorships; and for another three (budget, environment, and taxes), there are linkages for

[26] Percentages are not the most appropriate comparison for House introductions, since the denominators tend to be quite low. When I compare the raw volume of introductions and cosponsorships, I find eleven links for introductions and eleven for cosponsorships (Sulkin 2009b).

cosponsorships but not introductions.[27] Thus, relationships emerge both for relatively easy cosponsorships and for more effort-intensive introductions, and, for the Senate, such relationships are more widespread when introductions and cosponsorships are combined than when we consider either of them separately.

Normatively, these initial findings might be best characterized as heartening for the House, but somewhat disconcerting for the Senate. That a winning House candidate mentions an issue serves as a signal that he or she will be particularly active on it, but the same choice by a Senate candidate is a weaker indicator of his or her relative commitments. In the next chapter, I explore some explanations for these differences. Before doing so, though, it is useful to investigate variation in the signaling power of different types of appeals (i.e., positive versus negative, specific versus vague). Any potential differences across appeals are important in and of themselves for assessing the quality of campaign discourse and the role of campaigns in the representative process. In addition, to the extent that House and Senate candidates' appeals differ in a systematic way, this may also contribute to the aggregate chamber differences in follow-through on appeals.

THE EFFECTS OF RHETORICAL DIFFERENCES

The measure of campaign discussion in the models in Table 3.3 was a simple dummy variable for whether or not the candidate raised the issue. However, as I argued in Chapter 2, the strength of the linkages between campaign appeals and legislative activity may vary with the language that candidates employ when talking about issues. Using just the dichotomous indicator of discussion therefore could mask differences in the signaling power of appeals. My hypotheses about rhetorical differences were that claims that candidates make about themselves should serve as better indicators of their interests and later activity than claims that criticize the opponent, and that the linkages between appeals and legislative priorities could also vary with specificity, tense (i.e., referencing the past or future), and the prominence of an issue, although the directions of the expectations for these features was less clear.

To investigate these possibilities, I use the same basic models, but I vary the measure(s) of campaign discussion. For example, to determine whether there is a difference in the signaling power of positive versus negative

[27] Also, once again for corporate regulation, there is a significant negative relationship between mentioning the issue and subsequent activity on it.

appeals, I first replaced the dummy variable for having mentioned the issue at all with a dummy for having mentioned the issue in reference to oneself, and then with a dummy for having discussed the opponent on the issue. Unsurprisingly, because virtually all candidates mention themselves when talking about an issue, the first set of analyses yields the same results as those in Table 3.3; for fifteen issues in the House and six for the Senate, candidates who mentioned themselves in reference to the issue were subsequently more active on it in Congress than those who did not.

Using the "mention opponent" dummy variable, however, leads to a very different conclusion. For the Senate, there are significant linkages for only two issues: candidates who criticized their opponents on Medicare and consumer issues were more active on those issues in Congress. For the House, there are three significant linkages (for civil rights, defense and foreign policy, and consumer issues), but for consumer issues, the relationship is negative, such that candidates who attacked their opponents on the issue were *less* active on it than those who did not.

The conclusion here is clear. As expected, appeals that attack the opponent on an issue provide less information about candidates' legislative priorities than claims they make about themselves. For instance, winning House and Senate candidates who discuss their views on the environment are more active on it than those who do not discuss it, but just criticizing the opponent's positions or actions on environmental policy does *not* signal that the candidate himself or herself will be active on the issue.[28]

More generally, these results confirm that the appropriate starting place for assessing whether rhetorical features of claims matter is to control first for whether or not the candidate mentioned his or her views on an issue. Then we can incorporate indicators of the rhetorical feature of interest (e.g., specificity, prominence, etc.) into the models to determine whether they offer additional predictive power about legislators' subsequent levels of activity. As such, to explore more fully the relationship between rhetoric and follow-through, I begin with the models from Table 3.3, but in addition to the dummy for having mentioned an issue in reference to oneself, I add an indicator of whether the opponent was mentioned, whether the claim was specific, whether it referenced the past, whether it referenced the future, or how prominently the issue was featured. The

[28] This is not to say that negative appeals do not convey any information. Criticisms of the opponent may provide truthful assessments of his or her record or positions, and may even imply that the candidate will take the opposite position, but they do not indicate that the candidate intends to pursue the issue.

results from these analyses are summarized in Table 3.4. In the interest of space, and for ease of comparison, the table presents only the coefficient on the rhetorical feature of interest. Those that are statistically significant are presented in bold. As before, these coefficients reflect the difference in the proportion of candidates' subsequent agendas devoted to an issue for those who discussed the issue in one way versus those who discussed it in another.

The first column presents the findings for having mentioned the opponent. As shown, after including the control for whether a candidate mentioned himself or herself, the effects of discussing the opponent are even further dampened (i.e., relative to the results discussed previously). For both the House and Senate, there is only one significant relationship: among Senate candidates, those who criticize the opponent on Medicare are more active than those who do not, but, among House candidates, those who attack the opponent on consumer issues are less active on it than those who do not.

I use a similar approach to investigating whether the specificity of appeals matters. In these models, summarized in the second column of Table 3.4, the additional rhetorical variable of interest is a dummy for whether at least one of the appeals a candidate made about himself or herself on an issue was specific. The results show that, for House candidates, there are only two issues for which specificity serves as a predictor of activity above and beyond raising the issue. The two issues are children's issues and civil rights, which are among the least mentioned by candidates. For another two issues (moral issues and taxes), specificity is *negatively* related to follow-through, such that candidates who made specific appeals were less active than those who were vague. For the Senate, there is a similar pattern – three issues (consumer issues, jobs and infrastructure, and Medicare) for which specific claims signal higher levels of subsequent activity and two issues (agriculture and budget) for which specificity is negatively related to later attention.

For virtually all issues, then, variation in the specificity of appeals made by candidates has no relationship with their later activity. Thus, for instance, House candidates who discuss an issue such as crime are more active on it than those who do not, but laying out detailed plans for dealing with it does not serve as a stronger signal than just saying that one wants to "make our neighborhoods safer."[29] This is contrary to the conventional

[29] In Chapter 5, I explore whether candidates who make specific claims are more likely to introduce or cosponsor legislation that deals with the particular dimensions of the issue they raised. For now, though, my interest is in their volume of activity on an issue.

TABLE 3.4 *Effects of Rhetorical Features of Campaign Discussion*

	Opponent?	Specific?	Past?	Future?	% of Ads?	Ad Time?
House						
Agriculture	-.97(1.02)	-.33(1.05)	.38(1.06)	1.06(.89)	-.00(.01)	-.00(.05)
Budget	.37(.27)	-.60(.51)	-.15(.35)	.26(.33)	.01(.00)	**.02(.01)**
Campaign Finance	-.19(.23)	-.21(.28)	.07(.30)	–	**.01(.00)**	.01(.02)
Children's Issues	.17(.75)	**1.41(.32)**	.70(.52)	**.51(.30)**	.00(.01)	.01(.02)
Civil Rights	1.04(.99)	**3.62(1.22)**	–	.02(1.13)	-.01(.01)	-.02(.01)
Consumer Issues	**-.93(.42)**	-.57(1.89)	1.65(1.31)	**-1.57(.51)**	.01(.01)	.02(.01)
Corporate Regulation	.43(.60)	.30(.51)	.07(.48)	.02(.63)	.01(.01)	.01(.03)
Crime	.01(.45)	-.74(1.22)	-.69(.58)	.33(.69)	.00(.01)	-.02(.02)
Defense & Foreign Policy	3.67(2.30)	.85(1.44)	2.23(1.62)	.24(2.15)	-.02(.02)	-.02(.03)
Education	-.10(.52)	-.06(.47)	.43(.51)	.24(.61)	**.01(.01)**	**.03(.01)**
Environment	-.23(1.37)	-.83(1.33)	-.61(1.37)	**3.36(1.71)**	.01(.02)	.08(.05)
Health	-1.23(.82)	1.01(.80)	-.62(.96)	-.36(.96)	**.03(.01)**	**.05(.02)**
Jobs & Infrastructure	.58(.63)	.51(.60)	-.47(.83)	.31(1.03)	**.02(.01)**	.02(.01)
Medicare	.56(.63)	.62(.61)	.40(.56)	-.39(.53)	.01(.01)	.02(.02)
Moral Issues	.34(1.21)	**-5.61(3.04)**	2.00(1.85)	**-6.00(1.34)**	.02(.03)	.04(.03)
Social Security	.15(.17)	.05(.14)	.39(.24)	-.20(.15)	-.00(.00)	-.00(.01)
Taxes	-.27(.70)	**-1.49(.79)**	**-2.02(.81)**	.59(.82)	**.05(.01)**	.04(.03)
Welfare	-.51(.42)	-.07(.38)	-.37(.46)	**-1.00(.20)**	-.00(.01)	-.00(.02)
Senate						
Agriculture	-1.70(1.80)	**-2.08(1.24)**	-.18(1.40)	-1.97(1.36)	.04(.02)	.09(.07)
Budget	-.21(.33)	**-.95(.35)**	**-.70(.41)**	-.39(.36)	-.00(.01)	-.03(.03)
Campaign Finance	-.11(.36)	.91(.73)	.91(.73)	-.92(.85)	-.04(.10)	-.15(.27)
Children's Issues	-.21(.93)	–	.31(.55)	.01(.58)	.00(.01)	-.00(.03)
Civil Rights	1.11(1.71)	1.84(1.30)	-1.01(1.71)	–	.00(.04)	-.00(.07)
Consumer Issues	1.63(.98)	**2.20(.95)**	**2.10(.85)**	1.02(.91)	.01(.02)	.00(.04)

TABLE 3.4 (*cont.*)

	Opponent?	Specific?	Past?	Future?	% of Ads?	Ad Time?
Corporate Regulation	.38(.52)	−.12(.52)	.02(.52)	.54(.68)	.04(.05)	.08(.17)
Crime	−.21(1.02)	−2.19(2.27)	−.50(1.16)	1.12(1.26)	.01(.02)	.01(.06)
Defense & Foreign Policy	−.70(1.70)	−2.77(1.98)	−1.24(1.64)	1.77(1.74)	**.05(.03)**	.02(.05)
Education	.63(.65)	1.25(.95)	.73(.63)	.10(.59)	**.04(.01)**	.05(.04)
Environment	.37(1.40)	−3.13(3.26)	1.49(1.83)	.45(2.05)	**.08(.04)**	**.20(.08)**
Health	−.57(1.22)	2.61(1.87)	.90(1.41)	−.03(1.31)	.01(.03)	.01(.05)
Jobs & Infrastructure	−.38(1.30)	**2.16(1.25)**	1.81(1.74)	.67(1.28)	**.04(.03)**	.06(.05)
Medicare	**2.46(.74)**	**2.04(.90)**	**−1.38(.82)**	−.30(.76)	.00(.02)	.03(.05)
Moral Issues	−.95(1.23)	1.22(1.87)	1.84(2.19)	−.97(1.93)	.01(.05)	.10(.11)
Social Security	.18(.16)	.09(.17)	.04(.20)	−.13(.16)	.00(.01)	**.03(.02)**
Taxes	−.65(.61)	.10(.80)	.12(.69)	.03(.70)	.02(.02)	.04(.04)
Welfare	−.88(.88)	1.09(.68)	.71(.77)	−.09(1.16)	−.01(.03)	.02(.07)

Note: Cell entries are OLS regression coefficients with standard errors in parentheses. Separate models were estimated for each issue, with the dependent variable in each the percentage of legislators' agendas devoted to an issue. Independent variables include controls for election year and whether a candidate raised the issue in reference to himself or herself, plus the indicators of rhetoric noted at the top of each column. (For several, there were no candidates who made that type of appeal.) Bold indicates that the coefficient is significant at $p < .10$.

wisdom that specificity is a signal about candidates' sincerity and level of commitment to an issue, and suggests that the decision to be specific or vague is a function of other strategic considerations. I explore this hypothesis in more depth in the next chapter.

What about the tense used when candidates talk about issues? Does a claim about what a candidate *has done* in the past or *will do* in the future serve as signal about subsequent action? The analyses summarized in columns three and four are designed to answer these questions. In column three, the additional variable added to the model was a dummy for whether or not the candidate referenced the past on an issue, and in column four, it was for whether the candidate talked about the future. The basic conclusion that I draw from these analyses is that neither of these variables appears to be a strong predictor of post-campaign activity. For Senate candidates, having referenced a past action on an issue is a significant predictor of activity for three issues (budget, consumer issues, and Medicare), but for budget and Medicare, the effect is negative, such that candidates who discussed the past were less active on them than those who did not. For the House, there is one significant linkage, for taxes, but there again the relationship is negative.

It may not necessarily be a surprise that referencing the past is not a predictor of future activity, but it comes as more of one that making claims about what one *will* do also fails to offer much predictive power. For the Senate, there are no issues for which a discussion of future intentions is an indicator of activity above and beyond mentioning the issue. For the House, there are five significant linkages (for children's issues, consumer issues, environment, moral issues, and welfare), but for three of them, the relationship is negative. Candidates who talk about the future on consumer issues, moral issues, and welfare are less active on those issues than those who do not. In Chapter 4, I explore why discussing future plans is not linked to higher activity (i.e., above and beyond just mentioning the issue). One possibility is that candidates' decisions to invoke the future (or the past) are a function of their seniority or electoral status (i.e., as incumbents or challengers/open seat candidates), rather than the strength of their intentions to act.

There is one final feature of discussion to consider: the prominence given to an issue in a candidate's campaign discourse. This feature differs a bit from the others since it reflects not how a candidate talks about an issue, but the relative place of that issue in his or her overall campaign agenda. It seems reasonable to expect that candidates who devote more attention to an issue in their campaign might also devote more attention to it in office, though, as discussed in Chapter 2, relative prominence might be more a function of candidates' agenda size, the number of ads they air, and so on. Including a continuous measure of attention may also enable me to identify effects that I missed out on with the dichotomous indicator. Particularly for the Senate, where candidates discuss a larger set of issues, the latter may be too blunt a measure to capture the linkages between campaign and legislative priorities.

However, the results in the last two columns of Table 3.4 indicate that this is not the case. Column five summarizes the results of a series of models in which the measure of prominence is the percentage of a candidate's ad airings that feature an issue. In column six, the measure of prominence is the "advertising time" variable for each issue (which also takes into account the number of issues mentioned in each ad). As shown, there are some slight differences in the patterns between the two, with more relationships emerging for the percentage of airings measure (for five of the eighteen issues in the House and four in the Senate) than for the advertising time measure (three issues in the House and two in the Senate). Thus, although there is some tendency for those who feature an issue prominently to follow through at higher rates, overall, talking about an issue a lot does not serve as a stronger signal about later activity.[30]

For the House, this finding can once again be interpreted as normatively good. Just because a candidate does not feature an issue in all of her ads does not indicate that she is not sincere about actively pursuing it. Time and space constraints may mean that an issue can be discussed only in passing, but even this is enough to serve as a signal that it is a priority. For the Senate, however, the conclusion is more pessimistic, since taking into account the prominence of issues does not help to reconcile the relative lack of responsiveness to campaign appeals for winning candidates for that chamber. For most issues, even candidates who feature a particular issue prominently are no more active on it than their peers who focus on other issues.

CONCLUSIONS

What general conclusions should be drawn from the findings in this chapter? First, and perhaps most importantly, promise-keeping linkages

[30] If I use the prominence measures *instead* of the dichotomous measure (i.e., rather than in addition to it), only one more issue is significant (i.e., there are linkages between campaign appeals and legislative activity for seven issues rather than six).

are very widespread for the House, but are less so for the Senate. Put simply, at least when it comes to predicting legislators' agendas, House campaigns carry more information about winners' likely activity in office than do Senate campaigns. Second, for both chambers, variation in the way candidates talk about issues does not matter as much as the conventional wisdom might lead us to expect. Positive claims candidates make about their own interests in an issue do serve as stronger signals about the content of subsequent activity than do criticisms of the opponent, but specific appeals, references to past accomplishments, discussion of future plans, and prominent treatment of an issue do not offer additional information about winning candidates' likelihood of following through on that issue once in Congress. The next chapter addresses why.

4

Mechanisms Underlying Promise Keeping

Two important findings emerge from the analyses in Chapter 3. First, linkages between campaign appeals and legislative activity are widespread, but are more common among members of the House of Representatives than among senators. Second, for members of both chambers, certain types of appeals serve as stronger and more consistent signals about legislative activity than others. What produces these patterns?

To begin, it is useful to return to the causal story about the mechanisms underlying promise keeping that I outlined in the introductory chapters. My argument was that appeals should serve as signals about activity to the extent that they are a function of legislators' relative levels of interest in an issue. If legislators choose to focus their campaigns on those issues they particularly care about (and *only* those issues they particularly care about), then we should see strong links between the content of their campaign agendas and the content of their subsequent legislative agendas and, hence, high levels of promise keeping. If, however, they select some or all of their themes for reasons that are not connected to their interest in and commitment to these issues, then fewer relationships should emerge. Along the same lines, among the group of candidates who talk about an issue, variation in the types of appeals they make should offer additional information about their future activity only if choices about language (i.e., positive versus negative, specific versus vague) are related to the intensity of their interest in it.

To this point, I have not tested these hypotheses, nor have I detailed the assumptions behind them. Among the most important of these is that "interest" can be measured in a valid and meaningful way. My basic approach in this chapter will be to identify potential indicators of issue interest and then to assess their relationships with representatives' and senators' campaign appeals and their post-campaign legislative activity. My expectation is that measures of interest will do an equally good job of explaining legislators' policy-making activity in the House and Senate, but will be stronger predictors of House candidates' campaign appeals than Senate candidates'. For example, I anticipate that legislators' levels of interest in education policy should predict the amount of attention representatives and senators devote to education in office, and should explain whether or not a House candidate discusses education, but should *not* be linked to whether or not a Senate candidate does so. Similarly, given the patterns of findings in the previous chapter, I do not expect variation in interest in education to be what drives some of the candidates who talk about it to offer specific appeals, reference the past or the future, and so on.

MEASURING ISSUE INTEREST

How should we measure legislators' relative levels of interest in an issue? One option would be to ask them (i.e., "How important is issue X to you?"), but such self-reports present a number of problems for validity and pose challenges for data collection, particularly when one wants to look back to previous elections and congresses. In addition, in studying promise keeping, I am concerned with a particular type of "interest" – that which is manifested in some tangible way during a campaign and/or in office. If deep down a legislator cares about consumer issues, but never does or says anything about it, then this interest is peripheral to understanding the linkages between appeals and activity. The flip side of this definition is that "strategic" interest in an issue *does* count as interest. If the legislator who actually is most concerned about consumer issues instead talks about agriculture in her campaign and advocates for agricultural policy in office because she hails from a rural district, she has done what she implied she would do and thus has kept her promises.

As such, rather than asking legislators about their interests, a more appropriate and practical way of tapping them is to identify indicators of their behavior that should be correlated with their relative levels of commitment to an issue. For those who are incumbents, the strongest indicator is the extent of their past records on an issue. To build their careers, most legislators specialize, at least to some degree, so it is reasonable to claim that a legislator who has been particularly active in the past on an issue such as crime (i.e., as indicated by the percentage of his or her agenda in the previous term devoted to it) is more interested in the issue than one who has paid little or no attention to it. Of course, it is important to acknowledge that there is clear circularity to the reasoning here; I am assuming that legislators are interested in an issue because they have demonstrated that they are interested in the issue. For purposes of predicting the content of appeals and for assessing differences between the House and Senate, though, this circularity does not pose a problem, since I am not making a causal argument. Instead, I simply want to test the previously raised hypotheses raised by comparing the degree of association among interest, activity, and appeals for representatives versus senators and by assessing the relationships between interest and the nature of the rhetoric used in appeals.

Nonetheless, it is useful to supplement the past record measure with other indicators of legislators' likely interest in an issue that skirt this circularity problem a bit more, and so I also consider their previous committee assignments, their party identification, and characteristics of their constituencies. I expect that all other things equal, legislators who serve on committees that have jurisdiction over an issue should be more likely to be interested in it. Such interest could arise in several ways. It could be a simple signal about priorities because the legislator requested that particular committee, but it is also the case that legislators tend to become invested in the issues that their committees deal with, even if a committee was not originally their first choice (Fenno 1973). In the analyses that follow, the committee variable is a dummy for whether or not the legislator served on at least one committee with jurisdiction over a particular issue.[1]

Party should also be an indicator of interest because of the longstanding differences in the issue foci of Democrats and Republicans, deriving from their historical commitments and the concerns of their base constituencies (Petrocik 1996).[2] We might then expect party members to be more

[1] Committee jurisdictions do not always map easily on to the issue scheme I use here, so to determine which committees match which issues, I examined the patterns of referrals for introduced bills. If more than 20 percent of bills on an issue were referred to a given committee, I coded that as a committee that corresponded to the issue. Most issues were addressed in multiple committees. For each issue in the scheme, I noted whether the legislator served on a committee that had jurisdiction for that issue. Legislators received a code of one if they served on one or more relevant committees and zero if they did not serve on a committee dealing with the issue.

[2] Across the time period I examine, Democrats in both chambers devote more attention to civil rights, children's issues, consumer issues, health, Medicare, and welfare, and Republicans in both chambers devote more of their agendas to the budget, moral issues, and taxes. In addition, in the House, Democrats devote more attention to education and the

interested in pursuing issues that their party "owns." I assume, for instance, that the average Democrat is more interested in the environment than the average Republican, and the latter is more interested in defense and foreign policy than the former.

Finally, it is likely that legislators who have "high-demand" constituencies on particular issues should be more interested in those issues (Adler 2000; Adler and Lapinski 1997). For example, those who come from districts or states with large numbers of senior citizens should be more concerned about Medicare and Social Security policy than those who come from districts with few elderly residents, and those from largely rural constituencies should be more interested in agriculture than those from urban areas. In the analyses that follow, my indicators of constituency demand are drawn from 2000 Census data, which I use to identify characteristics that correspond to each of the issues in the scheme.[3] The measure for the agriculture, crime, and environment models is the percentage of the district or state that is rural/urban; for the children's issues and education models, the percentage of children under eighteen; for the civil rights model, the percentage of nonwhite residents; for the defense model, whether or not there is a military base in the district (for the House) and the percentage of armed forces personnel and veterans in the state (for the Senate); for the Medicare and Social Security models, the percentage of the district or state age sixty-five or older; for the jobs and infrastructure model, the percentage of the district in blue-collar and service professions; for the welfare model, the percentage below the poverty line; and for the budget, campaign finance, consumer issues, corporate regulation, and taxes models, the median income of the district or state (in thousands of dollars).[4]

If these measures of past record, committee and party affiliations, and constituency characteristics are indeed valid indicators of interest, then

environment than do their Republican colleagues, and the latter devote more attention to agriculture, corporate regulation, and jobs and infrastructure. Interestingly, in the House, it is Democrats who devote more attention to defense and foreign policy, but in the Senate, it is Republicans who do so. (Differences were assessed using paired samples t-tests, where the feature of interest is the proportion of legislators' agendas devoted to an issue. All differences are significant at $p < .10$.)

3 For the 1998 and 2000 election cycles, I use the 2000 data. The Census Bureau recalculated these district characteristics following redistricting, and I use these values for the 2002 election sample.

4 The fit between these characteristics and the issue category is more natural for some issues than for others (i.e., percentage senior citizens and Social Security/Medicare compared to median income and consumer issues), so it is likely that the strength of the relationships will vary.

they should be strong predictors of the content of legislators' congressional agendas. To confirm this, I conducted a series of ordinary least squares (OLS) regression analyses (with separate models for each of the eighteen issues), presented in Table 4.1. My dependent variable is the percentage of the sampled legislators' post-campaign legislative activity (introductions plus cosponsorships) devoted to an issue. Because the independent variables (i.e., indicators of preexisting interest) must be measured prior to the start of each term, the analyses are limited to the 305 House winners and 54 Senate winners who were incumbents running for reelection in the campaigns studied and so have previous records and committee affiliations.[5]

The results demonstrate convincingly that these measures of interest do a good job of predicting the content of legislators' activity in office. Perhaps unsurprisingly, activity in the previous term has the strongest and most consistent relationship with subsequent activity – there are significant linkages for sixteen of the eighteen issues in the Senate and all eighteen in the House, and, at the level of individual issues, the magnitude of these effects is relatively comparable across the chambers. (The coefficients reflect the effect of a 1 percentage point increase in previous legislative attention to an issue on the proportion of a legislator's agenda devoted to that issue in the next term.) Committee assignments offer additional predictive power for nine issues in the House and six in the Senate (for a seventh, there is a negative relationship), party is a significant explanatory factor for eleven issues in the House and ten in the Senate, and constituency characteristics are predictors for four issues in the House and three in the Senate.

Thus, as expected, representatives' and senators' policy-making activity is relatively *equally* predictable – the same indicators of interest explain activity in both chambers. Legislators' choices about attention allocation in their House and Senate activity are a function of their previous policy commitments, institutional assignments, partisan leanings, and the nature of their constituencies.[6] To determine whether my hypotheses about the mechanisms underlying promise keeping and the House–Senate difference in the strength of the linkages between appeals and activity are correct, I

[5] As noted before, some representatives appear in the sample in multiple election years. To account for this, I cluster the standard errors on the legislator. I also include controls for election year in both the models for the House and the Senate.

[6] These are, of course, correlated with one another, so if I analyzed them separately, more linkages with activity would appear. For instance, if constituency characteristics alone are included in the models, there are seven significant linkages for each chamber.

TABLE 4.1 *Effects of Issue Interest on Legislative Activity*

	Past Activity	Past Committee	Constituency Characteristic	Democrat?
House				
Agriculture	.57(.08)***	.32(.44)	.024(.005)***	−.32(.17)*
Budget	.47(.05)***	.30(.14)**	.002(.006)	−.29(.12)**
Campaign Finance	.26(.04)***	−.12(.14)	.002(.005)	−.14(.09)
Children's Issues	.47(.04)***	−.07(.10)	−.006(.014)	−.03(.07)
Civil Rights	.76(.13)***	−.10(.17)	.005(.006)	.80(.23)***
Consumer Issues	.38(.06)***	.93(.20)***	−.001(.010)	.06(.14)
Corporate Regulation	.49(.07)***	.47(.22)**	.039(.012)***	−.14(.21)
Crime	.54(.05)***	1.55(.63)**	.003(.007)	.28(.24)
Defense & Foreign Policy	.58(.05)***	1.21(.53)**	.640(.460)	2.00(.46)***
Education	.51(.12)***	1.96(.77)**	−.002(.048)	.80(.22)***
Environment	.67(.06)***	.89(.36)**	.027(.007)***	.19(.31)
Health	.61(.05)***	1.11(.53)**	.024(.019)	1.96(.45)***
Jobs & Infrastructure	.48(.05)***	.50(.45)	.016(.027)	−1.29(.35)***
Medicare	.59(.05)***	.55(.42)	.040(.046)	1.13(.30)***
Moral Issues	1.10(.04)***	.16(.27)	–	−.78(.20)***
Social Security	.48(.05)***	−.09(.11)	.056(.020)***	−.01(.11)
Taxes	.52(.06)***	2.89(.69)***	−.004(.018)	−3.89(.51)***
Welfare	.38(.06)***	.19(.17)	.011(.014)	.51(.12)***
Senate				
Agriculture	.57(.06)***	−.51(.68)	.005(.014)	.16(.42)
Budget	.22(.07)***	−.33(.19)*	.021(.017)	−.71(.19)***
Campaign Finance	.23(.10)**	.10(.23)	−.010(.016)	.23(.18)
Children's Issues	.38(.10)***	.68(.33)**	.022(.061)	.31(.24)
Civil Rights	.56(.08)***	−.49(.31)	.014(.008)*	.68(.31)**
Consumer Issues	.11(.11)	1.35(.28)***	.036(.024)	.53(.28)*
Corporate Regulation	.30(.18)	−.32(.34)	.060(.035)	.52(.30)
Crime	.41(.09)***	3.35(.83)***	.013(.019)	−1.20(.54)**
Defense & Foreign Policy	.57(.12)***	.67(1.30)	.094(.339)	−2.16(1.09)*
Education	.50(.13)**	.62(.68)	−.113(.166)	.69(.62)
Environment	.80(.11)***	.55(.97)	.012(.032)	−.09(.85)
Health	.57(.10)***	3.04(.89)***	.120(.074)	−.93(1.00)
Jobs & Infrastructure	.35(.12)***	1.39(1.20)	.41(.14)***	2.65(1.03)**
Medicare	.40(.10)***	−.86(.82)	.161(.156)	1.54(.55)***
Moral Issues	1.00(.14)***	−.03(.46)	–	−1.23(.56)**
Social Security	.26(.10)**	.42(.26)	−.017(.046)	.07(.17)
Taxes	.36(.09)***	2.68(.83)***	.025(.047)	−1.33(.65)**
Welfare	.40(.09)***	1.14(.35)***	−.045(.049)	.90(.33)***

Note: Cell entries are unstandardized OLS regression coefficients with standard errors in parentheses. There are separate models for each issue, with the dependent variable the percentage of legislators' agendas in office devoted to each issue. Independent variables include past activity, past committee assignments, relevant constituency characteristics, party, and election year (not presented).

*** = p < .01;** = p < .05;* = p < .10.

need to assess whether these interest variables have *different* relationships with House and Senate candidates' campaign agenda choices. As discussed previously, I anticipate that indicators of interest should be strong predictors of House candidates' campaign agenda choices, but only weak predictors of Senate candidates' issue selections.

ISSUE INTEREST AND CAMPAIGN AGENDAS

Testing this hypothesis is quite straightforward. To do so, I simply replicate the analyses in Table 4.1, but instead of using post-campaign activity on an issue as the dependent variable, I use a dummy variable for whether or not a candidate mentioned each issue in his or her campaign. Figure 4.1 summarizes these results for the House and the Senate. The second panel for each chamber illustrates the relationship between past activity on issues and the content of campaign appeals, and, for purposes of comparison, the first panel shows the relationship between past activity and subsequent activity (i.e., the results from Table 4.1). These analyses reveal a clear difference in the factors explaining House and Senate candidates' agenda choices. House winners' decisions to raise issues are more strongly related to their past records (for half of the issues, past activity is a significant predictor of appeals), but the same holds true for only four issues in the Senate. This general pattern also holds for the relationships among constituency characteristics, party, and appeals.[7] In short, there is much less of a relationship between these interest variables and the content of Senate candidates' campaign agendas. Put another way, House winners' appeals are more predictable: if we know what issues incumbents have been active on in the past and consider the nature of their districts, we can make accurate guesses about what they will talk about in their campaigns. Knowing the same pieces of information about a senator provides us with less insight into what he or she will highlight. Thus, for the House, the same factors that explain activity explain campaign agendas, but for the Senate, there is a disjuncture, and it is this disjuncture that explains why promise-keeping linkages are much rarer among senators than representatives.

[7] I do not present the full specifications, as doing so would take up several pages. However, I find that constituency characteristics are significant predictors of campaign appeals for ten issues in the House compared to one in the Senate and party is for seven issues in the House compared to one in the Senate. After I control for past activity, past committee assignments are independent predictors of campaign appeals for only a single issue in the House and Senate.

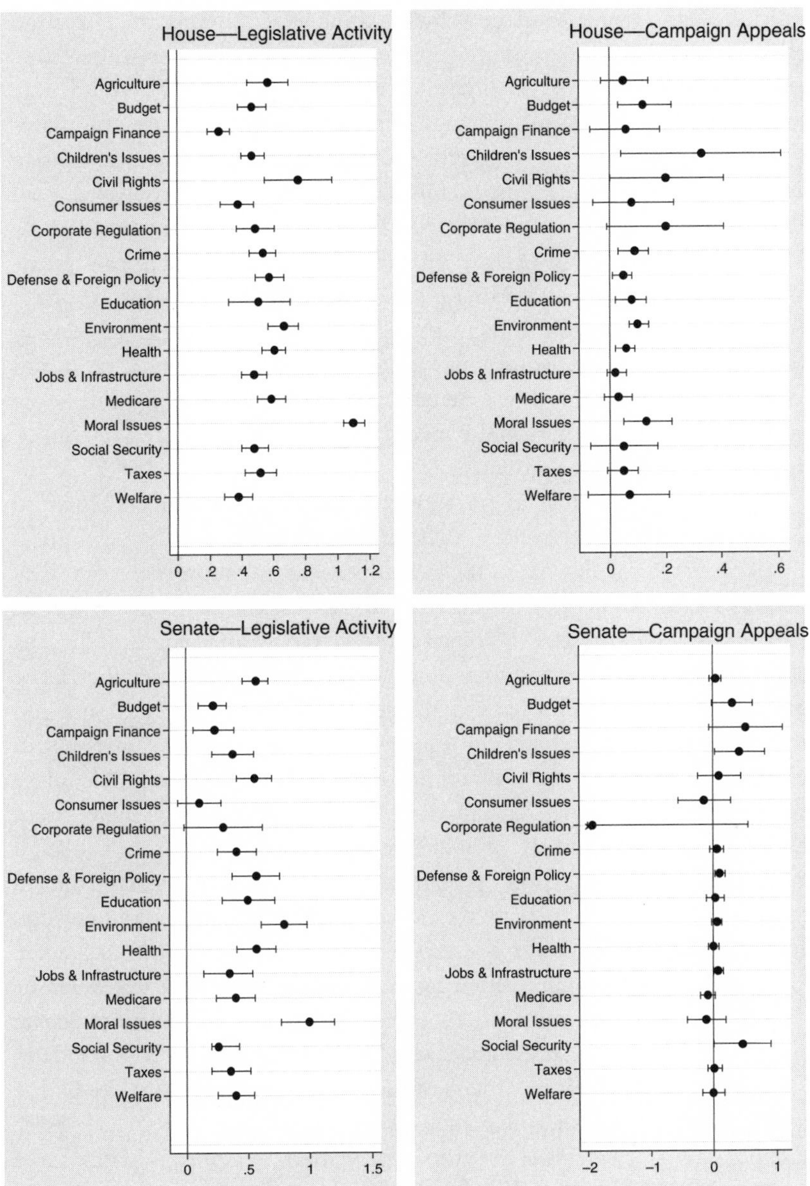

FIGURE 4.1 The Relationship between Past Activity and Subsequent Activity/ Campaign Appeals

Note: The figure summarizes the results of a series of regression analyses where the dependent variable is either a representative's or senator's percentage of activity devoted to an issue or whether he or she raised that issue in the campaign. The dots represent the coefficient on the primary independent variable of interest – the percentage of activity in the previous congress that each legislator devoted to each issue. Lines represent the 90 percent confidence intervals.

Why might this be the case? Why are there looser connections between senators' policy priorities and the content of their campaign appeals? One fairly obvious culprit is the difference in the scope of House and Senate candidates' agendas. As we saw in the previous chapter, Senate candidates typically discuss three to four more issues, on average, than do House candidates. Thus, while House members may highlight only their first-level priorities, senators may also talk about their second-order priorities, so that the choice to discuss an issue is a weaker signal. Senators are also more likely than their peers in the House to be generalists, active across a variety of issues, so they may have less clearly identifiable priorities, resulting in more diffuse agendas. Thus, the weaker linkages between interest and appeals likely emerge because Senate candidates' agendas include some issues that are of less personal concern to them, not because they fail to mention issues they care about.

For example, senators may feel more compelled to use their campaigns to discuss pressing national issues, both because of the higher profile of their races and because the smaller size of their chamber makes it more likely that they will play some role in policy making about those issues (for a similar argument, see Atkeson and Partin 2001). When I compare House and Senate candidates' relative amounts of attention to issues, I find support for this hypothesis. For most issues, there is not a large difference in the propensity of House and Senate candidates to raise them. However, for more prominent issues, a difference emerges. For instance, in the 2002 elections, the first to take place after the terrorist attacks of September 11, 2001, 54 percent of winning House candidates talked about defense, which represents a big jump from 1998 and 2000, when only about 10 to 15 percent did. However, this is much less than in the Senate sample, where 74 percent of the candidates talked about defense. Similarly, the Patients' Bill of Rights was a big issue in Congress in the late 1990s and figured prominently in the 2000 election cycle. In that year, 51 percent of House winners talked about health care, but 89 percent of Senate winners did. Thus, when presented with a high-profile issue, Senate candidates may choose to discuss it regardless of their own predilections, while House candidates may do so only if the issue is of real interest to them.

What this all suggests is that the appeals that Senate candidates make are less likely to indicate what they will do in the future because they are noisier signals about their true priorities.[8] However, although this is likely the most important factor at work, it may not be the only reason for the

[8] As I have noted before, this does not mean that their appeals are untruthful or even uninformative (i.e., it is useful for constituents to know how a candidate voted on the

relative lack of promise-keeping linkages for senators. They also simply may be less responsive than their peers in the House, perhaps because they face more heterogeneous constituencies and so face a more difficult task, or perhaps because they perceive less benefit from following through on their appeals (or less cost from failing to do so). Another possibility is that characteristics that lead legislators to be less likely to follow through on their promises are more prevalent among senators than representatives. If, for instance, levels of follow-through are related to electoral vulnerability, seniority, ideological extremity, or party, then differences across the chambers in the distribution of these features could manifest themselves in aggregate differences in promise keeping. I explore the factors driving individual variation in promise keeping in Chapter 6, but in the remainder of this chapter I investigate explanations for the variation in the signaling power of different types of appeals.

DIFFERENCES BY LANGUAGE

If the reason that Senate candidates' appeals are less likely to signal their legislative action is that they are less closely related to their interests, it follows that the reason that most rhetorical differences are not linked to follow-through is that decisions about *how* to discuss an issue are also unconnected to candidates' levels of interest in an issue. For example, if this conjecture is correct, the lack of findings for specificity (i.e., that those who make specific appeals about an issue are no more active on it than those who make vague appeals) should also mean that those who talk about an issue such as agriculture in a specific manner have the *same* levels of preexisting interest in it as those who talk about it in a vague way.

To confirm this, I evaluate the strength of the linkages between interest and various rhetorical choices. Some of these tests require that the analyses be limited to the group of candidates who raised an issue, and given the low Ns for most issues, it is not possible to estimate models with all of the independent variables from the analyses in Table 4.1 and Figure 4.1. Instead, I opt to use bivariate analyses where one variable is the proportion of legislators' previous agendas devoted to an issue (which in the preceding models was shown to be the strongest predictor of subsequent activity and the content of appeals) and the other is a feature of candidates' rhetorical choices on it.

Patients' Bill of Rights), but that observing their campaigns is less likely to enable a voter to infer what the candidate would pursue in the next term.

For the first sets of analyses, presented in columns one and two of Table 4.2, I conducted a series of t-tests where the grouping variable is either whether or not a candidate talked about his or her actions on an issue or whether or not a candidate referenced the opponent.[9] Thus, the question of interest is whether incumbent candidates who raise an issue or criticize their opponent on it have more of a record on it than those who do not. As shown, the results for mentioning oneself largely correspond to those from Figure 4.1. For thirteen issues in the House and six in the Senate,[10] candidates who raised the issue in reference to themselves had more extensive past records than their peers who did not discuss the issue. Consider, for example, the issue of agriculture. House candidates who discussed their own interests in this issue had devoted, on average, about 5 percent of their previous legislative agenda to it, compared to about 3 percent of for those who did not discuss agriculture. The difference for the Senate is 6.4 percent versus 3.8 percent. (Recall that every percentage point difference translates to about two activities for representatives and five for senators, so these differences are meaningful in magnitude.) In contrast, mentioning the opponent does not appear to be a function of interest; for only a single issue in each chamber do we see candidates with a more extensive record more likely to raise the issue in reference to the opponent. This means that, for virtually all issues, the choice to attack on an issue has little or nothing to do with legislators' own interests in and records on that issue.

What about other features of rhetoric? To explore the relationships among interest, specificity, and tense (i.e., referencing the past or future), I limited the sample to candidates who raised the issue in reference to themselves and ran a series of t-tests comparing the proportion of candidates' past attention to an issue for those who did and did not make a specific appeal about it (column three), did or did not mention the past (column four), and did or did not discuss the future (column five). As is clear from the patterns in the table, the conclusion to be reached from these analyses is that there are relatively few relationships between interest and rhetorical choices. In general, among the group of candidates who discuss an issue, having a comparatively extensive record on it does not make one more likely to offer specific appeals about it, to talk about the future, or to

9 In these and the other analyses, the cells in the table are blank if there were not enough candidates in a group to conduct systematic analyses (i.e., for agriculture in the House, only one candidate referenced the opponent).

10 For a seventh issue in the Senate, there is a negative relationship, such that candidates who mentioned corporate regulation had less of a record on it than those who did not.

TABLE 4.2 *Interest and Rhetorical Choices*

	Own	Opponent	Specific	Past	Future	Ad Time	% of Ads
House							
Agriculture	**5.0/3.0**	–	5.0/5.0	5.1/5.0	–	–.06	–.03
Budget	**2.3/1.5**	1.9/1.7	2.4/1.5	2.6/2.2	**3.4/2.1**	**.22**	**.19**
Campaign Finance	2.1/1.7	1.1/1.7	2.3/1.6	2.3/1.6	–	.23	.37
Children's Issues	**1.8/1.1**	.7/1.1	2.1/1.1	**3.1/.9**	–	–.23	–.35
Civil Rights	**4.6/2.1**	–	5.8/3.8	–	–	–.02	.08
Consumer Issues	**4.1/2.6**	3.9/2.7	4.5/3.2	4.2/4.1	–	.06	–.03
Corporate Regulation	2.1/1.7	2.2/1.8	–	2.2/2.1	–	–.10	.34
Crime	**7.0/5.9**	5.9/6.2	**6.6/8.6**	6.7/7.0	7.2/6.9	**–.25**	–.18
Defense & Foreign Policy	**18.2/15.1**	**21.9/15.8**	18.5/17.9	**20.7/17.5**	19.9/18.1	.05	.04
Education	**5.7/4.6**	5.2/5.4	5.8/5.6	6.0/5.7	5.9/5.8	.10	.10
Environment	**10.7/7.8**	8.7/8.3	10.3/11.7	10.3/10.5	9.5/10.4	.15	**.26**
Health	**13.0/10.6**	11.5/11.7	13.1/12.0	13.8/12.7	11.5/13.1	**.28**	**.20**
Jobs & Infrastructure	16.2/16.2	17.0/16.2	16.5/15.6	15.8/16.3	16.2/16.2	–.02	–.08
Medicare	**6.7/6.0**	7.1/6.3	6.8/6.6	7.0/6.5	7.1/6.6	.04	.06
Moral Issues	**5.2/2.9**	4.3/3.0	4.6/5.8	6.6/4.7	–	.21	**.47**
Social Security	2.0/2.0	2.2/2.0	2.2/1.9	**2.4/1.9**	**1.7/2.1**	.00	–.18
Taxes	**9.5/7.0**	9.1/7.9	**8.5/10.6**	**8.3/10.3**	9.2/9.5	**.19**	**.37**
Welfare	2.6/2.6	1.6/2.6	**3.0/2.3**	3.6/2.6	–	.22	–.03
Senate							
Agriculture	**6.4/3.8**	–	6.8/5.2	5.8/6.6	–	.44	**.56**
Budget	**2.0/.9**	**3.3/1.2**	2.3/1.3	1.1/2.3	2.2/2.0	.20	.20
Campaign Finance	**2.7/1.1**	1.1/1.1	–	–	–	–	–
Children's Issues	**2.3/1.3**	–	–	1.0/3.0	–	–.40	–.12
Civil Rights	2.5/2.5	–	**3.6/.3**	–	–	.21	.27
Consumer Issues	2.6/2.6	–	**3.2/1.5**	**3.7/1.7**	–	.10	.23
Corporate Regulation	**.9/1.4**	–	–	–	–	.45	**.98**

TABLE 4.2 (*cont.*)

	Own	Opponent	Specific	Past	Future	Ad Time	% of Ads
Crime	7.1/6.5	7.0/6.8	7.1/5.0	8.3/6.7	–	.04	.02
Defense & Foreign Policy	**19.2/14.2**	16.6/16.4	19.1/16.7	21.6/17.9	**24.3/18.3**	–.11	.19
Education	5.6/5.1	5.5/5.5	5.7/4.5	5.2/5.8	5.3/5.8	.19	**.30**
Environment	10.2/9.0	9.0/9.4	9.6/15.4	8.7/10.7	7.3/10.7	.27	.32
Health	13.1/10.9	14.0/12.2	13.1/13.5	**15.6/12.0**	10.2/13.4	.09	.02
Jobs & Infrastructure	16.4/15.7	16.3/16.4	16.3/16.8	14.5/17.2	15.9/16.5	.12	**.52**
Medicare	5.6/5.3	5.7/5.5	**6.1/3.4**	**7.3/4.9**	5.8/5.3	.21	.15
Moral Issues	1.5/2.7	1.8/2.5	1.6/1.4	2.5/1.2	–	.34	.21
Social Security	1.5/1.2	1.9/1.3	1.5/1.5	**2.5/1.2**	1.4/1.6	.27	–.05
Taxes	**6.7/4.2**	3.9/5.9	6.6/6.9	6.0/7.0	4.7/6.8	.24	**.43**
Welfare	3.3/3.3	2.4/3.4	3.6/2.8	4.0/3.0	–	.04	–.35

Note: Columns one through five present the proportion of legislators' previous agendas devoted to an issue by group (i.e., whether it was mentioned by the candidate himself or herself or not, or by the opponent or not), with differences assessed using independent samples t-tests. Columns six and seven present Pearson correlation coefficients for the relationship between advertising time on an issue, the percentage of ads that feature an issue, and the proportion of legislators' past activity devoted to it. For some rhetorical features for some issues, the *N*s were too low to permit systematic comparisons. Bold indicates significant ($p < .10$) relationships.

reference the past. Significant differences emerge for only a handful of issues, and are not always in the predicted direction. For example, House candidates who made specific appeals about crime had less extensive past records on it than those who made vague appeals, and those who referenced the past on taxes had been less active on it in the previous term than those who did not.

The same conclusion holds for issue prominence. In the final two columns of the table, I report the correlations between past record and the amount of advertising time devoted to an issue (column six), and the percentage of a candidate's ads that feature the issue (column seven), when the sample is limited to candidates who raised it. The relationships are stronger for the latter measure, emerging for five issues for each chamber, but that is still less than one-third of the issues. Thus, candidates' relative levels of interest in issues seem to have only weak relationships with how prominently they feature them in their advertising. For instance, Senate candidates who talked about the budget had more extensive records on it than those who did not raise it, but the relative prominence of the issue in their previous legislative agendas does not explain its place in their campaign agendas.

If variation in interest does not explain these choices about language, then what does? I hypothesized in Chapter 2 that they might instead be a reaction to contextual factors related to the candidate and the race (see also Kahn and Kenney 1999; Sides 2006; Sulkin, Moriarty, and Hefner 2007). Given what we know about what motivates candidates to "go negative," for example, we might expect candidates in close races to be more likely to criticize their opponents on issues. When I compare candidates in races categorized as "tossups" by the *Cook Political Report* with those in less competitive races, I find that this is indeed the case. Winning House candidates in tossup races averaged 2.8 issue mentions of the opponent compared to .9 for those in other races ($t = 6.4$, $p < .01$), and winning Senate candidates in tossups average 5.2 issue mentions of the opponent compared to 1.5 for non-tossups ($t = 5.7$; $p < .01$). These findings hold even after controlling for the overall size of candidates' agendas, which are also larger for winners in tossups (5.9 issues versus 4.7 for the House, $t = 3.2$, $p < .01$; and 8.9 versus 7.1 for the Senate, $t = 2.6$, $p < .01$).[11] This finding

[11] They also raise more issues in reference to themselves. For the House, the difference is 5.1 issues for tossup candidates compared to 4.5 for others ($t = 1.9$; $p < .10$), and for the Senate, the difference is 8.1 issues for tossup candidates compared to 6.9 for others ($t = 1.9$; $p < .10$).

that agenda size is a function of the closeness of the race may also help to explain the relatively weak associations between issue interest and the amount of campaign attention devoted to an issue. In general, the more issues a candidate raises, the less attention can be devoted to each one, so the prominence of any issue is related more to the scope of a candidate's agenda than to his or her level of interest in it.

The competitiveness of their races has more mixed relationships with candidates' tendencies to offer specific appeals or to reference the past or the future. I find that winners in tossup races do not offer specific appeals on a greater proportion of their own issues (68 percent for both groups for the House and 76 percent for tossups versus 77 percent for others in the Senate). However, the specificity of appeals is significantly negatively related to eventual vote shares (with those who make specific appeals on a high proportion of their issues receiving lower vote shares, $r = .10$ and $.07$, $p < .10$).[12] This suggests that candidates may respond to close contests by offering more specifics about their plans, perhaps in an effort to contrast themselves with the opponent.

Candidates in tight races are also no more likely to mention the past on one of their issues (40 percent of House tossup candidates do, compared to 44 percent of non-tossups, and 70 percent of Senate tossups do, compared to 63 percent of non-tossups), but they *are* more likely to reference the future (60 percent versus 30 percent for the House, $t = 4.1$, $p < .01$; 85 percent versus 57 percent for the Senate, $t = 2.3$, $p < .05$). However, rather than being influenced by the competitiveness of the race per se, these choices may be affected more by the status of the candidate as an incumbent or nonincumbent.[13] More precisely, the decision to discuss the future may be based on the fact that one does not already have a record to discuss, and so must rely on claims about what one will do, rather than what one has done or is doing. For both chambers, I do find significant differences in the propensity of new and returning members to discuss future plans. In the House, only 24 percent of incumbent winners referenced the future on at least one of the issues they mentioned, compared to 65 percent of winning challengers and open seat candidates ($t = 7.6$, $p < .01$). In the

[12] I do *not* assume that this relationship is causal (i.e., that making specific appeals lowers vote share).

[13] Competitiveness is, of course, correlated with candidate status because winners who were not incumbents were most often in close races. If I include both tossup status and incumbent status in the models for future and past discussion, the closeness of the race is not a significant predictor, but status is (except for past discussion for the Senate, where neither is).

Senate, 50 percent of incumbents discussed the future, compared to 92 percent of nonincumbent candidates ($t = 3.5$, $p < .01$).

A similar logic holds for discussion of the past. Among House candidates, 49 percent of incumbents compared to 28 percent of new winners referenced the past on at least one of their issues ($t = 3.5$, $p < .01$). In the Senate, there is no difference between these groups (64 percent versus 65 percent), but this may be due to the fact that many new senators have prior experience in the House of Representatives or other offices and so can draw on that when making their appeals.

Although these analyses are intended as illustrations rather than conclusive tests, they do provide strong support for the argument that while the content of appeals may be linked to candidates' individual policy interests (particularly for representatives), rhetorical features of those appeals are a function of contextual factors and, as such, do not provide much additional insight into candidates' likely priorities in office.

DO CAMPAIGNS MATTER?

These analyses confirm the story about promise keeping I developed in earlier chapters. When candidates' choices about issue content and language are linked to their interests in an issue, they serve as good signals about subsequent activity. When there is a looser connection between preexisting interest and the content and rhetoric in appeals, we see less follow-through.

What do these findings tell us about the role of campaigns and how they matter? To return to the language of Chapter 1, is the correspondence between appeals and activity entirely a function of the endogeneity inherent in the selection of campaign and legislative priorities, or can campaigns also serve as *independent* sources of information about what legislators will do, above and beyond what we might infer from other factors?

As a first step in answering this question, I model promise-keeping linkages using an instrumental variables framework that explicitly treats appeals as endogenous. In particular, I use a two-stage least squares regression analysis that enables me to evaluate the relationship between appeals and activity after "purging" the joint effect of issue interest on both. In the first stage (which approximates the analyses summarized in Figure 4.1), whether a candidate mentioned an issue is the dependent variable, and the independent variables include the "interest" indicators used in previous analyses, controls for election year, and, as an instrument, the number of issues raised by the candidate (since the larger the agenda, the higher the probability of raising any given issue).[14] For the second stage, the dependent variable is the proportion of legislators' agendas devoted to an issue. The independent variables include the same set as in the first stage (though the committee variable is the current assignment rather than the previous one), plus the instrumented appeal variable.

Figure 4.2 illustrates the primary relationship of interest from these analyses: the effect of appeals on subsequent activity. As expected, after taking into account the fact that interest affects both campaign and legislative agendas, there is no additional influence of appeals on the content of activity. Thus, appeals do not usually provide independent information about legislators' priorities. A constituent who had paid close attention to what the representative had done in the past would be able to predict what he or she would do in the future, even in the absence of the campaign. Normatively, this is not a bad thing; it means, particularly for the House, that candidates' appeals are often sincere and informative about their priorities. Very few constituents carefully follow what their elected representatives do in office but may tune in to the campaign, which can provide them with the information they may need to make good choices. Equally important, as discussed at length in Chapter 1, promise keeping does not require an independent effect of campaigns – just that legislators' priorities in office correspond to what they said they would do in their campaigns.

However, it would be premature to conclude based on these results that campaigns *never* provide unique information or are not themselves meaningful. For instance, they are often the only source of information that voters have about the potential policy priorities of newly elected legislators. When I replicate the basic analyses from Chapter 3 (i.e., asking whether candidates who raised an issue are subsequently more active on it than those who do not) but limit the sample to first-term representatives and senators, I find significant linkages for nine of the eighteen issues for the House (agriculture, children's issues, civil rights, consumer issues, crime, education, environment, Social Security, and taxes) and three for

[14] The total issues variable is a significant predictor of mentioning the issue for seventeen of the eighteen issues, but has little to no relationship with subsequent attention to the issues, so it is a good instrument. Because the endogenous variable (the campaign appeal) is dichotomous, I use the procedures outlined in Wooldridge (2002, 623–5). I first estimated a series of probit models for appeals, calculated the predicted values, then used these (instead of a dummy for having mentioned the issue) in a 2SLS instrumental variables regression.

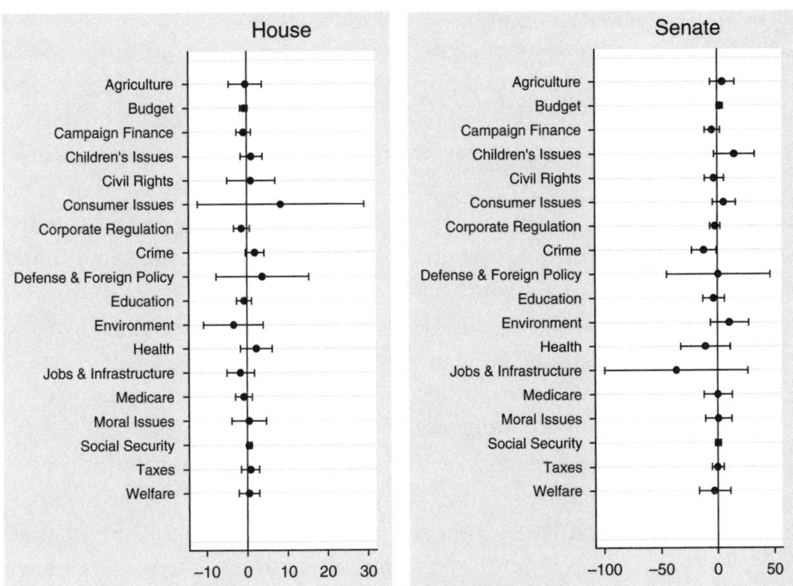

FIGURE 4.2 The Independent Effect of Appeals on Activity
Note: The figure summarizes the results of the second stage of a 2SLS instrumental variables regression where the dependent variable in the first stage is whether a candidate raised an issue and the dependent variable in the second stage is the proportion of the candidate's subsequent activity devoted to it. Independent variables in stage 1 include past activity, past committee assignments, constituency characteristics, party, election year, and the size of the candidate's agenda. Independent variables in stage 2 include past activity, committee assignment, constituency, election year, and the instrumented appeals variable from stage 1. The dots present regression coefficients on the instrumented appeals variable for stage 2, with the lines representing the 90 percent confidence intervals.

the Senate (children's issues, consumer issues, and Medicare). In addition, nearly all of the coefficients are positive (seventeen of the eighteen for the House and thirteen for the Senate), with many of these hovering near significance. This is important to note because the N, particularly for the Senate, is quite low (only twenty-seven legislators).

It is also the case that aggregating across all representatives or all senators, as I have done throughout the analyses in this and previous chapters, may miss out on some important dynamics. This approach assumes that having mentioned an issue will have the same relationship with later activity for all types of candidates. However, it is reasonable to think that, for any given issue, there are two groups of candidates: those who were predisposed to have raised it, based on past records, party, constituency characteristics, and so on, and those who were not. Does raising an issue signal something different for one of these groups than the other? For example, if a candidate who should *not* have been expected to raise the issue does, does this mean that he or she is more committed to it? Or, instead, does this indicate insincerity or some sort of strategic error?

To address this, I compare the levels of subsequent legislative action on each issue for four categories of candidates: (1) those who were predicted to have raised the issue and did; (2) those who were predicted to, but did not; (3) those who were *not* predicted to and did not; and (4) those who were not predicted to, but did. To the extent that differences emerge between groups one and two and between groups three and four, it suggests that under certain circumstances campaigns can indeed provide additional information about legislators' policy intentions.[15]

For these analyses, I took the probabilities from the instrumental variables regression specifications (i.e., the relative likelihood that each candidate would raise each issue), split them at the means,[16] and ran separate analyses for those candidates above the mean (those predicted to have raised the issue) and below the mean (those less likely to have raised the issue). For each group, I do t-tests where the variable of interest is the proportion of a legislator's agenda in the next term and the grouping variable is whether or not the candidate actually mentioned the issue in reference to himself or herself. The results are presented in Table 4.3.

A very interesting pattern emerges here. For candidates who were predisposed to mention the issue, there are often important differences in the volume of subsequent legislative action on an issue between those who did raise the issue and those who did not. For nine issues in the House (agriculture, children's issues, environment, health care, Medicare, consumer issues, civil rights, taxes, and corporate regulation) and five issues in the Senate (children's issues, jobs and infrastructure, Medicare, consumer issues, and taxes),[17] those who mentioned the issue engaged in significantly more activity on it. For the group of candidates who were *not* supposed to raise the issue, there are many fewer differences – only two for the House (agriculture and environment) and none for the Senate.

[15] In contrast, the analyses in Figure 4.2 in essence combine into single categories groups one and four and groups two and three. Accordingly, we should then see relationships between appeals and activity only if the effects of having mentioned an issue swamp all of the other things that may explain activity on it. This assumes a very large effect, and there is reason to expect that it may be more subtle.

[16] I get the same pattern of results with other splits (e.g., along the median).

[17] For a sixth issue, corporate regulation, those who raised it engaged in less activity.

TABLE 4.3 *Differences in Subsequent Activity Levels on an Issue for Candidates Who Were and Were Not Predicted to Have Raised an Issue*

	House Predicted to Have Raised	House Not Predicted to Have Raised	Senate Predicted to Have Raised	Senate Not Predicted to Have Raised
Agriculture	**4.9/3.5**	**4.7/2.6**	4.3/3.2	3.4/2.7
Budget	1.8/1.6	1.6/1.1	1.1/1.5	.3/.6
Campaign Finance	1.3/1.1	–	–	–
Children's Issues	**1.9/1.2**	1.5/.9	**1.9/1.0**	1.6/1.1
Civil Rights	**5.3/2.8**	–	2.3/3.2	–
Consumer Issues	**3.4/2.5**	–	**3.6/2.2**	–
Corporate Regulation	**2.1/1.3**	2.3/1.6	**.9/1.3**	–
Crime	6.9/6.5	6.0/6.4	7.0/6.3	3.9/7.6
Defense & Foreign Policy	20.0/18.9	17.6/15.8	21.3/20.4	16.8/17.9
Education	6.0/5.7	5.4/4.8	4.8/3.8	4.3/4.6
Environment	**11.4/8.2**	**8.0/6.4**	10.5/9.4	11.0/8.2
Health	**13.2/10.9**	10.6/9.8	13.8/13.7	12.9/10.4
Jobs & Infrastructure	15.1/14.5	15.1/15.0	**16.3/14.1**	16.0/16.3
Medicare	**6.5/5.5**	5.9/6.1	**5.8/3.8**	5.6/5.0
Moral Issues	6.3/5.1	2.7/3.1	2.9/2.6	2.4/4.2
Social Security	2.1/2.0	2.0/1.9	.9/.9	.9/.9
Taxes	**9/8/7.2**	7.5/6.3	**5.5/1.8**	4.8/3.8
Welfare	2.8/2.7	2.3/2.6	3.3/3.0	3.9/3.3

Note: The cells present the percentage of legislators' agendas devoted to an issue for four different groups of candidates: those who were predicted to have raised it in the campaign and did, those who were predicted to have raised it and did not, those who were not predicted to raise it but did, and those who were not predicted to have raised it but did not. The first entry in each column is the percentage for the group who did raise the issue and the second is the percentage for the group who did not. Differences in means are assessed via independent samples t-tests. For some issues, the Ns were too low to permit systematic comparisons. Bold indicates a significant ($p < .10$) difference.

Several important conclusions can be drawn. These results indicate that appeals that come out of nowhere are not meaningful; when a candidate with no apparent reason to discuss an issue does, this does not tell us anything about his or her actual intentions about the issue. However, for candidates who do have reason to mention an issue, whether or not they actually do so is often informative. In short, on many issues, candidates who should have raised the issue and did are subsequently more active than their similarly predisposed peers who chose not to feature the issue in their campaigns. Another way of thinking about this is that a candidate's choice *not* to discuss an issue can be a signal. For instance, imagine that a constituent's district and state both have relatively large numbers of senior citizens and his or her representative and senator both have been very active on senior issues. However, if one talks about Medicare in his campaign and the other avoids it and discusses other issues, this indicates that the latter will probably not be as active in pursuing the issue of Medicare in the next term.

Although these effects do not occur for all issues, they do occur for many, and the differences are particularly impressive because they emerge from aggregate analyses, which mask variation in follow-through at the level of individual legislators. Even with past record and constituency characteristics held constant, it is unlikely that all legislators engage in promise keeping at similar rates. Instead, it is probable that some are highly attentive to their previous campaign themes and others less so. Exploring this individual variation is the task of Chapter 6. First, though, I pause in the next chapter to explore in more detail the nature and quality of representatives' and senators' follow-through on their campaign issues.

5

Promise Making and Promise Keeping on Defense and Environmental Issues

The investigations thus far have demonstrated the value of an agenda-based approach to understanding promise making and promise keeping. Compared to position-based models, which assume that candidates use their campaigns to stake out their stances on a variety of issues, my conceptualization more accurately captures the real-world behavior of candidates, who often focus on their priorities, but more rarely offer specifics about their positions on policies relating to those priorities. For example, they may say that they will work to preserve the environment, but do not offer details on how they will vote on amendments to the Clean Air Act, policies regarding hazardous waste, or proposals to set aside land as wilderness.

Although this lack of specificity is often criticized by both pundits and scholars, I have argued that it is not by itself normatively problematic. The results in Chapters 3 and 4 demonstrate that specificity is not a strong indicator of sincerity, with vague and more detailed appeals serving as equally good predictors of the content of winners' later activity. In addition, because few introduced measures will reach a final passage vote, and because candidates cannot usually anticipate in advance what those might be, broad appeals that discuss a candidate's general orientation on an issue can be just as informative as many specific appeals (i.e., those about a policy that never gets a vote, or that was the focus of attention in a *previous* congress), enabling voters to infer how that candidate will behave once in office. Moreover, in many if not most cases, voters themselves may care most that important issues be addressed and problems solved, without being wedded to the particulars of the policies to do so.

This is not to say that it impossible to imagine scenarios in which an agenda-based conception of promise keeping might be misleading. My underlying assumption throughout this book has been that legislators are generally honest – that, to use the previous example, if they say in their campaigns that they want to preserve the environment and then proceed in office to introduce and cosponsor measures on the topic, those measures are intended to aid the environment (taking into account, of course, that there may be differences of opinion about how best to do this). What, though, if many candidates purposely lie? For instance, what if it is common for candidates who say that they want to preserve the environment actively pursue measures in the next congress designed to reduce penalties for polluting or to open up protected wilderness land to commercial development? In a situation like this, we could observe a high level of correspondence between legislators' campaign and governing priorities (i.e., because they talked about the environment and then acted on it), but the follow-through would not be sincere, and it would be wrongheaded to claim that promises were kept.

Put another way, when I argue that voters are open to a variety of solutions to an issue, this is only within a reasonable set of bounds. Even vague claims typically have some implied direction to them, especially when considered in light of a candidate's partisanship, and we should assume that voters wish to see behavior that aligns with the underlying spirit of the appeal made in the campaign. If their legislator claims to be pro-environment (and if they agree with her on this stance), they should in most cases be equally happy if she works on policies regarding pollution, conservation, or hazardous waste, but should not be equally pleased if she engages in activity that would be thought of as clearly anti-environment.

A priori, we should not be overly concerned about "spurious" responsiveness being widespread because there is little incentive for candidates to behave in this manner. Most of the candidates I study are incumbents who come into their campaigns with records that constrain their appeals. A legislator with a history of supporting cuts in defense spending would come under immediate and harsh criticism if he claimed in the campaign to be strongly pro-defense, and would run the risk of alienating current supporters who agreed with his prior stance on the issue (see Sellers 1998). If he wanted to reach out to new voters, a better option would be to ignore the issue and instead talk about a theme likely to be supported by both current supporters and the constituents he hopes to win over.

Nevertheless, it is at least theoretically possible that legislators sometimes dissemble, claiming to be supportive of efforts that in reality they work against. Thus, to bolster my arguments about the value of agenda-based promise keeping, it is important to establish that most follow-through is genuine. Exploring in a more nuanced way the relationship between the appeals that candidates make and what they actually do on those issues in office can also offer further insight into the nature and quality of promise keeping. Accordingly, my analyses in this chapter are designed to provide a more in-depth understanding of the links between campaign appeals and legislative behavior. More specifically, I examine the bills introduced by legislators who had made specific claims about an issue, assessing the extent to which the content of these measures aligns with the content of their claims. Then I ask how my agenda-based measure of promise keeping maps on to more traditional position- or vote-based measures. In particular, does having made an appeal on an issue signal legislators' relative positions on policies related to it? (That is, are those who make an appeal about the environment more "pro-environment" than those who do not talk about the issue?) If so, then observing legislators' priorities, even if expressed in a vague way, can tell us not just what they will be active on, but can also offer information about the positions they will take.

These investigations do not lend themselves to the same approach that I have used in previous chapters. There are simply too many combinations of candidates/legislators and issues to make examining all of them feasible. Instead, I opt for more detailed analyses of promise making and promise keeping for two issues: the environment and defense and foreign policy. I have a number of reasons for choosing these issues. Perhaps most importantly, there is variation in partisan ownership. The environment has traditionally been a Democratic theme and defense and foreign policy a Republican one (Petrocik 1996; Sides 2006). This enables me to evaluate how legislators' party affiliations condition their follow-through. These issues also both fall in the middle of the spectrum of popularity and salience, so there are enough legislators discussing them to allow for comparisons, but they were not so salient that everyone raised them.[1] Deciding to discuss defense or the environment therefore was a matter of conscious choice on the part of candidates. In addition, although there is some overlap (twelve senators raised both defense and the environment, as did forty representatives), this pairing of issues brings in different legislators. Finally, as shown later in this chapter, for those who made specific

[1] Ninety-six representatives and forty-two senators in the sample discussed defense (in reference to themselves) and sixty-seven representatives and twenty-eight senators discussed the environment. As I have noted before, there was a big jump in attention to defense in the 2002 elections (the first after the 2001 terrorist attacks), but even then, about one-quarter of the Senate sample and one-half of the House sample did not discuss the issue.

appeals about these issues, there is clear variation in content of those appeals (i.e., they did not all call for the *same* specific policy), which should provide for stricter tests of follow-through.

DO WINNING CANDIDATES DO WHAT THEY SAID THEY WOULD DO?

I begin by examining the degree to which the content of legislators' activity in office on defense or the environment matches the specific content of their campaign claim(s) about these issues. For instance, if a candidate speaks of the need to protect defense jobs, do his or her introductions on defense deal with this component of the issue? Strong linkages at this level would indicate clear commitments on the part of legislators to following through on their promises. On the other hand, we have seen that specificity is largely a reaction to the competitiveness of a race, so detailed appeals may be less a roadmap for the future than examples intended to illustrate in a concrete way a candidate's more general interest in an issue. In this case, we might see high levels of activity on the issue, but not necessarily on the component of it discussed in the campaign.

To assess this, I return to the campaign appeals of the eighty-one legislators who talked about defense in a specific manner and the seventy-two who did so for the environment and divided their claims into more narrow categories. These claims fall fairly naturally into about six or seven categories for each issue, which are shown in Table 5.1. For the environment, they include conservation (topics such as establishment of parks and wilderness areas, protecting plant and animal species, preserving coastlines and wetlands, etc.), pollution (of air and water), hazardous waste and solid waste disposal, land use, water infrastructure (the creation of water projects), nuclear issues, and drilling (for oil and gas). For defense and foreign policy, they include military bases and defense jobs, specific defense programs, homeland security and terrorism, foreign policy, immigration, and veterans and military personnel (the Department of Veterans Affairs [VA], military pay and benefits, programs for families, etc.).

I find that most candidates who talked about an issue referenced only one dimension or component of it, but some discussed multiple themes. Not surprisingly, this is more common in the Senate (where 40 percent discussed two or three dimensions of defense and 35 percent discussed two or three dimensions of the environment) than in the House, where about one-quarter of those who talked about the environment discussed two themes and only 15 percent of those who talked about defense mentioned two.

TABLE 5.1 *Subdimensions of Appeals on Defense and the Environment*

	# of House Candidates	# of Senate Candidates
Defense		
Mentioned?	96	42
Made Specific Appeal?	47	34
Talked about:		
Bases/Jobs	12	6
Defense Programs	5	11
Terrorism/Homeland Security	4	9
Foreign Policy	4	5
Immigration	1	3
Veterans & Military Personnel	25	14
Environment		
Mentioned?	67	28
Made Specific Appeal?	49	23
Talked about:		
Conservation	20	10
Pollution	14	8
Hazardous & Solid Waste	6	3
Land Use	3	2
Water Infrastructure	12	4
Nuclear Issues	5	3
Drilling	1	2

How much follow-through do we see on these specific dimensions? When I use the same six- or seven-category scheme to code winning legislators' introductions,[2] I find that in the Senate, 76 percent of legislators engaged in at least one introduction on defense that corresponded to the content of their appeal,[3] and that the same holds true for 70 percent of legislators for the environment. The percentages for the House are lower – 46 percent for defense and 55 percent for the environment. For that chamber, though, we must remember that introductions are undertaken more rarely and that it is common for legislators to engage in none at all on an issue. When I limit the denominator to representatives who made at

[2] I focus on introductions rather than cosponsorships because they provide for a more stringent assessment of follow-through and because doing so makes the recoding task more manageable.

[3] Interestingly, for defense, these patterns do not appear to differ pre– and post–September 11. Almost all of the increase in attention to defense in the 2002 elections is the result of more candidates making vague appeals about the issue. Later in this chapter, I take up in more detail what having made a claim about the issue (vague or specific) indicates about a legislator's likely positions on votes on defense.

least one introduction on defense or the environment (i.e., so the question is whether their activity on an issue addresses the specific theme), the percentages approximate those for the Senate – 68 percent on defense and 77 percent on the environment.

Are these numbers high or low? The answer depends upon one's perspective. The results indicate that the vast majority of candidates do indeed engage in activity on the specific policy they mentioned in their campaigns. As such, even if those candidates who make specific claims are not more active in office on an issue than those who make vague appeals, specific appeals remain valuable for predicting activity because we can be relatively confident that the details of a specific claim will be reflected in one or more introductions undertaken by the winning candidate once in office. However, it is still the case that between one-quarter and one-third of candidates who make a specific appeal on an issue and then act on that issue fail to address the particular dimension of that policy raised in the campaign.

Importantly, my requirements for determining whether an appeal-introduction match exists are fairly strict – the appeal and activity must clearly fall within the same subcategory. For instance, in 2002, Senator Gordon Smith (R-OR) noted in his campaign that he had worked to stop drilling in Alaska, but he introduced no measures in his next term related to this. Nonetheless, he was very active on measures about energy efficiency, and there is a logical connection there (i.e., more efficient use of energy should reduce the need for oil and gas). Because there was not a one-to-one match between the appeal and those introductions, though, he is identified as not having followed through on the specific nature of his claim. Thus, my estimates are conservative, particularly when we consider that some introductions are very difficult to classify by dimension. Relaxing the rules about whether an introduction relates to a campaign appeal would likely lead to even higher assessments of responsiveness.

We can therefore safely conclude that it is very common for winners to introduce measures in office that reflect the policy areas raised in their specific claims about an issue. Does this one-to-one follow-through dominate their activity on that issue, or do they also introduce legislation on other dimensions of it? When I investigate the patterns of activity for those who engage in multiple introductions on an issue, it becomes clear that the answer is the latter. In the House, where introductions are fewer in number, a little less than one-third of legislators focus solely on the specific dimension of the environment or defense raised in their campaigns. In the Senate, where introduction levels are higher, almost no one limits his or her activity on an issue to the particular dimension he or she raised in the campaign – there is only one case of this for defense and one for the environment.

That said, an expectation that promise keeping would be of higher quality if legislators did focus solely on the specifics of their appeals is probably misguided. To see why, consider the environmental claim made by Ron Wyden, the other senator from Oregon, in his 1998 Senate campaign. In that race, he ran an ad that informed voters that he had "protected our drinking water at Bull Run Watershed." In the next term, he introduced twenty bills on the environment, including nine on the specific theme of water infrastructure. Two of those bills were specifically about the Bull Run Watershed, producing as close an alignment as is possible between appeals and activity. The first of these bills was introduced in the 106th Congress, which immediately followed Wyden's reelection. That bill (S 2691, "A bill to provide further protections for the watershed of the Little Sandy River as part of the Bull Run Watershed Management Unit, Oregon, and for other purposes") passed in the Senate, but did not make it out of committee in the House. Wyden subsequently reintroduced it in the 107th Congress (where it was S 254). In that congress, the House version of the bill (HR 427, introduced by Representative Earl Blumenauer [D-OR]) passed both chambers and became law.

This example highlights several points that we need to consider when evaluating promise keeping. First, and perhaps most ironically, Wyden had a second bill on Bull Run only because the first attempt failed. Had his measure or a similar one been successful in the 106th Congress, he probably would not have introduced a bill dealing with Bull Run in the 107th. Thus, if we assume that more activity always equals more follow-through, we run the risk of discounting the contributions of more successful members or of forgetting that lawmaking is ultimately about problem solving.[4] Indeed, this may be one reason that we see fewer systematic links for senators between campaign appeals and the volume of subsequent activity on an issue. As a group, they may be more effective at making policy on their priority issues, and so may not require a large number of introductions or cosponsorships to demonstrate their commitment.[5] Second, as I

[4] To some extent, this logic holds for all of the analyses I have undertaken, but is really only an issue for the specific appeals–introductions match. For instance, for the more general link between appeals and activity on the environment, even if one environmental issue is solved to a legislator's satisfaction, there are always more to address.

[5] I follow up on this possibility in Chapter 8, where I explore the policy implications of promise keeping.

just intimated, we need to think about what Wyden might have intended to communicate with his appeal about Bull Run. Was that one policy salient enough that he wanted to imply that it would be the sole focus of attention, or did he use it to signal his general interest in water infrastructure issues (the subject of seven of his other bills) or, even more broadly, to provide it as just one specific example of his commitment to issues involving Oregon's natural resources? This latter interpretation seems perhaps the most reasonable (particularly since his claim referenced his past rather than future action on Bull Run) and, in fact, eight of his other environment bills dealt with the conservation and protection of forests and wilderness land.

IS FOLLOW-THROUGH GENUINE?

If Wyden is typical of his colleagues in the House and Senate, this suggests that follow-through on campaign appeals is genuine. However, my focus thus far has still been primarily on the overall content of bills rather than the particular direction of the policy proposed in them (though it is hard to believe that "a bill to provide further protections" actually eroded protections). Is there any evidence that representatives or senators make introductions that are contrary to the spirit of their campaign claims? Or, viewed another way, does evidence exist that they make campaign appeals that are misleading about their true intentions on an issue?

As a caveat, I should note that it is sometimes difficult to determine the intent or effects of a very specific measure on an issue from the full text of a bill, much less from its title. Nonetheless, reading through the titles and descriptions of the bills sponsored by members of the sample who discussed the environment and/or defense gives a good sense of whether the proposed legislation matches the implied direction of the members' claims. Take, for instance, the measures introduced by the twenty-five representatives who talked about veterans and military personnel in their campaigns. Sixteen of them followed through with some introduction activity on this issue in their next terms, producing a total of forty-four bills or joint resolutions on this dimension of the topic.[6] In the interest of transparency, and to illustrate what the content of introduced measures looks like, I have listed these bills in Table 5.2. They run the gamut from Department of Veterans Affairs health matters to tax policies involving military personnel

[6] Twenty-one of these were introduced by a single member in the 108th Congress: Lane Evans (D-IL), who was the ranking Democrat on the Veterans Affairs Committee.

TABLE 5.2 *Bills on Veterans' Issues by Members of the House Sample*

Congress	Bill	Sponsor	Description
106	HR 9	Buyer, Stephen	A bill to express the sense of Congress that a comprehensive effort is required to revitalize and sustain the all-volunteer force and address the decline in the quality of life for members of Armed Forces and their families and to provide a 4.8 percent increase.
106	HR 1020	Snyder, Vic	A bill to amend title 38, United States Code, to establish a presumption of service connection for the occurrence of hepatitis C in certain veterans.
106	HR 4335	Snyder, Vic	A bill to amend the Internal Revenue Code of 1986 to provide that hazardous duty pay of members of the Armed Forces shall not be taken into account in computing the earned income credit.
106	HR 5048	Kanjorski, Paul	A bill to amend chapter 171 of title 28, United States Code, with respect to the liability of the United States for claims of military personnel for damages for certain injuries.
107	HR 1962	Buyer, Stephen	A bill to amend title 10, United States Code, to modify the time for use by members of the Selected Reserve of entitlement to certain educational assistance.
107	HR 2886	Frost, Martin	A bill to amend title 10, United States Code, to authorize the award of the Purple Heart to civilian employees of the Department of Defense who are killed or wounded by a terrorist attack.
107	HR 3254	Buyer, Stephen	A bill to amend title 38, United States Code, to provide for a partnership between the Department of Veterans Affairs and the Department of Defense to develop and disseminate education and training programs on the medical responses to the consequences of terrorist activities.
107	HR 4510	Kanjorski, Paul	A bill to amend chapter 171 of title 28, United States Code, with respect to the liability of the United States for claims of military personnel for damages for certain injuries.
107	HR 4852	Weldon, Dave	A bill to amend title 38, United States Code, to provide for the geographic allocation of funds made available to the Department of Veterans Affairs for medical care on a basis that better reflects the veterans population of different regions of the country and that accounts for significant shifts in the veterans populations in those regions, and for other purposes.

TABLE 5.2 (*cont.*)

Congress	Bill	Sponsor	Description
107	HR 5084	Buyer, Stephen	A bill to amend title 38, United States Code, to improve accountability of research corporations established at Department of Veterans Affairs medical centers.
107	HR 5359	Kanjorski, Paul	A bill to rescind the Department of Veterans Affairs memorandum of July 18, 2002, in which Directors of health service networks in the Department of Veterans Affairs are directed to ensure that no marketing activities to enroll new veterans occur within their networks.
107	HR 5590	Hayes, Robin	A bill to amend title 10, United States Code, to provide for the enforcement and effectiveness of civilian orders of protection on military installations.
108	HJ Res 41	Evans, Lane	Disapproving the rule submitted to Congress by the Department of Veterans Affairs on January 22, 2003, with the title "VA Acquisition Regulation."
108	HR 58	Edwards, Chet	A bill to restore health care coverage to retired members of the uniformed services.
108	HR 533	Evans, Lane	A bill to amend title 38, United States Code, to provide for health benefits and certain other benefits to be furnished by the Department of Veterans Affairs to any individual who has spina bifida and is the natural child of a veteran who, while in military service, was exposed to a herbicide agent.
108	HR 761	Evans, Lane	A bill to amend title 38, United States Code, to authorize the Secretary of Veterans Affairs to provide adapted housing assistance to disabled members of the Armed Forces who remain on active duty pending medical separation.
108	HR 813	Kanjorski, Paul	A bill to rescind the Department of Veterans Affairs memorandum of July 18, 2002, in which Directors of health service networks in the Department of Veterans Affairs are directed to ensure that no marketing activities to enroll new veterans occur within their networks.
108	HR 1193	Hayes, Robin	A bill to amend title 10, United States Code, to provide permanent authority for certain chaplain-led family support programs of the Department of Defense.
108	HR 1256	Evans, Lane	A bill to amend title 38, United States Code, to provide for the annual placement of memorials honoring the service in the Armed Forces of veterans who, at the time of death, were homeless or indigent.

TABLE 5.2 (*cont.*)

Congress	Bill	Sponsor	Description
108	HR 1257	Evans, Lane	A bill to amend title 38, United States Code, to make permanent the authority for qualifying members of the Selected Reserve to have access to home loans guaranteed by the Secretary of Veterans Affairs and to provide for uniformity in fees charged to qualifying members of the Selected Reserve and active duty veterans for such home loans.
108	HR 1309	Evans, Lane	A bill to amend title 38, United States Code, to provide improved prescription drug benefits for veterans.
108	HR 1374	Evans, Lane	A bill to amend chapter 1606 of title 10, United States Code, to increase the amount of basic educational assistance for members of the Selected Reserve, and for other purposes.
108	HR 1565	Baldwin, Tammy	A bill to establish a National Center for Military Deployment Health Research in the Department of Health and Human Services to provide an independent means for the conduct and coordination of research into issues relating to the deployment of members of the Armed Forces overseas, and for other purposes.
108	HR 1681	Evans, Lane	A bill to amend title 38, United States Code, to allow for substitution of parties in the case of a claim for benefits provided by the Department of Veterans Affairs when the applicant for such benefits dies while the claim is pending, and for other purposes.
108	HR 1712	Evans, Lane	A bill to amend the Small Business Act to establish a development program for small business concerns owned and controlled by qualified service-disabled veterans, to reauthorize the programs of the National Veterans Business Development Corporation, to establish a Government-wide procurement goal for small business concerns owned and controlled by veterans, and for other purposes.
108	HR 1713	Evans, Lane	A bill to amend title 38, United States Code, to improve benefits under the Montgomery GI Bill by establishing an enhanced educational assistance program, by increasing the amount of basic educational assistance, by repealing the requirement for reduction in pay for participation in the program, and for other purposes.

TABLE 5.2 (*cont.*)

Congress	Bill	Sponsor	Description
108	HR 1838	Evans, Lane	A bill to amend title 38, United States Code, to revise the presumptions of service-connection relating to diseases and disabilities of former prisoners of war.
108	HR 1906	Evans, Lane	A bill to amend title 10, United States Code, to revise the Transition Assistance Program for persons separating from active duty in the Armed Forces to make that program mandatory for all separating members and to provide for the furnishing to such members of information about homelessness.
108	HR 2126	Edwards, Chet	A bill to recognize the importance of the Veterans Administration Medical School Assistance and Health Manpower Training Act of 1972 in addressing shortfalls in the number of physicians and other health care professionals employed in the health care system of the Department of Veterans Affairs, to reauthorize the program of grants to medical schools affiliated with the Department, and for other purposes.
108	HR 2318	Evans, Lane	A bill to amend title 38, United States Code, to provide for an assured adequate level of funding for veterans' health care.
108	HR 2349	Evans, Lane	A bill to authorize certain major medical facility projects for the Department of Veterans Affairs.
108	HR 2445	Evans, Lane	A bill to amend title 38, United States Code, to make permanent the requirement for the Secretary of Veterans Affairs to provide nursing home care to certain veterans with service-connected disabilities and to expand eligibility for such care to all veterans with compensable service-connected disabilities.
108	HR 2569	Edwards, Chet	A bill to improve benefits for members of the Armed Forces and veterans and for their dependents and survivors.
108	HR 2829	Baldwin, Tammy	A bill to amend title 38, United States Code, to improve compensation benefits for veterans in certain cases of impairment of vision involving both eyes.
108	HR 2970	Sanders, Bernard	A bill to authorize the disinterment from the Lorraine American Cemetery in St. Avold, France, of the remains of Private First Class Alfred J. Laitres, of Island Pond, Vermont, who died in combat in France on December 25, 1944, and to authorize the transfer of his remains to the custody of his next of kin.

TABLE 5.2 (*cont.*)

Congress	Bill	Sponsor	Description
108	HR 3018	Evans, Lane	A bill to amend title 10, United States Code, to permit members of the Selected Reserve the use of Reserve Montgomery GI Bill education benefits for payment for licensing or certification tests.
108	HR 3387	Evans, Lane	A bill to amend title 38, United States Code, to improve health care programs of the Department of Veterans Affairs and to extend certain expiring authorities.
108	HR 3392	Evans, Lane	A bill to amend title 38, United States Code, to make certain improvements in the procedures for adjudication of claims for benefits under laws administered by the Secretary of Veterans Affairs.
108	HR 3413	Evans, Lane	A bill to amend title 38, United States Code, to prohibit additional daily interest charges following prepayment in full of housing loans guaranteed by the Department of Veterans Affairs.
108	HR 4172	Evans, Lane	A bill to amend title 38, United States Code, to codify certain additional diseases as establishing a presumption of service-connection when occurring in veterans exposed to ionizing radiation during active military, naval, or air service, and for other purposes.
108	HR 4423	Edwards, Chet	Making appropriations for the Department of Veterans Affairs for the fiscal year ending September 30, 2005, and for other purposes.
108	HR 4424	Edwards, Chet	Making appropriations for military construction and family housing for the Department of Defense for the fiscal year ending September 30, 2005, and for other purposes.
108	HR 5047	Edwards, Chet	A bill to amend title 38, United States Code, to increase the maximum coverage under the Servicemembers' Group Life Insurance and Veterans' Group Life Insurance programs from $250,000 to $500,000.
108	HR 5244	Evans, Lane	A bill to improve programs for the identification and treatment of Post-Traumatic Stress Disorder in veterans and members of the Armed Forces, and for other purposes.

to educational benefits to family support programs to rules regarding liability of the government to claims from military personnel and veterans.

The rule I use in determining whether a measure supports the interests of veterans is to ask whether, if one were a veteran, he or she would be pleased by the results of the bill if passed. (I include the further caveat not to consider the costs of these measures, since some veterans might oppose them for purely fiscal reasons.) Applying this rule, I find no cases in which the answer is no. From the titles alone, it is clear that most measures are intended to extend benefits to veterans, military personnel, or their families. For those in which the direction of the effect is not certain from the title (e.g., were the bills to amend policies "with respect to the liability of the United States for claims of military personnel for damages for certain injuries" designed to make it easier or more difficult for a member of the military to receive support for damages?), I investigated the text of the bill in more detail, once again finding no evidence that the policies would be detrimental to veterans and military personnel as a group.[7] Instead, if there were sins committed in promise keeping on this issue, they appear to be of omission (i.e., not engaging in activity on the theme at all) rather than commission.

An inspection of the patterns for other dimensions of defense and the environment yields the same conclusion: there are few differences in the general thrust of candidates' claims about the policy and their actions on it. For instance, candidates who said they wanted tougher rules on immigration introduced measures that offered further restrictions, and those who claimed to want to conserve wilderness or wetlands focused their legislative attention on the matter on measures to do so. Importantly, the effects seem to hold no matter the direction of the campaign claim. Not all who discussed the environment expressed conventional pro-environment views and not all who mentioned defense were hawkish. Some candidates who talked about the environment referenced rolling back restrictions on the use of public lands (i.e., to hunting and fishing or commercial use) and

[7] There are some measures that are purely commemorative or symbolic (though, in general, most of these are coded under the nonpolicy "government operations" category) and some redistributive bills in which the measure might help veterans in some districts at the expense of others. For instance, Dave Weldon's (R-FL) HR 4852 in the 107th Congress ("A bill to amend title 38, United States Code, to provide for the geographic allocation of funds made available to the Department of Veterans Affairs for medical care on a basis that better reflects the veterans population of different regions of the country and that accounts for significant shifts in the veterans populations in those regions, and for other purposes") likely had both supporters and detractors among veterans, depending on whether they liked the status quo or not.

some who talked about defense (particularly pre–September 11) touted their efforts to reduce spending on expensive weapons systems, and their actions align with their appeals as well. In 1998, for example, Senator Russ Feingold (D-WI) noted in his ad "Won't Fly" that he had eliminated the federal helium program "now that our soldiers travel a bit differently" and criticized his opponent for continuing to support the B-2 bomber after it had been shown to have problems. In line with this claim, Feingold went on in his next term to introduce measures terminating or rescinding funding for programs including the F/A-18E/F Aircraft Program, the D-5 Submarine-Launched Ballistic Missile Program, V-22 Osprey Program, and others.

In addition, as was the case with Wyden and the Bull Run Watershed, much of the time the links between appeals and the content of future activity correspond almost exactly. On environmental issues, Representative Shelley Berkley (D-NV) argued in her 2000 and 2002 campaigns that she would lead the fight against using Yucca Mountain as a nuclear waste site and introduced multiple measures to this effect; Senator Wayne Allard (R-CO) in his 2002 campaign touted his efforts to "keep Colorado's water from going outside our borders" and introduced seven bills on water infrastructure programs in Colorado; and Senator Ernest Hollings (D-SC) described his fight for protecting oceans and coastlines and, following his 1998 reelection bid, introduced measures to establish a National Ocean Council and a Commission on Ocean Policy, to amend the Coastal Zone Management Act to include more coastal areas, and to clarify the role of the National Oceanic and Atmospheric Administration (NOAA) in protecting ocean resources.

Similarly, for defense policy, we have seen that candidates who discuss veterans follow through with introductions to help them. Some further examples of close matches include Representative John Sullivan (R-OK), who in 2002 argued that he had worked to double the number of immigration officers in Oklahoma to fight terrorism and introduced a bill in the 108th Congress to establish a U.S. Immigration and Customs Enforcement field office in Tulsa; Representative John Mica (R-FL), who discussed airport security and introduced bills on the federal flight deck officer program, the establishment of programs to prevent threats to commercial aviation from portable surface-to-air missiles, and airport and airport perimeter security; and Senator Pete Domenici (R-NM), who claimed in 2002 to have saved Kirtland Airbase and in the next term supported more legislation to bring construction projects there.

These examples all bolster my argument that the vast majority of follow-through is sincere. Before moving on, though, it is important to select a very difficult case to analyze, one in which there is reason to believe based on other factors that at least some candidates' appeals might have been misleading. The possibility that jumps out across the campaigns and congresses I study relates to an environmental issue – air pollution. Twenty-two of the legislators in my sample, including Democrats and Republicans alike, spoke in their campaigns of pollution and the need to reduce it. During this time period, though, there were raging debates about the effects and actual intent of proposed changes to the regulations governing air quality, particularly pollution by power plants. Accordingly, it is useful to investigate the precise nature of the activities engaged in by those legislators who had made campaign appeals about pollution.

PROMISE MAKING AND PROMISE KEEPING ON CLEAN AIR

Early in his first term as president, George W. Bush announced his administration's plans to make adjustments to the Clean Air Act, which was originally passed in 1963 and had last been amended by Congress in 1990. The two proposals that received the most attention and criticism related to New Source Review and the Clear Skies Initiative. New Source Review involved provisions of the Act requiring that when power plants and refineries expanded or modified their facilities in a substantial way, they also upgrade their antipollution technology. Over time, the rules of the Environmental Protection Agency (EPA) about the distinction between major modifications and more routine maintenance had become more restrictive, and Bush proposed rolling them back, arguing that they inhibited efficiency and that the expense and time required by the review process led many companies to postpone projects that might be good for the environment. Environmental groups vehemently disagreed with the changes in rules, arguing that the end effect would be to enable companies to increase the overall amount of pollution they emitted.[8]

The Clear Skies Initiative, announced in February of 2002, focused on regulation of emissions from power plants, proposing a "cap and trade" plan. Under this plan, limits ("caps") would be placed on particular pollutants, most notably sulfur dioxides, nitrogen oxides, and mercury.

[8] For summaries of both sides of the argument, see the Environmental Protection Agency's fact sheet on New Source Review (Environment Protection Agency, 2002) and the press releases issued by the Sierra Club and League of Conservation Voters (e.g., Mund 2004).

Companies would then be issued permits to emit these pollutants up to the cap, and if they wished to go over them, would have to buy credits from other companies that polluted less than their caps. The Bush Administration argued that such a market-based solution would reduce pollution more quickly than standard regulations. Environmental groups again disagreed,[9] contending that it would permit the biggest companies (which were also the biggest polluters) to continue their behavior unabated – they'd simply have to buy credits, which would not constitute a big enough hurdle.[10]

The controversy thus centered on the underlying intent of the Bush Administration proposals. Did they just reflect a difference in opinion about the best methods for improving air quality, or were they actually designed to reduce restrictions and aid the owners of big power plants and refineries, many of whom had been contributors to Bush's campaign? Since many of the congressional advocates of these proposals were known to vote regularly against pro-environmental legislation (i.e., in the scorecards issued by the Sierra Club and the League of Conservation Voters), it was often argued that support for these measures did not align with a pro-environment stance.

From the perspective of promise keeping, the question is whether candidates who talked about pollution may have presented their views in a misleading way, suggesting that they wanted to increase restrictions, but then pursuing policies that did not necessarily do so. Evaluating this is difficult for a number of reasons. Although it is unlikely that commitment to air quality alone would lead one to support the Bush Administration's proposals, there was and remains honest disagreement about how best to reduce pollution, tracing back to fundamental ideological differences in beliefs about the role government should play. In addition, most of the proposals and actual changes to pollution rules did not occur through legislative action, but through the bureaucracy, promulgated through the Environmental Protection Agency. Indeed, a search in the Library of Congress's THOMAS site for "New Source Review" or "Clear Skies" yields only four House bills and joint resolutions on these topics in the 106th through the 108th Congresses and thirteen in the Senate in the 106th through the 110th, none of which progressed beyond committee. I

9 See Environmental Protection Agency (2009) for the EPA's information on Clear Skies and Willett (2003) for the Sierra Club's press release.

10 In the decade that has passed since these debates first raged, the politics of the issue have evolved such that pro-environment legislators often now advocate cap and trade, as it offers at least some restraint on emissions.

therefore opt for a multipronged approach, beginning by determining whether the fourteen representatives and eight senators who discussed pollution in their campaigns were sponsors or cosponsors of the seventeen measures on New Source Review or Clear Skies, then investigating their votes on related matters (if available), and finally exploring the content of their other introductions on air pollution.

Starting with the House, there was no legislation on either the Clear Skies Initiative or New Source Review until late in the 107th Congress, which is not surprising since the 106th and early 107th were before Bush's election, when these policies were not yet high on the agenda. In the 107th and 108th, though, Joe Barton (R-TX) introduced Clear Skies legislation (HR 5266 and HR 999) "by request" of the Bush Administration. The cosponsor for both of those measures was Billy Tauzin (R-LA), who is a member of the sample in both of the corresponding election years, but who did not speak of the environment in his campaigns. The 108th House also featured two measures dealing with New Source Review. The first, HR 3093, was introduced by Charles Bass (R-NH), and the second, HR 3133, was introduced by Mark Udall (D-CO). Neither of these measures supported the Bush Administration's stance on New Source Review. Udall's bill explicitly opposed the revisions by allowing states to impose stricter requirements. The intended effect of Bass's bill ("To amend the Clean Air Act to establish a national uniform multiple air pollutant regulatory program for the electric generating sector") is less clear on its face, but it was listed by the State Environmental Resource Center as a pro–clean air bill, in contrast to the Bush Administration's policies, which they classify as anti-environmental (State Environmental Resource Center 2003).

Bass was a member of the 2002 sample and discussed the environment, but not pollution (though, importantly, he had referenced it specifically in his 1998 campaign). He also had a more extensive record on the environment than many of his Republican peers, serving, for example, as a member of Republicans for Environmental Protection.[11] Udall, though not in the 2002 sample, was included in 1998 and 2000 and had discussed the environment in both of those campaigns. His measure was cosponsored by, among others, Dennis Cardoza (D-CA), a first-term representative and member of the sample who had specifically discussed air pollution

[11] Since leaving office in 2006, he remained active in power and air quality issues, and recently joined the board of directors of a company that develops biomass power plants (See Bass 2009).

in his 2002 campaign. (His ad "Tax Cuts" noted that "Cardoza passed the toughest air quality bill in the Valley's history.")

Thus, it appears that representatives who talked about pollution and were involved in measures dealing with New Source Review were in opposition to the Bush Administration's policies, such that their claims aligned with their activity. There were no votes in the House dealing with these issues, so it is not possible to use those to compare campaign and legislative action. However, these representatives' other introductions on air pollution also seem consistent with a pro-environmental stance. Four of the fourteen (Tom Allen [D-ME] and Brian Bilbray [R-CA] in the 106th; Allen and Charles Taylor [R-NC] in the 107th; and Dennis Cardoza [D-CA] in the 108th) talked about air pollution and introduced at least one measure dealing specifically with it or with the Clean Air Act. Of these, Allen had a long history of strengthening regulations on pollution and had actively opposed many of Joe Barton's Clear Skies legislative efforts (Janofsky 2005); his measures in the 106th and 107th all targeted reducing emissions. Cardoza introduced a measure to give a tax credit to clean fuel vehicles in areas where ground-level ozone levels were above standards, which seems in line with a clean air position. Bilbray too had a longstanding interest in environmental issues and a relatively pro-environmental record,[12] and his measures, most of which focused on reducing automobile emissions, also seem consistent with an antipollution claim.

The only case that is possibly suspect involves Charles Taylor (R-NC), but even there the situation is complicated. In his 2000 campaign, his ad "Neill and Sierra Club" claimed that he had "fought to clean our air" and had sponsored the "Great Smokies Clean Air Act," and criticized his opponent, Sam Neill, and the Sierra Club for opposing it. In the previous congress, he had indeed introduced a bill subtitled the "Great Smoky Mountains Clean Air Act" (HR 4859, "To reduce emissions from Tennessee Valley Authority electric powerplants, and for other purposes"). He sponsored this measure again in the 107th Congress, after the election in which he made the appeal. Critics of Taylor argued that these measures were not actually pro–clean air, since they targeted only a specific subset of polluters and because Taylor had repeatedly neglected to support

[12] For instance, Bilbray's score on the League of Conservation Voters' scorecard in the 106th Congress was 73 percent, compared to an average of 16 percent for the other Republicans in the sample that year. During a spell out of office in the mid-2000s, however, he did work as a lobbyist, and a power company was among his clients, a point of criticism from his 2006 challengers (Barone, Cohen, and Ujifusa 2008).

broader reforms at the national level. He also had a record of very low levels of support for environmental causes in general (e.g., a League of Conservation Voters score of only 3 percent in the 108th Congress), leading to more questions about the intent behind his measure (McLeod 2001). Accordingly, a voter who inferred from Taylor's campaign claim that he was unusually committed to air quality or to environmental protection would be incorrect. However, it should have been clear from other aspects of the ad, most notably his criticisms of the Sierra Club, that this was not his intent.

Thus, even on the potentially confusing or misleading case of air pollution, House candidates who said or implied that they were in favor of increased restrictions pursued such policies in office. Does the same pattern hold for the Senate? There are eight senators in the sample who discussed pollution in their campaigns (Peter Fitzgerald [R-IL] and George Voinovich [R-OH] in the 1998 election; Thomas Carper [D-DE], Rick Santorum [R-PA], and Paul Sarbanes [D-MD] in the 2000 election; and Tom Harkin [D-IA], Frank Lautenberg [D-NJ], and John Sununu [R-NH] in the 2002 election). Four of the eight (Carper, Santorum, Sununu, and Voinovich) participated as sponsors or cosponsors on one of the seventeen New Source Review or Clear Skies–related measures introduced in the Senate in the 106th through 110th Congresses.

Of these four, Carper was the most active, introducing bills in all three congresses of his term dealing with New Source Review (in the 107th, S 3135; in the 108th, S 843; and in the 109th, S 2724). These three measures were identical to each other and were the Senate counterparts of Charles Bass's House measure (i.e., "To amend the Clean Air Act to establish a national uniform multiple air pollutant regulatory program for the electric generating sector"). Carper also reintroduced the measure in the 110th Congress (as S 1177), and, in that congress, Sununu, a member of the 2002 election sample, was a cosponsor. As discussed previously, these bills were generally seen as pro-clean air and against the Bush Administration's changes to New Source Review rules, suggesting that Carper's and Sununu's campaign claims were sincere.

In contrast, the measures for which Santorum and Voinovich were participants were more in favor of Bush Administration proposals, or at least are harder to classify. Voinovich cosponsored two of James Inhofe's (R-OK) Clear Skies bills (S 485 in the 108th and S 131 in the 109th), actions that are clearly in line with the administration's preferences. In the 107th, though, Voinovich and Santorum were both cosponsors of S 60, a bill introduced by Robert Byrd (D-WV) that focused on clean coal technology and proposed an exemption from New Source Review for certain installation projects. New Source Review was not front and center in this measure, and it seemed more constituency-oriented, with a mix of Democrats and Republicans from coal states as cosponsors. Thus, it is not immediately clear on its face how the measure might map on to the broader debate. However, the Sierra Club viewed the bill as anti-environment, describing it as "a smudgy Valentine to the coal industry" that:

> has even less to do with pollution reduction than past clean-coal programs .... It would repeal provisions of the Clean Air Act for power plants with clean-coal technology, which could result in new "clean" coal plants that pollute more than plants built in the last ten years, and provide incentives to convert clean natural-gas burning plants to dirtier coal-burning systems. (Rauber 2001)

Based on these activities, then, we could argue that Carper and Sununu were on one side of the air pollution debate and Santorum and Voinovich on the other. This claim is bolstered by these legislators' vote decisions on a Senate amendment directly relevant to New Source Review. In response to rules changes published by the Environmental Protection Agency in December of 2002, John Edwards (D-NC) offered an amendment (S AMDT 67 in the 108th Congress) to the House's omnibus appropriations bill that asked that these changes be postponed until the end of the fiscal year. The intent of the amendment, according to the League of Conservation Voters, which selected this vote for its 2003 scorecard, was to institute a delay that "would have allowed the National Academy of Sciences to evaluate the impact of the proposed rule changes on levels of air pollution and the public's health – an analysis that the EPA had failed to complete" (League of Conservation Voters 2004, 18). The amendment was defeated by a forty-six–to-sixty vote. Among the supporters, though, were Carper and Sununu, as well as Lautenberg and Sarbanes. Fitzgerald, Santorum, and Voinovich voted against it, and Harkin did not cast a vote.

Their choices on this measure provide information about their preferences that helps to contextualize their other introductions on air quality. Fitzgerald, Santorum, Sarbanes, Sununu, and Harkin had no measures specifically about clean air (Fitzgerald, Harkin, and Sarbanes had referenced "clean air and water," in their campaigns and their pollution measures all addressed water) and Carper had no other introductions on air quality beyond the three anti–New Source Review measures discussed previously. Lautenberg, though, had two solidly pro–clean air bills dealing with renewable energy and greenhouse gas emissions,[13] and Voinovich introduced four bills.[14] Two of these (S 2362 in the 106th and S 1590 in the 107th) dealt with environmental review procedures and seem consistent with Voinovich's stance on New Source Review. Demonstrating how complicated all of this is, though, two more bills (S 1176 in the 107th and S 2233 in the 108th) focused on improving the quality of research done by the EPA (by appointing a deputy director of science and technology), and Carper, who voted against Voinovich's stance on New Source Review, was a cosponsor of these.

What, then, should we conclude about whether these senators' behavior matches their campaign claims? Again, for most, there seems to be a clear alignment. Carper's, Sarbanes', and Sununu's pollution claims line up with a pro–Clean Air stance. Fitzgerald and Harkin were not active on pollution, and seem best classified as examples of legislators who simply did not address their campaign claims. Santorum's case parallels Taylor's in the House. One of his 2000 ads ("Pop Up Video") claimed that "Rick wrote the Pollution Act." It is not clear exactly what this refers to (because there was no bill in his previous term called the "Pollution Act"), but it is most likely S 1521, in the 106th Congress, that proposed giving a grant to the National Environmental Policy Institute (NEPI) to develop a pilot program "relating to the use of telecommuting as a means of reducing emissions of air pollutants." Importantly, though, NEPI is a private entity that often takes an antiregulatory stance on environmental issues relating to businesses. Thus, this is another situation in which the claim is not technically incorrect, but in which a voter who inferred from it that the candidate was especially pro-environment would be wrong.

[13] These were S 1232 in the 109th Congress ("A bill to amend the Clean Air Act to increase production and use of renewable fuel and to increase the energy independence of the United States, and for other purposes") and S 1411 in the 110th ("A bill to amend the Clean Air Act to establish within the Environmental Protection Agency an office to measure and report on greenhouse gas emissions of Federal agencies").

[14] These bills are S 2362 in the 106th ("A bill to amend the Clean Air Act to direct the Administrator of the Environmental Protection Agency to consider risk assessments and cost-benefit analyses as part of the process of establishing a new or revised air quality standard"), S 1176 in the 107th ("A bill to strengthen research conducted by the Environmental Protection Agency, and for other purposes"), S 1590 in the 107th ("A bill to amend the National Environmental Policy Act of 1969 to improve the environmental review process that is associated with authorizations required under Federal law for construction, operation, or maintenance of energy facilities"), and S 2233 in the 108th ("A bill to amend the Environmental Research, Development, and Demonstration Authorization Act of 1979 to establish in the Environmental Protection Agency the position of Deputy Administrator for Science and Technology").

Voinovich's promise keeping on air pollution is the most difficult to assess because his activity in office includes some measures that were supported by environmental groups and some that were opposed by them. Nonetheless, it would be unfair to call his campaign claims misleading, since he does make clear where he comes down on the issue. In the 1998 ad, "Led Nation in Business," he said:

> Creating good jobs and protecting the environment. An architect of Ohio's EPA, he's done it without sacrificing the environment. Ohio's air and water are the cleanest they've been in over 20 years. He's proven he can balance a soaring economy with a cleaner environment. He'll do the same in the Senate.

Indeed, this is what his actual activity in his first Senate term appeared to do, and so we would be hard-pressed to argue that his claims were insincere, even though a casual observer might have missed the nuance.

CAMPAIGN APPEALS AND ROLL CALL VOTING

There appears to be very little evidence that candidates regularly lie or obfuscate by introducing legislation that contradicts their campaign appeals. This supports my arguments about the value of an agenda-based notion of promise keeping.[15] However, the analyses thus far have been necessarily limited to candidates who made specific appeals, such that there was some detailed content that could be matched (or not) with an introduction or vote. This is only a subset of the group of candidates who discuss any particular issue, and it may not be a representative one. It is possible that candidates who make specific pledges commit themselves more strongly to a point of view on an issue and so may have more to lose by diverging from it. If I were to expand the analyses to include all candidates, would I find a linkage between their choices to discuss an issue and their relative positions on it?

In other words, applied to the issues studied here, did those who talked about defense and the environment vote differently on these issues in office than those who did not raise them? Exploring this possibility helps to explain more of what it means for a candidate to choose to raise an issue, and also enables me to compare agenda and position-based conceptions of promise keeping. There are at least two reasonable hypotheses one

[15] Of course, my examination focused on only two issues, but there is no reason to think that this would be different for different issues, and, in fact, on issues mentioned more rarely, there is probably an even closer match (i.e., why would a candidate take the trouble to discuss consumer issues only to introduce measures that roll back protections?).

might propose about the relationship between mentioning an issue in the campaign and one's general position on that issue. Discussing an issue could indicate that one is more interested in it and hence will be more active, but not translate into systematic differences in position on policies related to that issue. Alternately, the intensity of interest in an issue that leads candidates to choose to discuss it could also mean that they hold different opinions on it (most likely by being more extreme) than their colleagues who forgo it in their campaigns in favor of other issues.

To determine which of these hypotheses is correct, I need a dependent variable that taps legislators' general positions on defense and the environment. The scorecards issued by interest groups such as the Center for Security Policy (CSP) (defense) and the League of Conservation Voters (LCV) (environment) provide good measures of this. These groups, like many other organizations, select a set of votes in each congress that they view as particularly important to their cause or emblematic of what they stand for and then report each representative's and senator's "score" on these votes on a scale of zero to one hundred.[16] My primary independent variable is whether or not the legislator had mentioned the issue in reference to himself or herself in the previous campaign. If the coefficient on this variable is significant, it indicates that candidates who discuss the issue differ systematically in their roll call voting from those who do not.

Figure 5.1 summarizes the results from a series of models designed to test my hypotheses, all of which are estimated using OLS regression. The dots represent the coefficient on having mentioned the environment (panel one) or defense (panel two), with the lines designating the 90 percent confidence intervals. Each coefficient is from analyses for a different group of legislators (i.e., in the House or Senate, just House/Senate Democrats, just House/Senate Republicans, etc.). Controls (not presented) include party (because voting scores tend to be largely bimodal, with partisanship explaining the vast majority of the variation)[17] and election year (since there are different numbers of votes in each year, the

[16] For the Senate, I average each member's score across the three congresses in the term. Complete CSP scores were not available for the 106th Congress. Thus, for analyses of defense, the 1998 sample is omitted.

[17] The mean LCV score for House Democrats is 79 percent, compared to 14 percent for House Republicans, and 77 percent for Senate Democrats, compared to 17 percent for Senate Republicans. As expected, the patterns for CSP scores are the opposite: House Democrats average 37 percent, compared to 85 percent for House Republicans, and Senate Democrats average 30 percent, compared to 85 percent for their Republican colleagues.

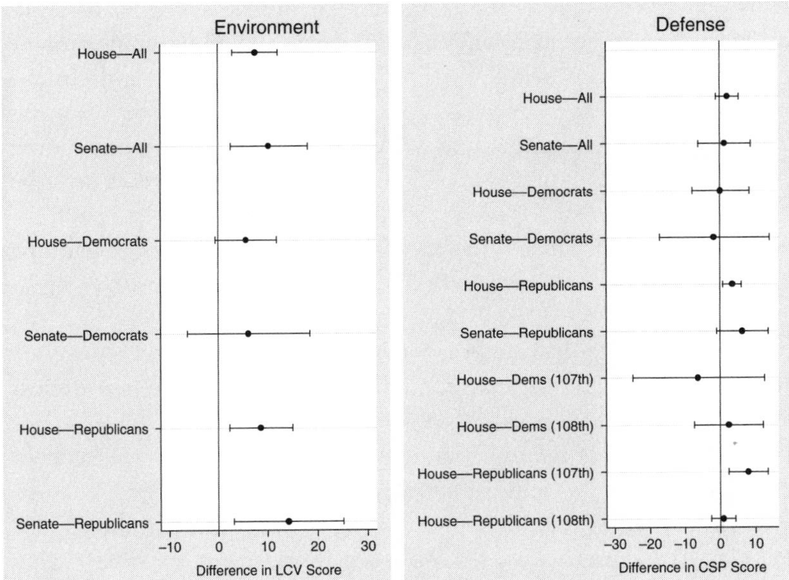

FIGURE 5.1 Campaign Discussion and Interest Group Scores on the Environment and Defense

Note: The dots in the figure represent OLS coefficients and the lines the accompanying 90 percent confidence intervals (although all differences are significant at $p < .05$). The dependent variable is members' vote scores on either the League of Conservation Voters or Center for Security Policy scorecards in the term following the election under study. Independent variables include whether a candidate mentioned the issue, party, and election year.

distribution of percentages is a bit different). For the House, I also cluster the standard errors on the legislator.

Do we see differences in roll call choices for those who raise an issue compared to those who do not? The first sets of results reveal that the patterns are consistent across chambers, but differ by issue. For the environment, in both the House and Senate, candidates who mentioned the issue went on to receive higher scores from the League of Conservation Voters. This finding is impressive because it averages across all candidates who raised an issue, and, as we know from the preceding discussion, a few candidates offered positions that were not clearly pro-environment, and this orientation was fairly easily discernible from their ads.[18] Thus, this

[18] When these legislators are removed from the sample and the analyses are rerun, the coefficients on having mentioned the environment are, as expected, larger.

tells us that a voter who observes a candidate talking about the environment in a way that seems pro-environment can be safe in assuming that the candidate is indeed pro-environment (at least by the standards of the League of Conservation Voters). The significant relationship between mentioning the environment and LCV scores also holds when I omit candidates who made specific appeals (so that the comparison is between those who made vague appeals to those who did not talk about the environment at all); indeed, the coefficients are even larger, suggesting that vague appeals are even *more* likely to signal support for environmental causes.[19]

While the same general patterns hold for defense, none of the effects are statistically significant, so that candidates who do and do not discuss defense (either vaguely or specifically) have indistinguishable Center for Security Policy voting scores. What might explain this difference between the environment and defense? One possibility is the nature of the issues. The environment is probably more unidimensional, such that the implied direction to a claim about it is fairly obvious. For defense, the situation is a bit more complicated. Legislators' Center for Security Policy scores reflect the extent to which they are hawkish, but many candidates focus their defense appeals on veterans, and it is not clear that support for policies to help veterans necessarily translates into support for defense programs, the war on terrorism, and so on. Similarly, appeals on foreign policy that call for aid for a particular country do not necessarily signal hawkish behavior either. Thus, "defense" as an issue encompasses some dimensions that are potentially at odds with one another, such that there is more heterogeneity in the issue positions of candidates who raise it.

To explore these possibilities in a bit more depth, I also broke out the sample by party, since Democrats and Republicans who talk about defense or the environment may differ from one another in their specific emphases and in their implied positions.[20] The models are summarized in the lower parts of the panels in Figure 5.1. For the environment, I find that in both

[19] This is likely because candidates who hold complicated positions on the environment and choose to raise it in their campaigns feel the need to offer some detail about the particulars of their views or actions. For instance, a candidate such as Charles Taylor is not going to say that he is "pro-environment," but instead will talk specifically about his activity on pollution.

[20] Ideally, to tap these differences, I would either explore a variety of different scorecards about defense or break out the sample by type of defense claim, but the N is too low for systematic analysis of the latter, and the CSP was the only scorecard available for the majority of the time period I am examining.

chambers, it is Republicans who drive the effect. House and Senate Republicans who discuss the environment in their campaigns vote more pro-environment in office than those who do not, but Democrats who do and do not discuss it do not differ significantly in their LCV scores. This makes sense: because the environment is a Democrat-owned issue, Republicans who trespass to discuss it are more likely to be outliers relative to their colleagues. For Democrats, though, it is not necessarily the case that we'd expect them to be significantly *more* pro-environment than their already pro-environment colleagues, though as shown in Chapter 3, they are significantly more interested in the topic, engaging in more activity on it.

If this logic also holds for defense and foreign policy, we should expect to see differences for Democrats but not Republicans. However, this is not the case. For the Senate, there is once again no relationship between appeals and voting scores. Perhaps this should not be unexpected, given that there is also no significant relationship between their appeals and their activity levels on defense. For the House, there is a relationship, but it is once again the Republicans for whom we see it – those who talked about defense voted more in line with the CSP's preferences. House Democrats who talked about defense, though, were no more or less supportive of the CSP than their colleagues who did not mention the issue.

We should interpret these results about defense with caution, since an obvious complicating factor is that the September 11, 2001, terrorist attacks occurred during this time period. This clearly changed the defense agenda, and may have changed voting patterns as well. Therefore, as a final step, I further broke out the sample by election year to investigate the relationships for defense mentions and voting in different congresses. I do this only for the House (since for the Senate, all of the sample years contained substantial periods of post–September 11 voting), comparing the voting of Democrats and Republicans who did and did not mention defense in the 2000 election and in the 2002 election.

These findings are revealing. As shown in the panel for defense, for Republicans, having mentioned defense in 2000 is a significant signal about voting in the 107th Congress – those who did so were more hawkish, going on to earn CSP scores about 7 percent higher than their peers who did not mention it. In 2002, though, when many more candidates discussed it, it loses its efficacy as a signal about position. For the Democrats, there is also variation across years. For the 2000 election sample, the relationship between having mentioned defense and CSP scores, although not significant, is negative. For 2002, though, the sign flips, and the coefficient is positive. These shifts likely reflect a difference in the types of candidates discussing defense pre– and post–September 11, as well as what they intended to signal when choosing to raise it.

CONCLUSIONS

The fundamental conclusion to be drawn from this chapter is that an agenda-based approach is a valid and meaningful way of conceptualizing promise making and promise keeping. Earlier analyses established that, particularly for the House, candidates who talk about an issue are more active on it in Congress than those who do not. We have seen here that for both chambers this activity nearly always aligns with the content of what candidates said they would do. More generally, there are often linkages between priorities and positions, such that candidates who choose to talk about an issue can send signals both about what they will be active on and what positions they will adopt on those issues.

Having established these patterns, my next step is to move beyond an issue-by-issue exploration of the linkages between appeals and activity to investigate differences in levels of promise keeping between and across legislators. In the next chapter, I seek to explain why some representatives and senators are more attentive to their campaign promises than others and to explore how they make choices about the location and timing of their promise-keeping activities.

6

The Who, When, and Where of Follow-through

The previous chapters have established the general outlines of the extent of the linkages between campaign appeals and legislative activity and their origins. Candidates, particularly for the House, often choose their campaign themes on the basis of their personal interests in and records on them, so their appeals on the campaign trail serve as accurate predictors about what their priorities in office are likely to be. Moreover, the content of legislators' promise-keeping bills aligns closely with the nature of their appeals. And, under certain circumstances, appeals can provide an independent source of information about the content of legislators' future activity, above and beyond what one might glean from an investigation of their past records or policy commitments.

To this point, my analyses have focused on investigating the presence or absence of appeals–activity linkages on an issue-by-issue basis. From a representational perspective, though, we should also be interested in representatives' and senators' promise keeping more generally. In this chapter, I push beyond asking whether those who make a promise about an issue are more active on it or whether there is correspondence between the content of a specific claim and the content of later activity to explore the broader dynamics of promise keeping and its place in legislative behavior. For instance, how much of legislators' agendas are devoted to their campaign themes? Do levels of promise keeping vary greatly across legislators? What explains why some are more attentive to their campaign themes than others? Are rates of responsiveness affected by legislators' electoral vulnerability, seniority, ideology, or institutional standing? Do legislators vary their follow-through across time within their terms or by activity type? Do these patterns differ by chamber, or are they similar for representatives and senators?

To answer these questions, I first need to identify overall measures of promise keeping at the level of individual members (i.e., a dependent variable or variables that capture their promise keeping across issues). The most obvious indicator of "keeping one's promises" is the number of introductions and/or cosponsorships legislators devote to the issues they raised in their previous campaigns. Are they very active on these issues or not? Take, for instance, Jim DeMint (R-SC) and Tom Tancredo (R-CO). In the 1998 election, they both raised the same three issues: education, Social Security, and taxes.[1] In the next congress (the 106th), DeMint engaged in forty-four activities on these issues and Tancredo engaged in fifty-seven. By this count, Tancredo would be judged the most responsive to his campaign appeals.

However, this assessment quickly becomes complicated. Due to differences in overall activity levels, DeMint's activity on his campaign appeals comprised 25 percent of his total agenda (of 173 policy-relevant activities), while Tancredo's was only about 20 percent (of his agenda of 288 activities). Thus, if relative responsiveness is the standard of interest, the conclusion about who was most faithful to his campaign promises is reversed – DeMint followed through more so than did Tancredo. Each of these measures has value, but, depending on the question one is asking, one may be more appropriate than the other. In the analysis in this and later chapters, I alternate between them.[2]

Table 6.1 presents data on these measures of promise keeping. The "count of activity" variables are calculated by summing all of a legislator's subsequent activities across the issues in his or her previous campaign agenda.[3] The denominator for the proportion calculations is the number of policy-relevant activities engaged in by the legislator (i.e., omitting governmental operations activities). In these and all of the analyses to

[1] That DeMint and Tancredo (both Republicans) discussed education and Social Security is another illustration of the point that issue ownership is not deterministic – as we saw in Chapter 3, every issue in my coding scheme was raised by at least one candidate from each party.

[2] Another possible indicator is the number or proportion of campaign issues on which a legislator took some sort of post-campaign action. For instance, if both candidates discussed two issues and devoted one hundred activities to them, but one performed fifty on each and the other performed one hundred on one and zero on another, we might judge the former to be more responsive. However, among members of the sample, there is little variation on this measure, so I opt instead for the number/proportion of activities, with controls for the total number of themes.

[3] All of these measures focus on promise keeping on issues candidates raised in reference to themselves.

TABLE 6.1 *The Prevalence of Promise Keeping in Legislative Activity*

	House of Representatives	Senate
Raw Counts of Campaign-Themed Activity		
Mean All Activities (Range)	77 acts (1–327)	295 acts (55–874)
Mean Introductions (Range)	4 (0–22)	47 (5–173)
Mean Cosponsorships (Range)	73 (0–324)	249 (52–740)
Campaign-Themed Activity as a Percentage of Policy Activity		
Mean All Activities (Range)	36.5 (2.1–84.2)	53.4 (12.4–91.7)
Mean Introductions (Range)	40.7 (0–100)	56.5 (6.4–100)
Mean Cosponsorships (Range)	36.3 (0–83.3)	53.2 (14.2–91.5)

follow in this chapter, the sample is limited to legislators who had raised at least one issue in reference to themselves (so that there is the potential for follow-through), and, for the Senate, who had completed a full term (since there is a considerable portion of the sample who did not). This includes 360 representatives and 71 senators.

Three important findings jump out from this table. First, there is considerable variation across legislators – some devote nearly all of their activities in office to their campaign appeals, while others are considerably less attentive to them. Second, within each chamber, rates of responsiveness are similar across activities. Legislators spend a roughly equal amount of their overall introduction and cosponsorship efforts on their campaign issues. Third, there is a noticeable House–Senate difference. Senators devote a higher proportion of their legislative activity to their campaign themes than do representatives. However, this is due almost entirely to the fact that, on average, they have more issues in their campaign agendas.

In reflecting on these patterns, it becomes clear that while these indicators do provide some useful information, by themselves they enable us to make only very crude assessments of relative responsiveness. Indeed, there are a number of factors that vary across legislators that could explain their volume of activity on a set of issues, but are not related to their levels of commitment to their campaign themes. The proportions capture the effects of differences in overall activity, which is the most obvious variable of this type, but there are also others. For instance, in comparing across legislators, we also need to take into account the fact that candidates, even within the same chamber, vary in the number of issues they raise. How, for example, might we make relative assessments about the promise-keeping activity of DeMint and Tancredo compared to that of David Price (D-NC), who, like them, talked about education, Social Security, and taxes in his 1998 campaign, but who also mentioned a fourth issue, health care? Because Price has more issues, it seems reasonable to expect him to engage in a higher overall volume of activity on his campaign agenda.

Equally important, issues differ in their salience, with some the subject of more legislation than others. This can be due to the relative popularity of an issue at a given time, to its amenability to legislative action (i.e., the scope of the issue, number of committees in which it is addressed, etc.), or to some combination of the two. For example, although Social Security was a high-profile campaign theme in the 1998, 2000, and 2002 elections, from a lawmaking perspective, it is fairly narrow, dealing with a single policy. As such, it was the focus of a relatively small number of introductions (in the House, fewer than one hundred per congress across the time period studied here). Compare this to an issue such as jobs and infrastructure, which received about eight times the amount of legislative attention.

These differences in aggregate issue attention should influence the raw amount of promise keeping we observe, as well as how we evaluate this activity in terms of relative responsiveness. Salience matters less for introductions, since the issues on which individual legislators choose to introduce and how much they do so is within their control. In contrast, the number of opportunities to cosponsor will vary depending on the salience of the issues raised. So, for example, had DeMint and Tancredo discussed jobs and infrastructure rather than Social Security, they would have had 749 more opportunities to cosponsor a campaign theme-related measure. We therefore should anticipate a higher volume of campaign-related activity for candidates who discussed higher-salience issues.

While it might be possible to combine all of these factors into a single index (i.e., a measure of promise keeping after taking into account differences in the size of campaign and legislative agendas and the salience of their content), the resulting variable would not be readily interpretable or particularly meaningful. Instead, when comparing across legislators, my approach will be to rely primarily on counts of activity as the dependent variable and then to control for factors such as the number of activities a legislator engages in, the number of themes from the campaign, and the salience of those themes. Doing so will enable me to evaluate the effects of the independent variables of interest (e.g., vulnerability or seniority) after taking into account these more "structural" differences between legislators and their agendas. Table 6.2 summarizes these structural variables.

The large ranges in the values of these variables across legislators support including them as controls. It is important to acknowledge,

TABLE 6.2 *Summary of Structural Control Variables*

Variable	Measured as	Range	Mean
# of Campaign Issues	# of issues the legislator raised in the previous campaign in reference to himself or herself	1–10 (H) 2–13 (S)	4.7 (H) 7.3 (S)
Policy Activities	# of all introductions and cosponsorships made by each legislator on nongovernmental operations matters	43–757 (H) 126–1,380 (S)	212.3 (H) 545.1 (S)
Salience	Total # of bills and resolutions introduced in Congress on a legislator's campaign themes (in the term following the election under study)	75–3,519 (H) 1,198–8,281 (S)	1,534.4 (H) 4252.7 (S)

though, that there are also strong theoretical arguments for *not* doing so and instead for focusing solely on comparing raw counts of promise-keeping activity. Legislators could almost always be more active if they wanted to (and so undertake more promise keeping), and, when constituents or potential challengers look to an incumbent's record to see whether a legislator has followed through on a campaign promise, they probably are more apt to consider the number of activities on an issue than the percentage of his or her agenda those activities comprise.[4] Along the same lines, it seems unlikely that a constituent expects less follow-through from his or her representative if that candidate discussed Social Security rather than a higher-salience issue such as jobs and infrastructure.

Nonetheless, I come down on the side of controlling for total activity levels because I recognize that there are some institutional constraints on activity. When I compare across legislators, accounting for total activity also provides a stricter test of relative responsiveness because it controls for the likelihood that, all other things being equal, legislators who are very active are more likely to introduce or cosponsor on any given issue. A similar logic applies to issue salience. Legislators should have a higher

[4] Constituents may care too about the importance of the activities. In Chapter 8, I investigate the policy effects of promise-keeping introductions.

probability of engagement on high-profile, high-activity issues, apart from their desire to demonstrate responsiveness.

EXPLAINING VARIATION IN PROMISE KEEPING

The central question, then, is whether the variation in promise keeping uncovered in Table 6.1 is due solely to structural factors, or whether it is also a function of more theoretically interesting characteristics of legislators, such as their electoral vulnerability, seniority, party, and ideology. As I discussed in Chapter 2, for each of these characteristics there are competing expectations about the direction that any effects of these might take, so if both are at work, they could wash each other out. Therefore, for any significant effects to emerge, the patterns in one direction will have to be fairly strong and consistent.

Electoral Vulnerability

The most common view in the literature on legislative behavior and representation is that more vulnerable legislators, who should be the most concerned about their reelection prospects, should also be the most likely to engage in high levels of reelection-promoting behavior. This argument suggests a negative relationship between vote shares in the previous election and subsequent levels of promise keeping, with more vulnerable representatives devoting more of their agendas to their prior campaign themes. As I argued earlier, though, this hypothesis presumes that legislators do not want to follow through on their appeals, and do so only because of electoral imperatives. If they raise issues at least in part because of their genuine interest in them, this logic unravels a bit. More generally, there is evidence that the causal relationship between vulnerability and behavior may go the other way, with electoral safety itself a function of savvy, responsive behavior in the past (Canes-Wrone, Brady, and Cogan 2002; Sulkin 2005). If similar dynamics are operating here, we will see a positive relationship between vote shares and promise keeping, with the safest representatives demonstrating the highest levels of follow-through on their appeals.

Seniority and Leadership Status

The same reasoning applies to the effects of seniority. If promise keeping has electoral advantages, these should be learned about over time, which may result in senior legislators following through at the highest rates. However, longer terms in office could mean that legislators have developed a stable "personal vote" through casework and constituency service and so are less reliant on their policy accomplishments for securing reelection. Seniority therefore may make members feel freer to pursue a variety of interests. It could also present them with a number of other responsibilities in the chamber that require their time and effort, leading them to display less commitment to their campaign themes. Thus, it is just as plausible that we would see a negative relationship between seniority and promise keeping, particularly after taking variation in electoral vulnerability into account. For similar reasons, I also explore the effects of institutional stature. My expectation is that leaders should be pulled in a variety of directions and so may devote less of their time to their previous campaign issues.

Party and Ideology

Legislators' party affiliations may also affect their levels of promise keeping. Although there is no reason to expect that, in general, members of one party would be more or less responsive than members of the other, it is possible that majority or minority status could matter. Each of the Senate terms in the sample (the 106th through 108th Congresses, the 107th through 109th, and the 108th through 110th) features a mix of Democratic and Republican majorities, but for all three House terms, Republicans were in control. This majority status may have provided institutional advantages for follow-through. On the flip side, because minority members have fewer venues for seeing their interests addressed, they may rely more on their introductions and cosponsorships for demonstrating their commitment to them (Koger 2003), resulting in higher levels of promise keeping. Regardless, if party matters in this way, I predict that there will be more of an effect in the House than in the Senate since the party in power was consistent in the former across the time period that I study.

Finally, ideological extremity could shape levels promise keeping. On one hand, ideologues may be more deeply committed to their campaign issues and so may pursue them more intently in office. On the other, commitment to issue *positions* may be different from commitment to issue *agendas*, and relatively extreme legislators may have strategic incentives to highlight in their campaigns issues that are not their true priorities but make them appear more moderate. Accordingly, we could

TABLE 6.3 *Factors Affecting Promise Keeping*

	House # of Promise Keeping Activities	**Senate # of Promise Keeping Activities**
Previous Vote Share	.006**	.006*
	(.003)	(.003)
Unopposed?	−.299*	−.051
	(.169)	(.175)
New?	.023	.132**
	(.040)	(.058)
Senior?	−.116**	.070
	(.048)	(.052)
Democrat?	.024	.014
	(.047)	(.050)
Ideological Extremity	−.107	−.007
	(.151)	(.180)
Leader?	−136**	.148*
	(.066)	(.081)
# of Campaign Issues	.056***	.035**
	(.013)	(.015)
Issue Salience	.001***	.000***
	(.000)	(.000)
Policy Activities	.004***	.002***
	(.000)	(.000)
2000 Election	.027	.026
	(.035)	(.051)
2002 Election	−.076*	.012
	(.039)	(.056)
Constant	1.900	3.093
	(.208)	(.262)
N	360	71
Log likelihood	−1566.62	−367.82

Note: Cell entries are negative binomial regression coefficients with standard errors in parentheses. The dependent variable is the number of promise-keeping activities engaged in by a legislator.
***= $p < .01$; **= $p < .05$; *= $p < .10$.

even see a negative relationship between extremity and levels of promise keeping.

To ascertain how vulnerability, seniority, institutional stature, party, and ideology are related to rates of promise keeping, I conduct negative binomial regression analyses, presented in Table 6.3. The dependent variable is a count of the number of introductions and cosponsorships undertaken by a legislator on his or her previous campaign issues, and the primary independent variables of interest include two measures of electoral security (the legislator's percentage of the major party vote share in the last election and a dummy variable for whether or not he or she was unopposed), two measures of seniority (a dummy for newly elected legislators and a dummy for "senior," which for the House reflects having served more than eight years and for the Senate reflects having served more than twelve years[5]), leadership status (a dummy coded one if the member was Speaker of the House, a majority or minority leader in the chamber, or a whip), party (a dummy variable coded one for Democrats and zero for Republicans), and ideological extremity (the absolute value of each legislator's common-space NOMINATE score, which ranges from about zero to one, where higher scores equal more extremism, either liberal or conservative). I also control for the structural variables discussed earlier (number of campaign issues, salience of those issues, and total policy activity) as well as election year, and, for the House, since some legislators appear in the sample in multiple election years, I cluster the standard errors on the legislator.

Who keeps their promises most faithfully? Is it the most electorally vulnerable or the least? Senior or junior members? Democrats or Republicans? Ideologues or moderates? Perhaps the most interesting findings relate to vulnerability. All other things being equal, the higher a legislator's vote share in the previous election, the *more* promise-keeping activities he or she engaged in during the next congress. However, these results, particularly in the House, are marked by an intriguing nonlinearity. The negative coefficient on "unopposed" means that legislators who faced no major party opposition in the previous election followed through on their appeals at lower rates than those who had a challenger.[6] This suggests that there is an element of truth in both of the competing hypotheses about the effects of vulnerability. While some vulnerability is necessary to induce responsiveness, for most legislators, more vulnerability does not mean more responsiveness. Instead, the legislators who are most attentive to their campaign appeals are those who fall in the middle in terms of vulnerability. They are neither in serious jeopardy of losing their seats, nor are they so safe that they are unconcerned about their reelection prospects. The magnitude of the effects is substantial: an increase in vote share from 50 to 70 percent is associated with an increase of about seven

[5] These cutoffs are chosen because they relatively equally divide the non-new members into two groups. If I were to use raw years in office as the measure, there are several outliers who would unduly influence the results.

[6] In interpreting these results, we should also keep in mind that unopposed candidates who nonetheless decide to campaign are a somewhat unrepresentative group.

promise-keeping activities in the House and about thirty-one in the Senate.[7]

The effects of seniority are also notable. In both chambers, there is evidence that more junior members are more attentive to their campaign themes. In the House, senior status is negatively associated with the number of promise-keeping activities engaged in by a legislator (about seven fewer activities on average), and, in the Senate, returning members undertake a lower volume of promise-keeping activities than their newly elected colleagues (about twenty-five fewer activities). Relatedly, in both chambers, leaders engage in less promise keeping than do rank-and-file members (a difference of about seven or eight activities in the House and thirty-five in the Senate).

Together, these findings indicate that vulnerability and seniority matter. All other things equal, relatively safe and relatively junior members tend to be the most responsive. However, there is no systematic effect of party or ideological extremity. Democrats and Republicans, ideologues and moderates, all engage in similar levels of attentiveness to their campaign themes. Finally, the structural controls largely work in the way predicted: representatives and senators with high levels of activity, those who had larger campaign agendas, and those who focused on high-salience issues tend to engage in a greater volume of activity on these issues.

PROMISE KEEPING BY TYPE OF ACTIVITY

Do these patterns hold when we separate out introductions and cosponsorships? The dependent variables in the analyses in Table 6.3 combine these activities into a single indicator of promise keeping, but as was obvious from the descriptive statistics about promise keeping in Table 6.1, when we aggregate activity across the issues in legislators' agendas, the difference in the volume of introductions and cosponsorships becomes quite large. Thus, while summing introductions and cosponsorships was justifiable when examining the appeals–activity linkages on an issue-by-issue basis, it is less so here. In short, the findings in Table 6.3 are driven largely by cosponsorships and it is possible that they may not also apply to introductions.

[7] These values are calculated using Tomz, Wittenberg, and King's CLARIFY (2003; see also King, Tomz, and Wittenberg 2000), and setting all variables at their means. In comparing the numbers for the House and Senate, it is important to contextualize them, as senators have longer terms and larger campaign agendas as targets for their follow-through.

I begin my exploration with a basic question: Are there differences in individual legislators' rates of promise keeping for introductions and cosponsorships? In other words, do they devote more of their introduction or cosponsorship agendas to their campaign themes? The answer to this question has theoretical implications for understanding legislative decision making and normative implications for assessing the quality of representation. Introductions are the more labor-intensive of the two activities because they require more than just signing on to an existing piece of legislation, and sponsors often take an active role in promoting their legislation (by seeking cosponsors, speaking on the floor, etc.). If legislators devoted considerably more of their cosponsorship agendas than their introduction agendas to their campaign themes, we might conclude that the responsiveness was less sincere than if promise keeping was evident at similar levels across both types of activities.

Given what we have learned about promise keeping thus far, there is little reason to expect that legislators would demonstrate follow-through on their campaign appeals through their cosponsorships but not their introductions. Results in Chapter 3 showed that there are strong correlations between the content of legislators' introductions and cosponsorships (so that those who engage in a high number of cosponsorships on an issue also tend to engage in a high number of introductions), and that on an issue-by-issue basis, promise-keeping linkages emerge just as frequently for both types of activities. However, these analyses do not tap whether individual legislators, on average, devote more of one activity than the other to promise keeping.

Since the comparison of interest here is *within* individual legislators' behavior rather than just across legislators, paired t-tests are the most appropriate tests, and because the volume of introductions and cosponsors differs so much, proportions provide for a better measure than raw counts. It is not necessary to control for other structural variables here, because factors such as agenda size and salience may differ across legislators, but are constant for an individual legislator, so the context in which he or she makes decisions about how to allocate introductions and cosponsorships is the same.

These analyses, summarized in Figure 6.1, reveal that, for both chambers, rates of promise keeping are, in fact, higher for *introductions* (for the House, 41 percent for introductions compared to 36 percent for cosponsorships, $t = 4.1$; $p < .01$; for the Senate, 57 percent for introductions compared to 53 percent for cosponsorships, $t = 2.2$, $p < .05$). Of course, in terms of raw numbers, this still amounts to more cosponsorships than

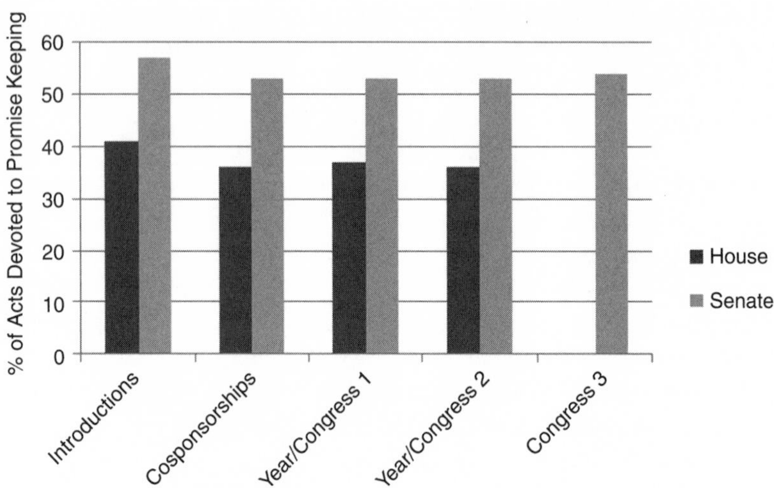

FIGURE 6.1 Rates of Promise Keeping across Activities and across Time

introductions, and these percentages may mask variation in the decision making of particular subgroups of legislators (a possibility I explore in more detail later in this chapter). These results do confirm, though, that when representatives and senators choose to follow through on their appeals, it is not just through the relatively easy activity of cosponsorship that they do so. This provides further evidence that promise keeping is a sincere and potentially consequential activity.

The next question is whether the same characteristics associated with high levels of promise keeping on introductions are also linked to high rates of responsiveness on cosponsorships. When I replicate the analyses from Table 6.3 for introductions and cosponsorships taken separately, I uncover no notable differences between the two for the House. In the Senate, though, I find that characteristics of individual legislators (i.e., seniority, vulnerability, leadership status, etc.) are stronger predictors of variation in cosponsorship follow-through than introduction follow-through. New members, safer members, and nonleaders devote more of their cosponsorships to their campaign themes, but these variables have no relationship with their volume of introductions on these issues. How should we interpret this finding? When combined with the previous results that showed that rates of promise keeping are higher on introductions than on cosponsorships, it actually suggests a positive, if tentative, conclusion: all senators are similarly responsive on their introductions, regardless of their vulnerability, seniority, or the like.

PROMISE KEEPING ACROSS TIME

The difference in the length of House and Senate terms is perhaps the most important distinction between legislative life in the two chambers. Because representatives serve two-year terms in the House, their next election is quickly upon them, so campaigning never really stops, and, with the exception of big exogenous shocks such as the terrorist attacks of September 11, 2001, the public and congressional agendas do not typically change much. In contrast, with terms three times as long, senators have more time to devote to goals other than reelection. Longer terms also mean that the issues they talked about in their campaigns as long ago as five or six years prior may have been resolved to their satisfaction or simply fallen from the scene by the time their terms reach their end.

These differing incentives and constraints may shape the distribution of promise keeping across legislators' terms. To assess this possibility, I once again use paired-samples t-tests, since the comparisons of interest are within individual legislators' behavior. For the House, the natural breakdown is between year one and year two of a term,[8] and, for the Senate, the breakdown is the congress within the term (i.e., the first, second, or third). For both chambers, my measure of promise keeping is the percentage of legislators' agendas devoted to campaign issues. This is more appropriate than raw counts because the volume of overall activity varies across legislators' terms – representatives are much more active in the first year of their terms (about 166 policy-relevant activities in year one compared to about 47 in year two, $t = 38.3$; $p < .01$), and senators' activity levels increase as their terms progress (from about 24 introductions in congress one to 28 in congress two to 32 in congress three, and from about 147 cosponsorships in congresses one and two to about 167 in congress three; all differences are significant at $p <. 01$).

The results for both chambers, summarized in Figure 6.1, indicate that relative levels of promise keeping are mostly invariant to time to election. House members devote about 37 percent of their agendas in year one to their campaign appeals, compared to about 36 percent in year two

[8] This breakdown is potentially a bit noisy for cosponsorships since it is based on when the cosponsored measure was introduced, not when a particular legislator decided to cosponsor it (i.e., some are "original" cosponsors who sign on to the bill at the time of introduction, and some sign on later). However, I get very similar results when I focus only on introductions, so I am confident that the dynamics across introductions and cosponsorships are similar.

(t =.40).[9] Breaking this out by activity type confirms that there are no differences in promise keeping in year one versus year two for cosponsorships, but that legislators do engage in slightly more promise keeping on introductions in their first year than in their second (41 percent compared to 35 percent of their agendas, t= 2.0; $p < .01$). However, given the low number of introductions, this percentage difference translates to a quite small difference in activities.

For the Senate, there are no differences in rates of promise keeping on either introductions (57 to 58 percent of senators' agendas in every congress) or cosponsorships (about 53 percent in each congress). This finding is in contrast to other work on Senate behavior, which shows that senators tend to become more reelection-oriented as time passes, moderating their roll call voting (Ahuja 1994; Bernhard and Sala 2006; Shapiro et al. 1990; Wright and Berkman 1986), attempting to increase the flow of appropriations (Shepsle et al. 2009), and attending to issues about which their previous challengers criticized them (Sulkin 2005). However, I do find that senators' *raw* volume of promise keeping increases over time, from fourteen to sixteen to eighteen introductions (all differences significant at $p < .05$) and from seventy-nine cosponsorships in congresses one and two to about ninety-one in congress three ($p < .01$).

Considering the raw volume of activity in the House also leads us to a slightly different conclusion. Given the differences in activity rates in year one and year two, 36 to 37 percent of representatives' agendas translates to an average of sixty promise-keeping activities in year one, but only about seventeen in year two. This suggests that representatives may be most devoted to their campaign promises right after the election, perhaps because they are freshest in their minds and/or because they want to demonstrate responsiveness early, before potential challengers have made the decision to run in the next election. Senators, on the other hand, may be less likely to act immediately on their appeals, but become more attentive to them as their terms progress and the next election looms nearer.

To better understand why legislators make the choices they do about when and where to engage in promise keeping, I explore in the next chapter the implications of decisions about location and timing. For instance, if there is an electoral payoff to promise keeping, we might expect more of these

[9] There are three representatives – Steve Largent (R-OK) and Joe Scarborough (R-FL) in the 107th and Ernie Fletcher (R-KY) in the 108th – who did not finish their terms. They are omitted from these analyses.

benefits to accrue to those who engage in relatively high levels early in their terms and/or who engage in follow-through on the more intensive activity of introductions.

As a preliminary step, it is useful to examine in more depth the relationships among vulnerability, seniority, and follow-through. We have seen in this chapter that safer and more junior legislators engage in higher rates of promise keeping. Do they also make different choices about the location and timing of their promise keeping? Perhaps most fundamentally, what explains why certain groups of members demonstrate the most follow-through on their appeals in the first place?

PATTERNS IN PROMISE KEEPING BY VULNERABILITY AND SENIORITY

I begin my investigation by breaking out the House and Senate samples into four groups of legislators: senior and vulnerable, junior and vulnerable, senior and safe, and junior and safe. The cutoff for vulnerability is a vote share in the previous election of less than 60 percent. I choose this figure because it breaks the samples relatively in half, although other vulnerability breakdowns yield the same substantive results. For seniority, I use the same cutoff as in the previous investigation: more than eight years for representatives and more than twelve years for senators.

Next, I replicate the paired samples t-tests for location and timing of promise keeping for each of these groups. Figure 6.2 illustrates the results for location. As shown, in the House, the overall introductions versus cosponsorships difference is driven by the behavior of junior members (both vulnerable and safe), who engage in relatively more promise keeping on their introductions. In the Senate, there is a similar result – for only the junior and vulnerable group is there more promise keeping on introductions than cosponsorships. All other groups engage in relatively equal amounts across both.

Figures 6.3 and 6.4 present the results for the timing of the promise-keeping decision. Figure 6.4 demonstrates that there are no differences across the groups for the Senate – junior and senior, vulnerable and safe all engage in relatively constant rates of promise keeping as their terms progress. For the House, though, as shown in Figure 6.3, the timing difference varies depending on the type of activity. With the proportion of introductions in year one versus year two, the difference emerges only for the junior and safe group, who engage in considerably more promise

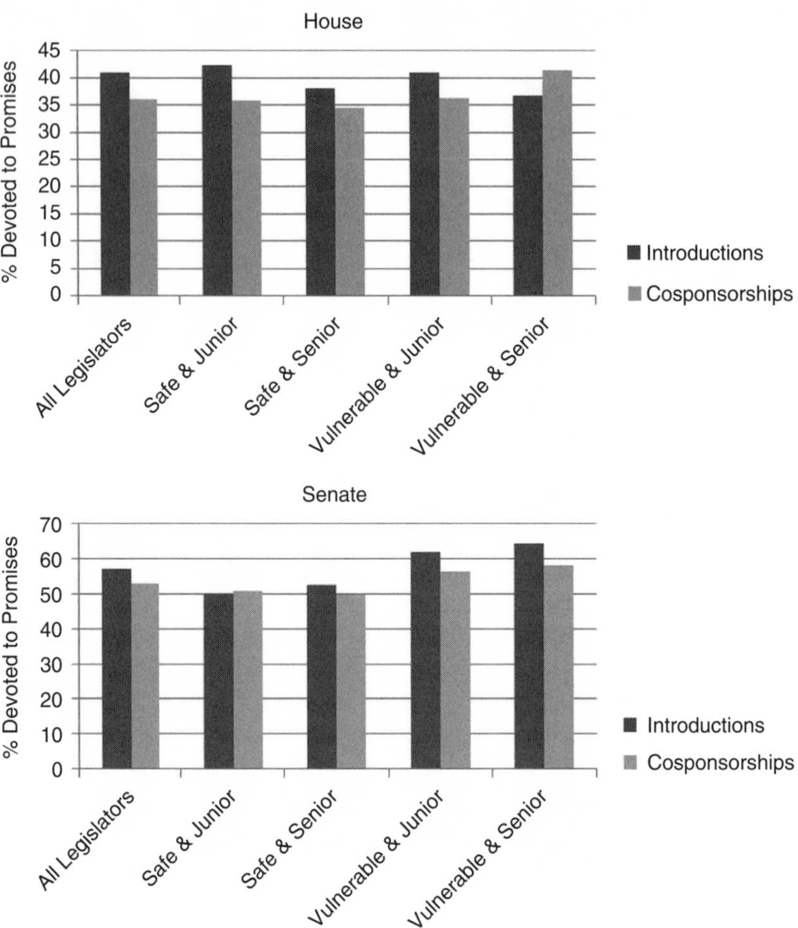

FIGURE 6.2 Promise Keeping on Introductions and Cosponsorships

keeping up front. However, when I examine instead the proportion of cosponsorships in year one versus year two, the rates are constant.

These results are admittedly a bit noisy, but one thread that carries throughout is that not only do relatively safe and relatively junior members typically engage in more follow-through on their appeals than their more vulnerable and/or more senior colleagues, they sometimes make different choices about when and where to demonstrate their responsiveness. The final task for this chapter is to examine *why* the linkages between appeals and activity are weaker for more vulnerable and more senior legislators.

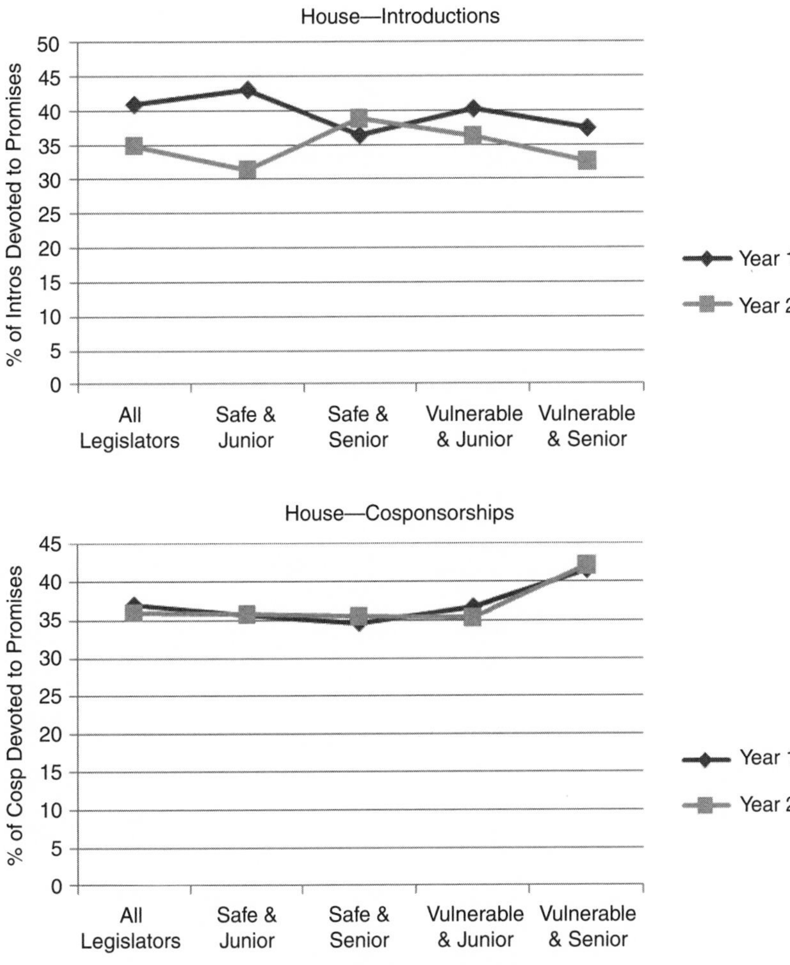

FIGURE 6.3 Promise Keeping across a Term in the House

There are at least two possible explanations for these patterns. One is that vulnerable and/or senior legislators are less sincere in their campaign appeals and therefore less likely to focus on their true priorities. The other is that they are just as likely as their safer, more junior colleagues to do so, but that, for some reason, once they are in office, they are less likely to follow through.

To distinguish between these explanations, one simple first check is to assess the relationship between past activity levels on issues (the measure of interest used in previous chapters) and the likelihood of relatively safe and

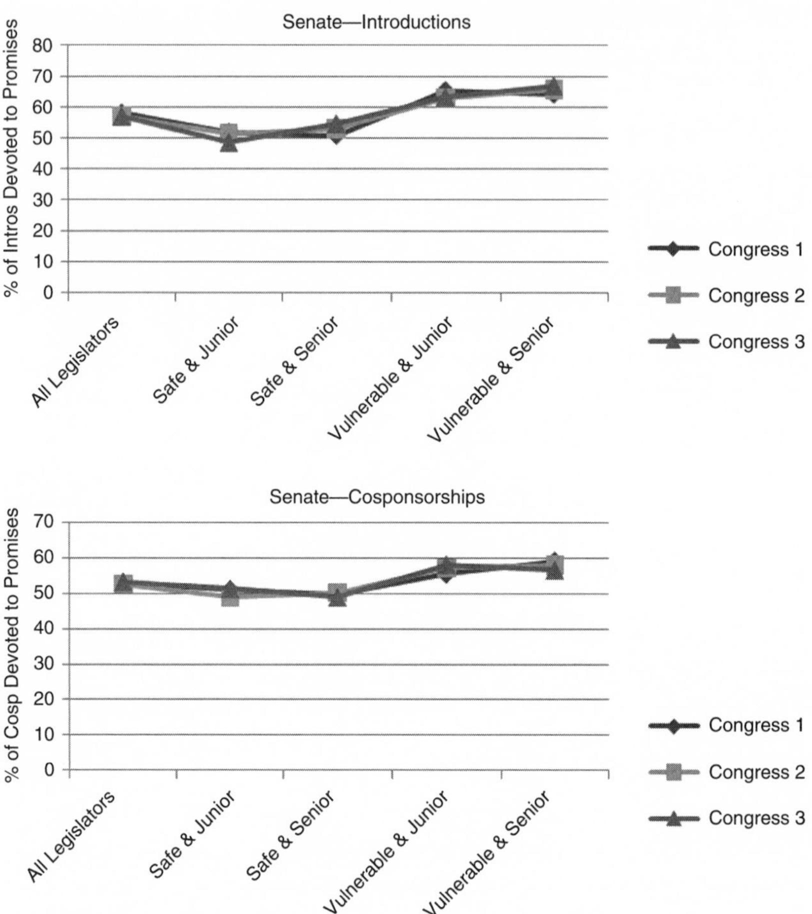

FIGURE 6.4 Promise Keeping across a Term in the Senate

relatively vulnerable and relatively junior and relatively senior legislators raising the issue. We saw in Chapter 4 that candidates, particularly those for the House, who discuss an issue tend have more extensive past records on it than those who do not. Indeed, it is this link between priorities and campaign appeals that is at the heart of promise keeping. Does this linkage hold equally for all legislators, vulnerable and safe, junior and senior?

To test this, I conduct a series of very simple bivariate regression analyses, where the variables are the percentage of legislators' agendas in the previous term devoted to each issue and whether or not they raised it in reference to themselves in the campaign. The coefficient in each model thus represents the difference in the proportion of the agenda on an issue for those who did and did not raise it.[10] For the House, I compare these results for four different groups of legislators: safe and junior, safe and senior, vulnerable and junior, and vulnerable and senior. If the reason that safer and more junior legislators follow through at higher rates on their appeals is that their appeals are more closely linked to their preferences, we should see the highest number of previous activity–campaign mention links for that group. Figure 6.5, which summarizes the results from these analyses (the dots represent the coefficient from each model and the lines the 90 percent confidence interval) reveals that this is indeed the case. For the safe and junior group, there are eleven issues for which candidates who raised the issue had been more active in the past than those who had not raised it. The same holds true for only five issues for the safe and senior group, three issues for the vulnerable and junior group, and two issues for the vulnerable and senior group. Thus, it appears that the linkages between intensity of interest in an issue and raising it in the campaign are much stronger for safe and junior legislators than for any of the other groups.

For the Senate, my approach to analysis is slightly different. Examining past activity requires limiting the sample to those who had been incumbents, which did not present problems for the examination of representatives' behavior, but which for senators makes the *N*s for the four groups too small for rigorous comparisons. Thus, I compare only two groups: safe versus vulnerable and junior versus senior. The results, presented in Figure 6.6, once again largely confirm expectations. There is no difference between junior and senior members (three significant links for each), but this is not a surprise. Recall from Table 6.3 that the indicator of seniority that was significant in predicting overall promise keeping was whether the legislator was new or not, and, after controlling for this, there were no differences between more and less senior legislators. We do, however, see a difference emerge for vulnerability. For safe members, there are six issues where there is a positive relationship between interest and campaign discussion, but only two such issues for vulnerable members.[11]

Thus, the campaign appeals of more vulnerable and, to some extent, more senior representatives and senators were less clearly tied to their past interests and priorities than were those of their safer and more junior

[10] The logic is a bit backward here, in that the campaign theme is really the dependent variable, but modeling it in this way enables us to compare the size of previous agendas on an issue for each group, which is the real feature of interest.

[11] For another issue, jobs and infrastructure, vulnerable candidates with more experience on the issue were less likely to mention it.

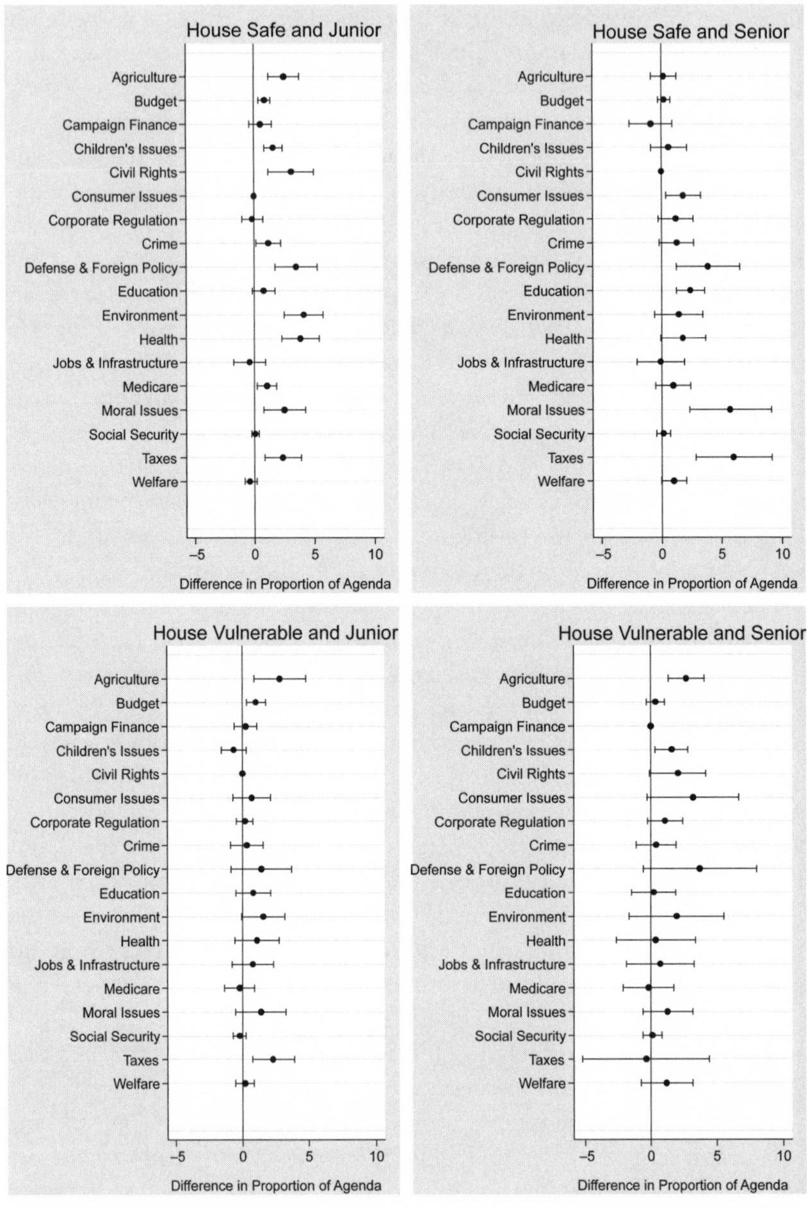

FIGURE 6.5 Vulnerability, Seniority, and the Interest–Campaign Theme Link for Representatives

Note: The figure summarizes the results of a series of bivariate regression analyses where the variables are the percentage of legislators' agendas in the previous term and whether they raised them in reference to themselves in the campaign. The dots represent the coefficients (the difference in the proportion of attention to an issue for those who did and did not raise it) and the lines represent the 90 percent confidence intervals.

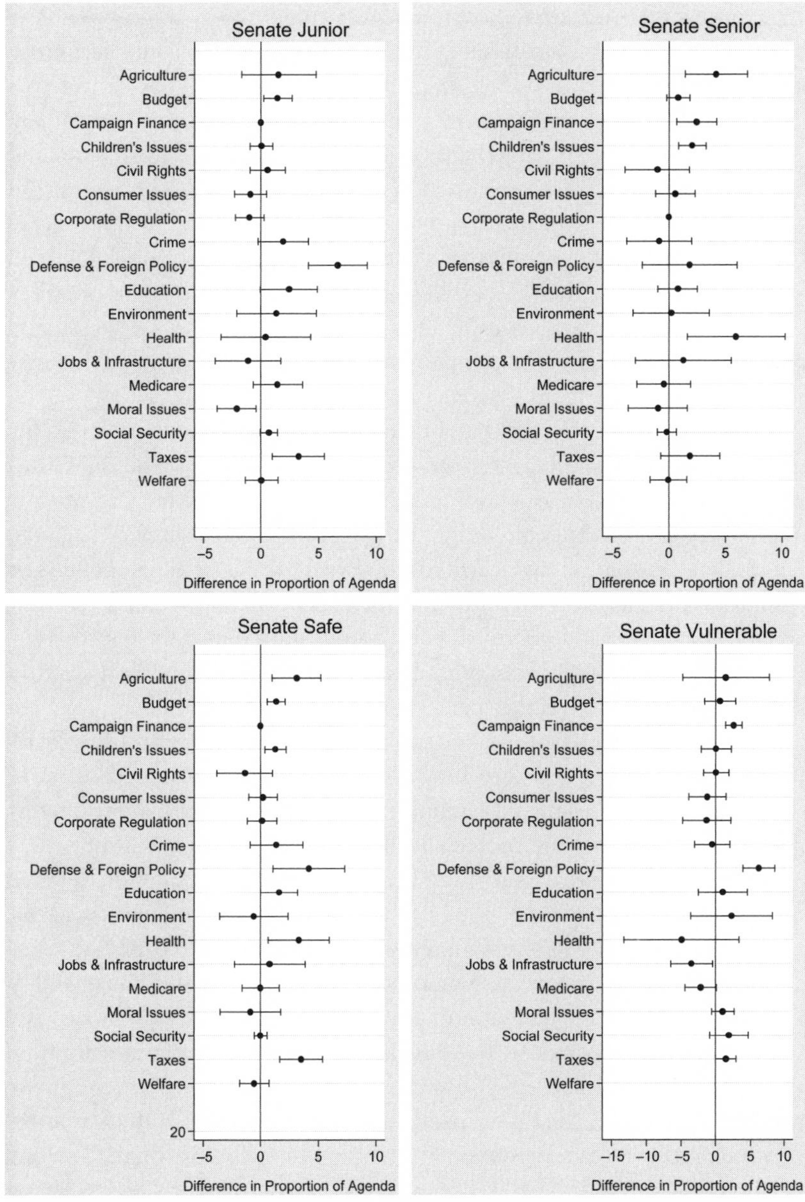

FIGURE 6.6 Vulnerability, Seniority, and the Interest–Campaign Theme Link for Senators

Note: The figure summarizes the results of a series of bivariate regression analyses where the variables are the percentage of legislators' agendas in the previous term and whether they raised them in reference to themselves in the campaign. The dots represent the coefficients (the difference in the proportion of attention to an issue for those who did and did not raise it) and the lines represent the 90 percent confidence intervals.

colleagues. It is important to note that safety/vulnerability could be either a cause or an effect (or both) here. Vulnerable legislators could feel compelled to talk about issues other than their own priorities in order to try to appeal to a broader constituency, or their choices to focus on nonpriority issues could make them vulnerable if they are viewed as less sincere or if they have engaged in less promise keeping in the past. Regardless of the reason, though, one important explanation for the lower rates of follow-through for these legislators is that their campaign appeals are less likely to be valid indicators of their underlying interests. Normatively, this provides yet more evidence that widespread incumbent safety is not necessarily indicative of a problem. The campaigns of safer members provide stronger signals about their later activity.

Is this the sole explanation for the higher rates of promise keeping for safer and more junior members? Or, if we hold interest constant, do we still see differences in levels of follow-through between vulnerable and safe (or junior and senior) members? To evaluate this, I conduct a series of negative binomial regression analyses where the dependent variable is a count of legislators' activities on an issue and the independent variables are past activity, the dummies for vulnerability and seniority, and the controls for total activity, number of campaign issues, salience of issues, and election year.[12] To the extent that the coefficients on vulnerability and seniority are significant, it means that these characteristics lead to more or less follow-through, even among legislators who were similarly predisposed to have raised an issue. The results are summarized in Table 6.4, and, in the interest of space, I report only the coefficients on vulnerability and seniority.

These findings reveal that after taking interest into account, relative safety or vulnerability does not offer additional predictive power about promise keeping. There is only one issue for the House (corporate regulation) and one issue for the Senate (crime) for which the vulnerability variable is a significant predictor of activity. The situation for seniority is a bit different. For the Senate, there is once again no real relationship (one issue where junior members follow through more and two where senior members do), but for the House, there is a bit of a pattern. Of the five issues for which seniority is a predictor of variation in follow-through, for four the direction of the effect is negative. Thus, for these issues, a senior legislator who talked about an issue is less likely to follow through than a junior legislator who discussed it, even if their past activity on the issue

[12] Each of the analyses is limited to candidates who had raised the issue in reference to themselves. Also, for the House, the standard errors are clustered on the legislator.

TABLE 6.4 *The Effects of Vulnerability and Seniority on Follow-through*

	House Vulnerability	House Seniority	Senate Vulnerability	Senate Seniority
Agriculture	−.052(.196)	−.082(.226)	−.448(.481)	.305(.464)
Budget	−.044(.179)	−.046(.165)	−.359(.366)	.018(.313)
Campaign Finance	.182(.302)	.286(.377)	–	–
Children's Issues	.407(.561)	.313(.134)**	−.269(.363)	−.092(.324)
Civil Rights	–	–	–	–
Consumer Issues	–	–	–	–
Corporate Regulation	−.318(.134)**	−.112(.153)	–	–
Crime	−.033(.083)	−.097(.105)	−.295(.172)*	−.344(.144)**
Defense & Foreign Policy	.037(.069)	−.187(.089)**	−.023(.168)	.074(.119)
Education	.013(.061)	−.170(.077)**	−.078(.164)	−.061(.123)
Environment	.109(.084)	−.110(.110)	−.113(.154)	.375(.092)***
Health	.028(.045)	−.088(.050)*	−.138(.101)	.045(.088)
Jobs & Infrastructure	−.022(.046)	−.078(.049)	.094(.168)	.177(.101)*
Medicare	−.039(.063)	−.120(.070)*	.232(.159)	.131(.129)
Moral Issues	.066(.220)	−.534(.348)	–	–
Social Security	−.009(.068)	.011(.081)	−.430(.405)	.032(.275)
Taxes	−.061(.078)	−.124(.110)	.085(.162)	.134(.138)
Welfare	.206(.203)	−.082(.199)	.008(.193)	−.114(.202)

Note: The cells summarize the results of a series of negative binomial regression analyses where the dependent variable is the number of activities each legislator engaged in on each issue. The independent variables include vulnerability (presented), seniority (presented), total activity, number of campaign issues, salience of campaign issues, and election year. The analyses are limited to legislators who had raised the issue in reference to themselves. For some issues, the *N*s were too low to permit estimation of the models.
*** = $p < .01$; ** = $p < .05$; * = $p < .10$.

was the same. This is suggestive of an additional post-campaign effect: once having made an appeal on these issues, senior members are less likely to keep their promises by being active on them. As discussed previously, this could be because senior members have more responsibilities and commitments, which may pull them away from their campaign themes.

CONCLUSIONS

This chapter has taken a (deceptively) simple question – "Who keeps promises?" – and complicated it considerably. Accordingly, it is useful to review the most important conclusions. First, levels of promise keeping vary a great deal across legislators, and this variation is systematic. Some is due to structural factors, such as the size of candidates' and legislators' agendas or the salience of their themes, but it is also a function of more theoretically interesting characteristics of legislators, most notably their vulnerability and seniority. Contrary to much of the conventional wisdom about representation, though, vulnerability does not necessarily induce responsiveness. Instead, in both chambers we see more promise keeping among relatively safe members. Interestingly, this appears to originate in their choices as candidates – safer incumbents are more likely to focus their campaigns on issues of real interest to them, while their vulnerable peers tend to diverge more.

This effect also explains some of the chamber-level differences in follow-through that we saw in Chapter 3. If safer members keep their promises at higher rates than their more vulnerable peers, then promise keeping should be more common in the chamber that has more safe members. House members, on average, have less to fear electorally than do senators, who are more likely to face experienced challengers, lose more often than their House colleagues, and, when they win, tend to do so by slimmer margins (Burden and Kimball 2002; Krasno 1994; Westlye 1991).

The results also demonstrate differences in the patterns of promise keeping across activities and within legislators' terms. Cosponsorships may require less effort than introductions, but we actually see more follow-through on the latter – legislators tend to devote a higher proportion of their introductions than their cosponsorships to their campaign themes. The difference in magnitude of this effect is not large, but it offers clear evidence against the claim that promise keeping is somehow solely symbolic: that legislators cosponsor measures on their campaign themes in an effort to appear responsive, but devote their real time and effort to other issues.

Similarly, in both chambers there is evidence that legislators consider the timing of the next election when making decisions about when to demonstrate their responsiveness. Legislators devote a relatively constant proportion of their activity to follow-through on their campaign appeals, but when I look at the raw count of promise-keeping activities, I find that House members engage in more in the first year of their terms, with a drop-off in the second year. Early promise keeping may be valuable in warding off potentially strong challengers, since the next election starts during the second year of their terms. Senators, on the other hand, engage in a higher raw amount of activity on their campaign issues as time passes and the next election grows nearer.

Thus, the analyses in this chapter go a long way toward explaining how and why legislators keep their promises. In Chapter 7, which explores the implications of promise keeping for legislators' electoral prospects and their career decisions, I provide more context for interpreting the strategic nature of the decisions about the location and timing of follow-through. These analyses help to complete the story about the motivations for promise keeping by investigating the other half of the electoral connection – how behavior in office shapes performance in the next election.

7

The Electoral Implications of Promise Keeping

The evidence presented over the past several chapters is consistent with a depiction of promise keeping as a reelection-oriented strategy. Legislators appear to choose campaign themes that are likely to resonate with their constituents and for which they can credibly claim interest and credit. Once they are in office, they follow through on their appeals, with almost all expending at least some time and effort on them, and many devoting a substantial portion of their legislative agendas to activity on these issues. Moreover, levels of promise keeping vary systematically with electoral vulnerability, and representatives' and senators' choices about where and when to engage in the most responsiveness correspond to electoral imperatives.

It is reasonable to conclude from these patterns that legislators choose to engage in promise keeping at least in part to help themselves electorally. However, it is also possible that the links we observe between characteristics of legislators and their promise-keeping behavior are mostly a by-product of good matching between a constituency and its representative or senator. If all legislators talk and act solely on their own interests, but for some of them these interests also align with those of the constituency (and this close match in interests means that the constituency is more favorable to the legislator), this could produce a positive relationship between vote share and subsequent levels of promise keeping.

In many ways, such a situation (what Burden [2007] calls "coincidental representation"; see also Fenno 1978, Parker 1992) is not normatively problematic. High levels of follow-through on appeals and close linkages between the interests of representatives and their constituents are good things, no matter how they arise. On the other hand, without stronger, more direct tests of the electoral implications of promise keeping, we cannot discern from the results thus far whether representatives and senators are actually rewarded for responsive behavior and punished for bad. Hence, we cannot say much about accountability.

Accordingly, the purpose of this chapter is to explore whether promise keeping itself pays off electorally. In other words, all other things being equal, do representatives and senators who devote more of their time in office to following through on their campaign appeals do better in the next election (measured a variety of ways) than those who engage in less follow-through? Even given the preceding caveats, there is clear reason to think that it should. We know that critics of the incumbent, particularly potential challengers, search actively for weaknesses they might be able to use in their campaigns, and a failure to keep promises provides them with ready ammunition. A lack of promise keeping could therefore have a direct effect on incumbents' future vote shares (i.e., if challengers highlight incumbents' failures on this dimension and this leads voters to be displeased with them) and/or an indirect effect if it encourages stronger, more experienced opponents to run, either in the primary or general elections.

Understanding the links between promise keeping and legislators' electoral fortunes is therefore central to evaluating how well elections work to promote responsive behavior and hold representatives and senators accountable for their past campaign promises. It also provides insight into the nature of legislators' decision-making processes, enabling me to assess the extent to which promise keeping is a conscious decision on their part and offering further evidence about how they balance competing goals. Exploring how levels of promise keeping are associated with legislators' career decisions should offer similar perspective, and so in the analyses that follow, I also investigate whether legislators who intend to retire or run for higher office differ in their behavior from their peers who plan to remain in the House or Senate for another term. My expectation is that to the extent that promise keeping is an electorally motivated activity with tangible payoffs, levels in office should affect the nature of the competition representatives and senators face in the next race and how well they do in that election, and should also be related to the choices they make about their political futures.

THE ELECTORAL CONNECTION IN LEGISLATIVE BEHAVIOR

Claims about the potential electoral rewards of various legislative activities are common in the literature on congressional behavior and representation, a legacy of Mayhew's (1974) arguments about advertising, position taking, and credit claiming. Moreover, nearly all political scientists who have interviewed legislators and their staffers about their decisions on roll call votes or agenda activities report a widespread belief that these choices are consequential and that missteps can damage electoral prospects (see, for example, Kingdon 1989; Koger 2003; Matthews and Stimson 1975; Schiller 1995). As one of the members of Congress interviewed by Kingdon in his study of voting decisions explained:

> I know that nobody will notice it right now. People never do. But it may be used against you in the next campaign. I learned that lesson in my first campaign for reelection .... You see, most people don't notice it. But your opponent will comb down through every aspect of your record, every vote you've ever cast.... (1989, 60)

Despite all this, actually *finding* strong, systematic effects of legislative activity on electoral fortunes has been fairly rare. Legislative scholars have paid the most attention to the links between roll call voting and reelection, particularly whether legislators who diverge from the ideological positions of their constituencies suffer at the polls (e.g., Ansolabehere, Snyder, and Stewart 2001; Canes-Wrone, Brady, and Cogan 2002; Erikson and Wright 2000) and whether taking the "wrong" position on particular high-salience roll call votes can harm legislators electorally (Bovitz and Carson 2006; Jacobson 1993). Although most of these studies uncover some relationship between roll call voting and future vote shares, the effects tend to be small and conditional (i.e., by only affecting the already vulnerable). Canes-Wrone, Brady, and Cogan (2002) summarize the state of the literature as "far from conclusive" that voting in office affects electoral outcomes (2002, 129).

Evidence that activities other than roll call voting yield a direct electoral payoff is also mixed. Many scholars have hypothesized that constituents should prefer highly visible and active representatives (see, for example, Fenno 1978), but studies of bill introductions and cosponsorships have found almost no link between the volume of legislators' activity and their vote shares in the next election (Johannes and McAdams 1981; Ragsdale and Cook 1987; Wawro 2000). Thus, legislators who are particularly active fare no better or worse at the polls than their less involved colleagues.[1]

[1] There is, however, some indication that the *content* of these activities matters more than the volume; for instance, legislators who address their previous challengers' critiques through their activity in office do better in the next election than those who ignore them (Sulkin 2005).

In sum, there is something of a disjuncture between the literature on legislators' motivations, which shows that reelection considerations are central to representatives' and senators' governing decisions, and the literature on the effects of activity in office, which finds only tenuous relationships between legislators' behavior and their future vote shares. How should we interpret this? Does it mean that legislators are just irrational when they worry that their activity could harm their reelection prospects? Are the latter two-thirds of Mayhew's assertion that legislators "think they can affect their own percentages, that in fact they can affect their own percentages, and furthermore that there is reason for them to try to do so" (1974, 33) incorrect?

Scholars have been careful to note that we cannot and should not make these inferences from the patterns. That there is little observable linkage between behavior in office and future vote shares does not necessarily mean that one does not matter for the other. It is undeniable that most legislators are overly concerned about reelection and so overestimate the likely consequences of their activity. But while legislative activity may only rarely be the decisive factor in a victory or loss, the fact remains that it sometimes is. Most legislators can point to cases where such activity legitimately seemed to make the difference, and "all of them can recall stories of 'safe' congressmen who are no longer congressmen" (Arnold 1990, 61). Further, even most seemingly secure legislators have had at least one close election in their careers, an experience that sticks with them. Given the importance they place on reelection, even if their policy activity in Congress only matters at the margins, this should be enough to induce responsiveness. As Fiorina (1974) explains:

> Granted, the overwhelming bulk of Congressmen are reelected. But, by the same token, never does a congressional election pass without leaving one or more Representatives and/or Senators consigned to political oblivion. There is always an example or two of a misstep that wiped out a political career. The costs of defeat are so enormous that the probability of defeat pales by comparison. Choosing discretion over valor, the representative votes as if the probability of his action becoming a campaign issue is unity. (124)

Indeed, if this is the case, legislators' reelection-oriented nature may be the *reason* few linkages emerge between activity and vote shares. If all representatives and senators care deeply about their electoral prospects and behave as such, then we simply do not see the whole range of possible behaviors. How, for instance, might representatives or senators behave if they were actively trying to minimize their vote shares? It is unlikely we have ever observed this, since "there is no congressman willing to make the experiment" (Mayhew 1974, 37).

The results in previous chapters provide support for this point; although not every legislator follows through on his or her appeals at the same high rates, there is little evidence of legislators actively going against their campaign promises. A representative or senator who says in the campaign that he or she will support legislation to increase border security does not then sponsor or cosponsor bills that make restrictions more lax. Similarly, candidates who claim to be pro-environment vote in line with the positions endorsed by environmental groups. If this pattern also applies to behaviors other than promise keeping, the lack of strong relationships between legislative behavior and vote margins may be due in large part to the fact that "reelection orientation" is closer to a constant than a variable, producing little meaningful variation in behavior.

Along the same lines, the previously cited studies of the electoral effects of legislative behavior nearly all focus on identifying constituency reactions to activity in office. But if legislators are adept at recognizing actions that would hurt them and so avoid behaving in this way, this should mute any relationship. Arnold (1990) argues that this "anticipatory" responsiveness is a central mechanism for representation. When faced with a decision, legislators ask themselves how likely it is that their constituents would notice (or, perhaps more accurately, how likely it is that it would be brought to their attention), and then how likely it is that, having noticed, they would care deeply enough for it to affect their vote choices. If they think the probability of both is high enough (and given their focus on reelection, the threshold for this is typically low), they avoid taking the potentially harmful action. Erikson, MacKuen, and Stimson (2002) make a similar argument, claiming that "rational anticipation" of constituent preferences is one of the key factors contributing to high reelection rates in the House (305–6).[2]

These arguments about anticipation provide a very compelling explanation for the lack of tangible effects of activity on reelection. If they are true, though, why would we see variation in a presumably reelection-oriented activity such as promise keeping? If all legislators care about their future prospects, shouldn't they all prioritize their campaign appeals in their legislative agendas? Not necessarily. It is likely that some representatives and senators are simply less savvy and so fail to recognize its

[2] Interestingly, they argue that this does not hold in the Senate and that responsiveness in that chamber is accomplished through electoral replacement.

benefits. Others may face constraints that limit their ability to respond. It is also possible that some legislators are skilled enough at making strategic calculations that they can calibrate their activity to enable them to both ensure their electoral security and attend to other interests or goals. In roll call voting, this could mean that some diverge from their constituencies to follow their own preferences when they know they can afford to (see Bianco 1994). This logic may not be as relevant to promise keeping as to other behaviors, since it assumes that there is a tension between doing what the constituency wants and doing what the legislator himself or herself prefers.[3] Nonetheless, time and resources are scarce, and there are almost always more things a legislator would like to accomplish than he or she can actually do. When legislators make choices about attention allocation, this strategic calculation (i.e., "How much do I need to follow through on my appeals to maintain my security?") could still apply. The outcome, then, should be to limit the amount of electoral punishment (and electoral reward) for their actions.

Overall, these arguments lead us to the expectation that the observable electoral effects of promise keeping are likely to be subtle and small in magnitude. Uncovering any effect at all should serve therefore as impressive evidence of its role in promoting reelection and democratic accountability. The next step, then, is to determine whether such effects exist. The analyses to come explore the relationships between representatives' and senators' levels of promise keeping and their performance on a variety of indicators of electoral success.

Although the most obvious of these indicators is incumbents' future vote shares, Table 7.1, which summarizes what became of the members of my House and Senate samples during (or, in some cases, before) the next election, suggests a number of additional possibilities. One of these is simply whether legislators win or lose. As shown, about 90 percent of the representatives and 80 percent of the senators in my sample ran for reelection, but while the vast majority of these (approximately 95 percent of House members and 88 percent of Senate members) were successful and returned to office, not all were. Fifteen House incumbents and nine senators fell short in their reelection bids. Another feature of potential interest is legislators' career decisions. Among the nonreturnees, most were

[3] The fundamental difference here is that legislators get to choose their campaign themes (and whether to respond to them), but do not normally have much influence over the issues on which they must take positions in roll call votes.

TABLE 7.1 *Electoral Decisions and Fortunes of the Sample in the Next Election*

	# of Representatives	# of Senators
Ran in Next Election	362	66
Lost Primary	5	0
Lost General	10	9
Faced Primary Opposition	53	30
Faced General Election Opposition	308	64
Experienced General Election Challenger	77	33
Did Not Run in Next Election	35	18
Died in Office	1	1
Retired	16	14
Ran for Higher Office	18	3

legislators who chose to retire or to run for higher office.[4] Does promise-keeping influence these choices or, perhaps more accurately, are these choices manifested in levels of promise keeping?[5] Finally, there is the presence and quality of opposition to consider. For those legislators who ran in the next electoral cycle, about 15 percent of the representatives and 45 percent of the senators faced primary challenges from members of their own party. In the general election, fifty-four members of the House sample and two members of the Senate sample were lucky enough to face no opposition, and of those who did have general election challengers, about one-quarter of representatives and one-half of senators ran against "quality" opponents with prior elected office experience.

PROMISE KEEPING AND VOTE MARGINS

I address all of these in turn, but I begin my investigation by examining the relationship between promise keeping and future vote shares. The general hypothesis is straightforward: if promise keeping yields a direct electoral payoff, we should see legislators who engage in more doing better in their next election than those who engage in less. As such, the dependent variable in my first set of models, presented in Table 7.2, is each

[4] Two of the legislators, Senator Paul Coverdell (R-GA) and Representative Bruce Vento (D-MN), died during their terms.

[5] For these indicators, promise keeping is probably more appropriately thought of as the dependent variable than the independent, since choices about whether to run or retire should drive responsiveness, rather than the other way around.

TABLE 7.2 *Does Promise Keeping Promote Reelection?*

	DV = Vote Share		DV = Won?	
	House	Senate	House	Senate
Promise-Keeping Acts	.054*	.054*	−.001	.013*
	(.030)	(.031)	(.004)	(.007)
Previous Vote Share	.698***	.292*	.045*	.079
	(.087)	(.154)	(.022)	(.068)
Seniority	−.144	.053	−.034**	.118
	(.106)	(.208)	(.016)	(.079)
Democrat?	.711	5.682*	-.413	–
	(1.610)	(3.366)	(.338)	
Ideological Extremity	10.896**	-7.610	1.113	3.023
	(5.281)	(12.425)	(1.353)	(2.193)
# of Campaign Issues	−.967*	−.428	.060	.375*
	(.535)	(1.068)	(.162)	(.225)
Issue Salience	.000	−.002	.000	−.001*
	(.002)	(.003)	(.001)	(.001)
Policy Activities	−.028**	−.036*	−.001	−.006
	(.012)	(.019)	(.001)	(.004)
2000 Election	1.296	-4.600	−.639	–
	(1.636)	(3.521)	(.405)	
2002 Election	−1.106	−4.164	−.419	−.051
	(1.870)	(3.679)	(.418)	(.596)
Constant	27.996	61.598	−.667	−2.891
	(6.539)	(17.626)	(1.407)	(4.776)
N	326	62	330	62
Pseudo/Adj. R^2	.23	.10	.19	.37

Note: Cell entries are OLS regression coefficients in the first set of models and probit coefficients in the second set (with standard errors in parentheses). The dependent variable is either legislators' percentage of the vote in the next election or whether the legislator won that election.
***= p < .01; **= p < .05; *= p < .10.

incumbent's percentage of the two-party vote in the next election.[6] The primary independent variable of interest is the number of promise-keeping activities (i.e., a count of the introductions and cosponsorships on campaign themes) that he or she undertakes. In addition, two types of control

[6] The difference in vote share between election one and election two for the House sample ranges from −32 to 48 and from the Senate sample from −45 to 46. This indicates that there can be considerable shifts in performance from election to election. If I exclude those who were unopposed in either of the elections, the ranges shrink to −21 to 23 for the House and −19 to 20 in the Senate, but still display impressive variation. Excluding the unopposed has little impact on the substantive results, so I include them. In later analyses, I examine whether high levels of promise keeping decrease the chance of facing opposition.

variables are necessary. The first relates to other characteristics of individual legislators that are likely to be associated with or to influence their future vote shares, including their previous vote shares,[7] their party, and their ideological extremity. The second includes those variables that are necessary to contextualize the raw number of promise-keeping activities, such as the total volume of legislative activity, the number of campaign themes, the salience of those themes, and the election year. As has been the case with the House sample in previous analyses, I cluster the standard errors on the legislator since some appear in the sample in multiple election years. Finally, because these analyses require that the incumbent be on the ballot in the next general election, they omit representatives who lost their primary bids.[8]

These results demonstrate that the amount of promise keeping that representatives and senators undertake has a clear effect on their subsequent electoral fortunes. Its relation to future vote shares is significant and positive, even after controlling for a variety of factors that should also explain them. More specifically, the coefficients indicate that, for both the House and Senate, every eighteen or nineteen additional promise-keeping activities are associated with a one-point increase in vote share. This may seem a modest effect, but since the average representative engages in about 77 promise-keeping activities per term and the average senator about 285, it is definitely meaningful in magnitude.

Is this effect enough to make the difference regularly between winning and losing? Not unexpectedly, my results reveal that the answer is no. Importantly, though, it is not necessarily a firm no. When I do some simple comparisons of the percentage of winners' and losers' agendas devoted to promise keeping, I find a significant difference for the House: winners in the next election allocated about 37 percent of their introductions and cosponsorships to their campaign themes, compared to only 27 percent for losers ($t = 2.0$; $p < .05$). For the Senate, the difference between the two, while in the same direction (53 percent for winners versus 50 percent for losers), is not significant.

Of course, these comparisons of means do not take into account all of the controls we might want to include, so I also conduct a more nuanced analysis that replicates the first set of models in Table 7.2, but uses a

7 Because I include this control, the coefficient on promise keeping is the same whether I use a dependent variable of future vote share or a dependent variable of change in vote share from election one to election two.

8 None of the sampled senators lost their primary election bids.

different dependent variable. Instead of vote share, it is a dummy for whether or not the incumbent won the next race. Interestingly, the results here, presented in the second set of columns in Table 7.2, are the opposite of what we found in the t-tests. For the House, there is no relationship between promise keeping and the probability of reelection. For the Senate, though, we do see a positive relationship – for those who choose to run again, the level of follow-through is a significant predictor of victory. However, this should be interpreted with caution since it was necessary to omit the party variable (all of the losers were Republicans) and one of the election-year dummies (there were no losers in 1998) in order to estimate the model.

But even if promise keeping is not often the decisive factor in clinching a win, the payoff for vote shares should certainly be enough to validate legislators' responsiveness and encourage them to continue to follow through on their appeals in the future. Winning may be the most important thing to legislators, but they are also concerned about doing so by wide margins, since close elections may be seen by others in the district or the state and beyond as signals about an incumbent's vulnerability. These interpretations can become self-fulfilling if they lead to stronger challenges the next time around (Mayhew 1974, 46). Engaging in high levels of promise keeping can help them to become safer, so representatives and senators are wise to devote substantial portions of their governing agendas to their campaign themes.

PROMISE KEEPING AND THE DECISION TO RUN

That promise keeping pays off is a critical, and perhaps even a bit surprising, finding. The effects are not overwhelmingly large, but they are on par with those of other activities such as roll call voting that are often assumed to matter for reelection. These findings also provide more evidence that looking for an electoral effect from the volume of activity alone is misplaced; *what* legislators introduce or cosponsor is often more important than just how much they do so.

Combined with the results from Chapter 6 that safer representatives and senators engage in higher levels of follow-through, these results also confirm that promise keeping clearly conforms to the dynamics of the broader electoral connection in legislative behavior. We observe safer (and perhaps more savvy) legislators keeping their promises at higher rates, this pattern of behavior then makes them even more secure in the next election, and they are returned to Congress with an incentive to continue it. Once having hit on a strategy that appears to pay off, legislators tend to persist in it (Fenno 1996; Hershey 1984; Kingdon 1968). In short, for those who plan to run again, promise keeping is an important component of the reelection arsenal.

What, though, of those who do not plan to remain in their current position? From Table 7.1, we saw that about one in ten of the legislators in the House sample and one in five of the Senate sample do not stand for reelection, choosing instead to retire or to run for higher office. How might these decisions manifest themselves in levels of promise keeping? Political scientists and economists have long been interested in the "last period problem" – theorizing about how elected officials might behave once the reelection constraint is removed, whether by retirement, a run for another office, or term limits (see, for example, Bender and Lott 1996; Carey 1998; Lott 1987; Rothenberg and Sanders 2000; Zupan 1990).

The empirical results in this literature have been contradictory. Some find that retirees and the progressively ambitious behave differently, either from their peers who stand for reelection or from their own past behavior (Francis and Kenny 1996; Herrick, Moore, and Hibbing 1994; Hibbing 1986; Rothenberg and Sanders 2000; Sulkin 2005), but others do not (Grofman, Griffin, and Berry 1995; Zupan 1990). These inconsistencies may arise, at least in part, because actually testing for last-period effects is fraught with complications, and different scholars have made different choices about how to deal with them. Some studies lump together retirees and those who run for higher office, but this may not be the best decision, since the dynamics might be different between, and even among, the two groups. In addition, if the decision to leave is what induces a change in behavior, pinpointing when this decision occurs is important, but it is also exceedingly difficult. Members of Congress who retire or run for higher office make the decision to not stand for reelection again at different points in the term, or even before the term begins.

These considerations provide an important backdrop for exploring the relationship between promise keeping and career decisions. They also suggest that to develop firm hypotheses about the direction of any possible effect, one must think first about why legislators choose to retire or run for higher office and how this might affect their promise-keeping calculations. In general, if legislators follow through on their appeals to please their current constituents and/or to ward off strong challengers, then once this is no longer a concern for them, they should undertake less promise keeping than their peers who know they must face reelection. On the other hand, if promise keeping has become habitual and/or if reelection is not a major motivation for it (e.g., if follow-through on campaign issues is driven almost entirely by legislators' own interest in those issues), then the decision to leave the chamber might not influence it.

The motivating assumption of work on the legislative manifestations of political ambition is Schlesinger's famous statement that "our ambitious politician must act today in terms of the electorate he hopes to win tomorrow" (1966, 6). In nearly all cases, the constituency for the office to which progressively ambitious legislators aspire differs from the one they currently represent, so these legislators might shift their behavior in ways that are likely to appeal to the new constituency. Applied to promise keeping, one could argue that those intending to run for higher office should engage in less follow-through on their previous appeals and instead introduce and cosponsor measures on the topics of most interest to their new constituency. However, this logic implies that they make the decision to run *after* the last election has taken place, and this is likely the exception rather than the rule. A representative who knows that a Senate seat is likely to become available in four to six years should start to change his or her behavior well before the term immediately preceding a Senate run, so the interests of the new constituency should *already* be incorporated into both his or her campaign appeals and legislative activity (see also Francis and Kenny 1996).

Thus, it is unlikely that we will observe lower levels of promise keeping for those who leave in the next election to run for higher office. We could even see higher levels among the progressively ambitious. One reason would be a selection effect, if they tend to be stronger, savvier legislators and hence, as a group, follow through more than their more vulnerable peers. In addition, their arguments for why they should get a promotion to a higher office may be based in large part on their past activity and reputation as a "good" representative who keeps his or her promises and has a sustained record of policy accomplishment. Indeed, a marked shift in priorities might open up a legislator to criticisms of "flip-flopping." These could all lead those who plan to run for higher office to be more attentive to their past promises than their peers who intend to stay in the House or Senate.

What about expectations for relative levels of promise keeping among soon-to-be retirees? Much of the same logic applies. If promise keeping is a conscious, reelection-oriented choice, then knowing that they do not have to face another election should lead them to engage in lower levels. Once again, this presumes that they decide fairly early on in the term of study that it will be their last, so that their decision to retire is manifested in their behavior.[9] If the decision comes later, or if other motivations for follow-through outweigh electoral considerations, then we may see no difference between retirees and those who run again.

Making predictions about retirees as a group is made even more complicated by the fact that there are at least two categories of retirees, each with different motivations and incentives. Although legislators typically frame their decisions to retire from public office as based on purely personal factors, scholars have shown that the high reelection rates we observe for incumbents may be a function of "strategic retirement," wherein representatives and senators who anticipate an uphill battle in their reelection bids choose to retire rather than face defeat (see, for example, Groseclose and Krehbiel 1994; Hall and Van Houweling 1995; Jacobson and Kernell 1983; Moore and Hibbing 1992; Murakami 2009). Jacobson and Kernell put this most colorfully, noting that "something about 1974 [the first elections following the Watergate hearings] made family men out of a disproportionate number of Republicans" (1983, 50).

Combining these "strategic" retirees and "sincere" retirees (who choose to leave because of age, health concerns, etc.) into a single group can lead to muddled results. One potentially important distinction between these legislators is when their decisions to retire take place. Although there is probably tremendous variation, on average, strategic retirees should decide later, after making every effort to improve their standing in the eyes of their constituents. Compared to those who run again, there may be less difference in their promise-keeping activity than in that of sincere retirees, who, if they decide earlier that they will be leaving, may devote their last terms in office to activities other than promise keeping.[10]

Thus, there are a number of competing expectations about how legislators' plans for their futures should influence their levels of promise keeping. How should we determine which of the hypotheses about progressive ambition and retirement are correct? My argument throughout this discussion has been that in most cases, it is the career decision that drives levels of promise keeping, rather than the other way around. The

9 Because the timing of the announcement of a retirement is strategic and is, at best, a noisy indicator of when the actual decision was made, it is almost impossible to pinpoint when representatives and senators make these choices.

10 One could also make the counterargument that sincere retirees, who are likely more senior, may be more in the habit of promise keeping, and/or that strategic retirees are vulnerable *because* of their inability or unwillingness to engage in high levels of responsive behaviors such as promise keeping. Nonetheless, the expectation that sincere retirees should demonstrate less than strategic retirees seems most reasonable.

most appropriate modeling strategy therefore is to consider the level of promise keeping to be the dependent variable, and the choice to run for reelection, to seek higher office, or to retire from public life as independent variables. As such, I simply replicate the "who keeps promises?" analyses from Chapter 6, but I add additional indicators of career decisions. In the first set of models, presented in Table 7.3, these include a dummy variable for "higher office," which for representatives includes the eighteen members who ran for the Senate or for governor. For the Senate, it includes three members who ran for president or governor (even though some might consider the governorship a lateral move).[11] For retirement, the measure is a dummy variable for leaving office with no (immediate) run for another office.

The results demonstrate that these choices are clearly related to levels of promise keeping. Even after taking into account other factors that might distinguish those who leave the chamber from those who run again (i.e., seniority, institutional position, vulnerability, etc.), we see that in both the House and the Senate, the progressively ambitious undertake significantly more follow-through than their peers who run for reelection to the chamber. In addition, House retirees engage in significantly less promise keeping, though there is no difference for Senate retirees. These findings underscore a point made by Rothenberg and Sanders (2000) – that it is important not to combine the progressively ambitious and retirees into the same group.[12]

For the reasons discussed previously, it may also be important to distinguish between strategic and sincere retirees. It is difficult to separate these groups cleanly, but one good indicator is seniority. A legislator who decides to retire after a single term is more likely to be doing so out of fear of defeat than one who does so after many years in office. Thus, in the

[11] These analyses likely underestimate the effects of progressive ambition, particularly on Senate behavior, since they do not single out legislators who seriously considered a run (and hence may have changed their activity), but did not ultimately decide to pursue it. Similarly, they do not capture differences in behavior between the truly statically ambitious and those who plan to run for higher office or retire in the near future, but not in the next election.

[12] My results also suggest that the dynamics for agenda-based activities such as promise keeping may differ from those for roll call voting. Rothenberg and Sanders (2000) find that ideological and participatory shirking increases for the progressively ambitious. However, their measure of participation is abstention rates on votes. One explanation is that members running for higher office are in Washington, DC, less, but, while casting a roll call vote requires that a member of Congress be in a specific place at a specific time, the process of introducing and cosponsoring legislation is more flexible.

TABLE 7.3 *Promise Keeping and Career Decisions*

	Model 1		Model 2	
	House	Senate	House	Senate
Higher Office	.340***	.313*	.314***	.310*
	(.090)	(.172)	(.092)	(.172)
Retire	−.239***	.006	–	–
	(.082)	(.058)		
Retire* Senior	–	–	−.326***	−.010
			(.080)	(.085)
Retire* Junior	–	–	−.186**	.018
			(.092)	(.075)
Previous Vote Share	.005*	.005*	.006*	.005*
	(.003)	(.003)	(.003)	(.003)
Unopposed?	−.266*	−.030	−.267*	−.028
	(.155)	(.175)	(.155)	(.174)
New?	.021	.122**	.025	.122**
	(.040)	(.057)	(.040)	(.057)
Senior?	−.110**	.055	−.099*	.061
		(.052)	(.05)	(.056)
Democrat?	.012	.028	.015	.028
	(.048)	(.050)	(.047)	(.050)
Ideological Extremity	−.115	.006	−.107	.006
	(.148)	(.176)	(.149)	(.175)
Leader?	−.089	−.138*	−.074	−.140*
	(.090)	(.080)	(.098)	(.080)
# of Campaign Issues	.054***	.039**	.055***	.039**
	(.013)	(.015)	(.013)	(.015)
Issue Salience	.001***	.000***	.001***	.001***
	(.000)	(.000)	(.000)	(.000)
Policy Activities	.004***	.002***	.004***	.002***
	(.000)	(.000)	(.000)	(.000)
2000 Election	.034	.043	.034	.043
	(.035)	(.051)	(.035)	(.051)
2002 Election	−.076**	.035	−.073*	.036
	(.039)	(.056)	(.039)	(.056)
Constant	1.921	3.139	1.905	3.135
	(.203)	(.258)	(.203)	(.259)
N	360	71	360	71
Log likelihood	−1562.14	−366.11	−1561.63	−366.07

Note: Cell entries are negative binomial regression coefficients (with standard errors in parentheses) where the dependent variable is a count of legislators' activities in office devoted to promise keeping.

***= $p < .01$; **= $p < .05$; *= $p < .10$.

second set of models in Table 7.3, I enter the retirement dummy variable separately for junior and senior legislators, using the breakdown (senior equals more than eight years in office for representatives and more than twelve years for senators) from earlier chapters.[13] As shown, there are indeed differences between these groups. In the House, the coefficient for both groups is negative, but it is larger for sincere retirees than strategic ones. In the Senate, neither coefficient is significant, but their direction corresponds to the pattern for the House – it is negative for sincere retirees, but positive for strategic ones. In short, representatives who plan to retire engage in less promise keeping than those who run again, and those whose retirements are likely planned the furthest in advance differ more in their promise keeping than those whose decisions happen later.

More generally, the findings about the relationships between promise keeping and career decisions provide further evidence that the decision to follow through or not is a conscious and at least partially electorally oriented one. Legislators react to career incentives and constraints in a systematic way, engaging in more or less promise keeping as their need to do so changes.

PROMISES AND ELECTORAL OPPOSITION

Thus far, then, we have seen that promise keeping is manifested in legislators' choices about their political futures and that it yields an electoral payoff, increasing the vote shares of those who choose to run for reelection. What we do not yet know is how the latter comes about. Is it a direct effect, or is it indirect, channeled through the presence and quality of the opposition that legislators face? Given most citizens' low levels of interest in and knowledge of politics, it seems unlikely that they would regularly monitor the behavior of their representatives and senators to determine whether promises are kept. Thus, it is most reasonable to hypothesize that much of the effect of promise keeping on vote margins is produced indirectly, by the reaction that following through on appeals (or the failure to do so) elicits from elites. And, as we have seen in the quotes from legislators throughout this chapter, this is their view on the matter as well. In short, as Arnold explains, "the fear is not simply that citizens will notice on their own when a legislator errs, but that challengers will investigate fully a

[13] This grouping has face validity – for both the House and Senate, "senior" retirees have previous vote shares about 4 percentage points higher than "junior" retirees, though these differences are not significant.

legislator's voting record and then share with citizens their interpretations of how he or she has gone wrong" (1990, 273).

By keeping their promises, legislators should be able to limit challengers' abilities to criticize them on this point,[14] and, perhaps more importantly, a legislator may be able to keep a challenger from running in the first place. Political ambition theory in general and work on challenger emergence in particular show that candidates, especially strong candidates, are most likely to make the decision to enter a race when circumstances are most favorable to them and a victory seems plausible (Jacobson and Kernell 1983; Schlesinger 1966). Many of these circumstances are outside the control of incumbents (e.g., widespread dissatisfaction with a presidential copartisan), but high levels of responsive behavior may provide them with some insulation from these trends and, in typical "localized" election years, may be the deciding factor in challengers' decisions about whether or not to run.

The dynamics and expectations for the relationships between promise keeping and challenges are a bit different for the House and the Senate. In the House, where uncontested races are common, strong incumbents may be able to ward off all opposition. For many, though, a more reasonable expectation is that the challenger they face will be less formidable. In the Senate, where uncontested races are rare, the strength of the challenger is the foremost consideration.

Scholars of congressional elections have devoted significant effort to identifying what makes for a quality challenger – one who can raise money, be seen as credible by voters and elites, run a savvy, well-organized campaign, and so on. The most important and consistent indicator to have emerged is whether or not a challenger has prior elected office experience. Challengers who have held office before do much better at the polls than their inexperienced peers, a phenomenon that applies to both the House and Senate and stretches far back into American history (see, for example, Carson, Engstrom, and Roberts 2007; Jacobson 1978; Squire 1989). The effect of this experience can be substantial. Jacobson (1990) finds that quality House challengers are successful (i.e., they win) four times as often as their inexperienced peers.

[14] Ideally, I would be able to investigate the challenger's rhetoric in each incumbent's next campaign to determine how their promise keeping activity shapes these critiques. Unfortunately, television ad appeals data for challengers are sparse (because few run televised advertisements), skewed highly toward competitive races, and, at the time of this writing, not yet publicly available for several of the elections I study.

Thus, in assessing the relationship between promise keeping and opposition, the questions for House incumbents are whether follow-through on appeals decreases the probability of facing a challenger at all and, barring that, whether it decreases the probability of facing an experienced challenger. For the Senate, I am interested in whether high levels of promise keeping decrease the likelihood of facing a challenger with any elected experience, but, because the range and scope of experience for Senate challengers is larger than for House challengers, I also ask whether promise keeping can deter "highly experienced" challengers, defined as those who are current or prior members of the House of Representatives.

It is also useful to consider the effects of promise keeping on the likelihood of primary election opposition. These should be stronger for the presence and quality of general election challengers (since members of the out party are always on the lookout for a chance to take the seat), but responsiveness to campaign appeals may also affect the decisions of an incumbent's supporters. In his discussion of presidential agendas, Kingdon (1984) noted that:

> Campaign promises do not affect the agenda simply because they were made. Rather, they are important because some significant part of the politician's electoral coalition remembers the promise and attempts to hold him to it, even accusing him of welshing and threatening desertion in the next campaign if he does not deliver. In the end, the mass public's awareness of the campaign issues is not as crucial to politicians as the satisfaction of the activist leaders that promises have been kept. (66)

Accordingly, it is also possible that a lack of promise keeping would elicit a challenge from a fellow copartisan.

Testing for such effects is straightforward. In these analyses, my primary independent variable is the number of promise-keeping activities undertaken by a representative or senator. For the House, my dependent variables are dummies for whether or not the incumbent faced a primary challenger in the next election; whether or not the incumbent had a general election opponent; and, for those who did, whether or not that challenger had prior experience. For the Senate, the dependent variables are facing a primary challenger, facing an experienced general election challenger, and facing a very experienced general election challenger. The controls in these models are identical to those used in the analyses in Table 7.2 (where the dependent variables were future vote share and whether an incumbent won the next race), with one exception: for the primary opposition analyses, I also include a control for whether he or she had a primary challenge in the previous election, as challenging the incumbent is more a norm in some districts, states, and regions than in others.

My results reveal that for the House, promise keeping has no effect on the probability of facing a primary challenger or a quality general election challenger, but it does significantly increase the probability of being unopposed in the next race. For the Senate, there is once again no effect on primary challenges, but highly responsive incumbents have a lower probability of facing an experienced general election challenger. However, among those who face quality challengers, promise keeping does not differentiate those who have very highly experienced challengers from those who face challengers with less experience.

I choose not to present the full probit results here, and instead illustrate the magnitude of the effects. To do so, I use the results to estimate the probability that a legislator will face opposition, run against a quality challenger, and so on, when all variables are set at their means and the percent of activities devoted to promise keeping is set at the median.[15] Then I recalculate these probabilities when all controls are set at their means, but the percentage of promise-keeping activities is set at the 80th percentile. These differences are presented in Figure 7.1.

The figure shows that a representative who undertakes an average amount of promise keeping has about a one in ten chance of being unopposed, whereas for one who engages in high levels of promise keeping this increases to a one in five chance. Along the same lines, the average senator has about a one in two chance of facing an experienced challenger, while a highly responsive one has only about a one in five chance. These are clearly large and meaningful differences, and are particularly impressive since the tests for them are strict – they control for many other factors that should also affect the nature of opposition, most notably the size of the incumbent's vote share in the previous election.[16]

[15] I use the percentage of promise-keeping activities rather than the raw number for these estimates because allowing the raw number of promise-keeping activities to vary while the total number of activities is set at the mean creates unrealistic scenarios (i.e., those in which the number of promise-keeping activities exceeds the total number of activities). The substantive conclusions about the significance of the relationships between promise keeping and opposition are identical no matter which measure of promise keeping is used.

[16] It is important to acknowledge that we should be careful about causal claims here; promise keeping may be part of a broader strategy of "responsive" behavior and so the coefficients may be capturing the effects of other activities as well and hence may overestimate the effect of promise keeping itself. Nonetheless, it is not likely that legislators disentangle these either, so to the extent that promise keeping is part of a broader strategy of responsiveness, it pays off and is rewarded.

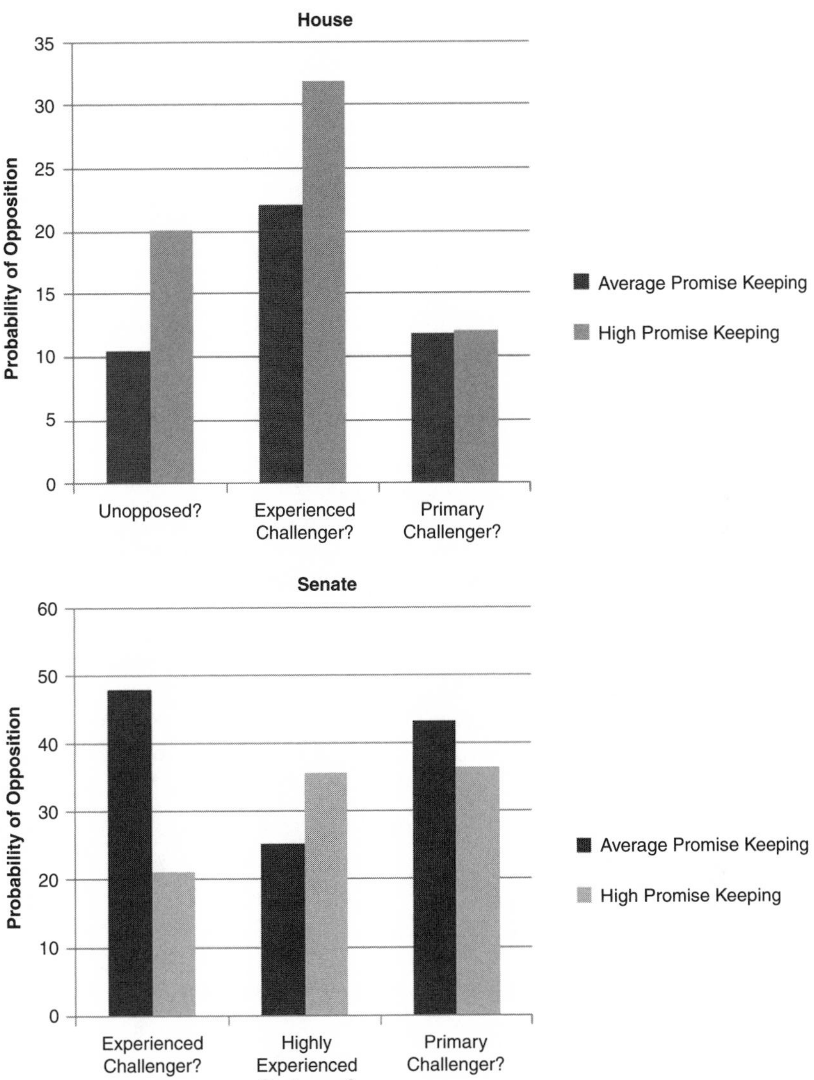

FIGURE 7.1 Promise Keeping and Electoral Opposition for the House and the Senate

Note: The figure presents the probability of facing an experienced challenger, a highly experienced challenger, and a primary challenger for those legislators whose levels of promise keeping put them at the 50th percentile (average promise keeping) and the 80th percentile (high promise keeping).

These results also confirm that much of the effect of promise keeping on future vote shares that we observed in Table 7.2 is likely indirect, a function of the presence and the quality of an incumbent's challenger. To assess this in a more rigorous way, I replicated the regression analyses summarized in that table, adding as an additional independent variable a measure of whether the challenger was (a) present and (b) experienced.[17] In the House, the inclusion of this variable negates the significant effect of promise keeping on vote shares. In the Senate, the size of the coefficient decreases, but remains significant. Thus, for representatives, the electoral benefits of promise keeping are almost entirely indirect, but for senators, there are both direct and indirect effects.

THE EFFECTS OF CHOICES ABOUT TIMING AND LOCATION OF PROMISE KEEPING

To this point, all of my analyses of the electoral implications of promise keeping have relied on the overall measure of legislators' follow-through on their appeals, aggregated across activities and across time. As the final step in my investigation, it is useful to break down this measure a bit to determine whether choices about the location and timing of promise keeping yield different effects. We saw in Chapter 6 that for the sample as a whole, there is not much difference in relative levels of promise keeping along these dimensions. Representatives follow through at about the same rates in year one of their terms as in year two, and there is no discernible variation for senators across the three congresses that constitute their terms.[18] Legislators in both chambers do devote more of their introduction agendas than their cosponsorship agendas to their campaign themes, but this difference is fairly small in magnitude.

However, these averages mask the fact that *individual* representatives and senators do differ in their choices about where and when to demonstrate their responsiveness. Some are much more responsive on one type of activity than the other, and some engage in constant levels of responsiveness across time, while others devote more attention to their promises early

[17] Instrumental variables regression would be a more rigorous approach (i.e., by directly assessing the effect of promise keeping on vote shares after purging its effect on opposition). However, there is no meaningful instrument that would affect the probability of opposition but *not* the size of vote shares.

[18] However, if we focus on the raw number of promise-keeping activities rather than the proportion, we do see a difference – a decrease for representatives in year two of their terms and an increase for senators in congresses two and three of theirs.

or late in their terms. These choices could impact the extent of the electoral payoffs that accrue from promise keeping. For instance, since introductions are generally more visible and more amenable to credit claiming than cosponsorships, we might expect legislators to get more bang for their electoral buck for their follow-through on the former than the latter. On the other hand, because introductions are undertaken more rarely, there may be more meaningful variation in the more prevalent activity of cosponsorship. (And given that cosponsorship weighs more heavily in the aggregate measures, the results from earlier analyses in this chapter are likely driven by the effects for them.) Similarly, although promise keeping on introductions would seem most likely to ward off strong challengers, high levels of follow-through on cosponsorships might be able to make up for a lack of responsiveness on introduced legislation, because such a record makes it hard for an opponent to claim that the legislator has ignored his or her promises.

What about the electoral effects of the timing of promise keeping? Differences in the length of House and Senate terms lead to slightly different expectations. With House terms, most potential challengers make their final decisions about whether or not to run in the first year of the term, so it seems likely that early promise keeping should do the most to ward them off and hence contribute to higher vote shares on Election Day. In contrast, for senators, the first congress following their election is quite far away from the next contest. We might therefore anticipate a more direct link between reelection fortunes and promise keeping that occurs later in the term.

To test these hypotheses, I replicated the analyses from earlier in this chapter for the relationships between promise keeping and future vote shares and the presence and quality of opposition, but instead of an overall measure of promise keeping, I break it out by activity (promise keeping on introductions versus promise keeping on cosponsorships) and time (year one versus year two for representatives and congresses one, two, and three for senators).

These findings are summarized in Figure 7.2, which presents the coefficient on promise keeping from each of these models (where promise keeping is measured as the count of activities on a legislator's previous campaign themes). The first panel illustrates the results when the dependent variable is vote shares. As shown, for both chambers, it is variation in follow-through on cosponsorships rather than introductions that drives the electoral effects. Thus, although legislators may engage in relatively more promise keeping on their introductions than their cosponsorships, it

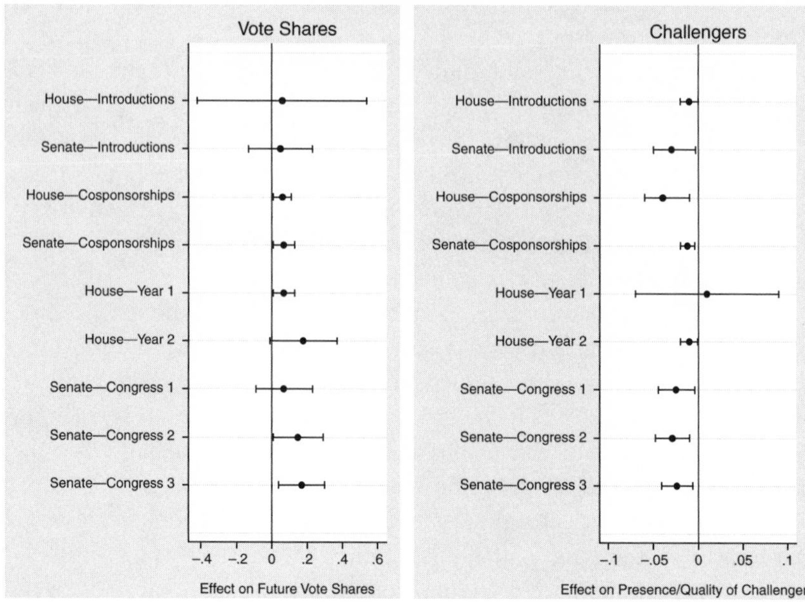

FIGURE 7.2 Variation in Electoral Payoffs by Timing and Location of Promise Keeping

Note: The figure summarizes the results of a series of regression analyses where the dependent variables are either a legislator's future vote share or the presence/quality of the challenger he or she faces in that race (presence for House members and quality for Senate members). The dots represent the coefficients on the primary independent variable of interest – the amount of promise keeping (as measured by a count of campaign-themed activities). Lines represent the 90 percent confidence intervals.

is responsiveness on the latter that tends to pay off more, at least when it comes to increasing vote shares in the next election. For timing, we see that early promise keeping appears to pay off more for representatives, but it is later promise keeping that does so for senators. This makes sense given the timing of the electoral cycle and potential challengers' decisions. Representatives who wait until the second year of their terms to act on their campaign appeals are too late to reap its benefits, but senators generally enjoy more payoff from the promise-keeping activities they engage in once the next election grows nearer and is more on the minds of elites and voters. In other words, front-loading their responsiveness and then moving on to other issues is not an electorally wise choice for them.

The second panel illustrates the results when the dependent variable is the presence of a challenger (for the House) and the presence of a quality challenger (for the Senate). For the House, we see that promise keeping on cosponsorships decreases the probability of facing opposition in the next election, but there is once again no significant effect for introductions (perhaps because they are just so low in number for most representatives). Interestingly, it is promise keeping in the second year of the term that is significantly related to opposition, with those with high levels less likely to face a challenger than those with lower levels.

For the Senate, the results for the quality of opposition are consistent – variation in levels of promise keeping for both types of activities and at all times in the term are significant predictors of the quality (or lack thereof) of the next challenger. By engaging in high levels of follow-through on their campaign themes, senators are able to ward off experienced challengers, no matter when or how they demonstrate their responsiveness.

CONCLUSIONS

That representatives' and senators' activity in office should affect their electoral prospects is a common hypothesis, but one for which confirming evidence has been somewhat elusive. The results here show, though, that promise keeping has a clear relationship with how well legislators do in the next election and with their decisions about whether or not to run in that election. Perhaps most importantly, incumbents who devote high proportions of their governing agendas to addressing their previous campaign themes achieve higher vote shares than those who devote less. Much of this effect is due to the reactions of potential challengers: highly responsive representatives are better able to forestall challenges altogether, and senators who engage in high levels of promise keeping significantly decrease their likelihood of facing a strong challenger. We also see that legislators' decisions about the next steps in their political careers are manifested in their choices about promise keeping. Those who plan to run again are more responsive than those who plan to retire, and those who wish to move up are even more attentive to their promises than those who intend to remain in their current office.

Taken together, these findings suggest that promise keeping is not coincidental, but is a conscious choice made by legislators. Thus, the reelection imperative encourages representatives and senators to remain focused on their campaign promises, and the system as a whole works to punish "bad" behavior and to reward responsiveness.

8

Promises and Policy Making

The results to this point have shown that promise keeping is widespread, that it varies in a systematic way across legislators, and that it both affects and is affected by their electoral prospects and their career decisions. These findings offer important insight into legislators' strategies and into the processes of responsiveness and accountability. As of yet, though, another piece of the puzzle remains largely unexplored – the policy implications of this activity. Do the measures that representatives and senators introduce and cosponsor on their campaign themes affect policy in a meaningful way? Or are these activities largely peripheral to lawmaking?

This is an issue that merits serious attention. As discussed in Chapter 2, there is a tendency in the literature on Congress to separate legislators' activities into two categories: those that are serious and policy-oriented and those that are symbolic and undertaken largely for electoral reasons. The critique is that the latter are mostly frivolous and insincere and take scarce time and resources away from general interest legislation and other efforts aimed at solving big problems. Throughout this book, I have made the argument (not unique to me – see, for example, Hall 1996) that these need not be mutually exclusive. There is no reason that a particular introduction or cosponsorship can fulfill one goal or the other but not both, and it is difficult, if not impossible, to classify individual measures as such, since their effects can be indirect and/or outside the control of the particular legislators who are involved with a piece of legislation. Moreover, of all of the phenomena related to representation, promise keeping seems the one where electoral and policy considerations should most clearly converge. Indeed, I have shown that promise keeping has its origins in candidates' choices to focus their campaigns on issues of particular interest to them, so that the process is driven by policy priorities, particularly for House members. In contrast, consider a story about promise keeping in which candidates choose campaign issues based on an exogenous factor (e.g., their prominence on the national scene) and then, having talked about them, feel compelled to demonstrate some sort of follow-through to ward off criticism about unresponsiveness. In such a case, their promise-keeping activity might be more halfhearted, because it is undertaken solely for strategic purposes.

Thus, the causal mechanisms underlying promise keeping are suggestive of a policy impact, as are the findings about its location. That legislators devote a larger proportion of their introductions than their cosponsorships to promise keeping supports the claim that it is a sincere activity with the potential for a direct influence on policy. Of course, because the content of appeals tends to match the content of activity, any laws that arise from promise keeping should also align with the claims made during campaigns.

Nonetheless, it is important to move beyond assuming a policy impact to test for one, and so in this chapter I take on this task. In doing so, I explore the direct and the indirect effects of promise keeping on the policy agenda and on policy outputs, at both the aggregate level and at the level of individual legislators. In particular, I examine the relationships between campaign and legislative agendas across congresses, evaluate the policy importance of promise-keeping measures, track the attention that sponsors devote to their campaign-themed and non–campaign-themed introductions and the fates of these measures in the legislative process, and assess how legislators' appeals condition their responses to unforeseen events. I choose to begin my investigation at the end, with those promise-keeping measures that became law.

PROMISE-KEEPING LAWS

It is hard to deny that the clearest evidence that legislators' promise-keeping activities have a lasting policy legacy is if they are passed into law. Across the time period I examine, that was the eventual fate of 33 of the House bills and joint resolutions and 107 of the Senate measures introduced by the sampled legislators on their campaign themes. These 140 bills were sponsored by twenty-six different representatives and forty-three senators and cross fifteen of the eighteen issue categories, including all of the most salient issues. (This is not surprising, since there were simply more bills on these issues to begin with.) The only issues for which we do

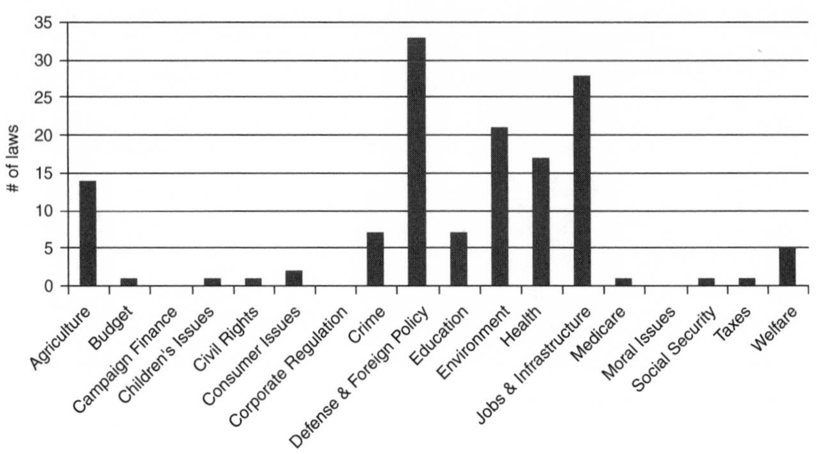

FIGURE 8.1 Promise-Keeping Laws by Issue Category
Note: The figure presents the number of promise-keeping bills in each issue area that became law.

not see any statutes are campaign finance, corporate regulation, and moral issues. Figure 8.1 presents the distribution of these laws across issue categories.

Like the vast majority of laws that are passed, many of these are minor, but a number do address major policy issues. For example, the 140 promise-keeping laws include multiple measures introduced on defense and disaster relief in the aftermath of the September 11 terrorist attacks and Hurricane Katrina. There are also laws dealing with such central national issues as the budget (Senator Bill Frist's [R-TN] S 2986 in the 108th Congress to increase the public debt limit); crime (Representative Sue Myrick's [R-NC] HR 2780 in the 106th Congress, which provided funding for programs to find missing adults); the foreign policy component of the defense category (Senator Richard Lugar's [R-IN] S 2781 in the 108th Congress to address the Darfur crisis); education (Senator George Voinovich's [R-OH] S 926 in the 108th Congress on student loan repayments); health care (Representative Roger Wicker's [R-MS] HR 717 in the 107th Congress, which amended the Public Health Service Act to provide for research on muscular dystrophy, and Senator Christopher Dodd's [D-CT] S 1789, also in the 107th, which focused on increasing the safety of prescription drugs used on children); Medicare (Senator Charles Grassley's [R-IA] S 2618 in the 108th Senate); and Social Security (Representative Clay Shaw's [R-FL] HR 743 in the 108th).

As we saw in earlier chapters, the link between the content of the measure and the content of the preceding campaign appeal is often quite strong. For instance, in his 2002 campaign, Representative Dave Camp (R-MI) spoke of promoting adoption and foster care, and in the next congress, his HR 3182 ("A bill to reauthorize the adoption incentive payments program under part E of title IV of the Social Security Act, and for other purposes") was passed into law. Similarly, in his campaign that year, Senator Tom Harkin (D-IA) talked about his support for the school lunch program, and subsequently introduced (and passed) S 870 ("A bill to amend the Richard B. Russell National School Lunch Act to extend the availability of funds to carry out the fruit and vegetable pilot program").

In addition to these promise-keeping laws on national-level policies, there are also a number of statutes that deal with issues that may not be especially important to the country at large, but do make a difference to a particular constituency. Along these lines, five representatives and six senators were the sponsors of laws that set aside land for wilderness or protected rivers or wetlands in their districts or states, and others passed bills that provided funding for hydroelectric projects, education grants to local districts, highways, and the like.

These laws all serve as tangible evidence of the policy legacy of promise-keeping activity. Even if having made a campaign appeal about an issue is not the sole reason that a legislator introduced a bill on it, it is still the case that campaign activity translates into a policy outcome. From the perspective of constituents and other observers interested in determining whether an incumbent has kept his or her promises, this is a sufficient and strong indicator of follow-through. It is important to note as well that by this measure, promise keeping is clearly more prevalent for senators than for representatives. Over half of the senators in the sample who ran for reelection in the next cycle could point to a law that originated with their promise-keeping activity. However, the same holds true for only about 7 percent of representatives. We might therefore characterize the House–Senate difference in follow-through as less promise-keeping *input* for the latter chamber (since the links between appeals and activity are fuzzier), but more *output*, since more of the legislators who make introductions on their campaign themes see them work their way into law.

Another important distinction between chambers is the partisan distribution of legislative success on promise-keeping bill introductions. In the House, the Republicans held the majority in all three congresses I study here, and only one of the thirty-three introductions from that chamber that passed into law was introduced by a Democrat.[1] Majority control in the Senate across the terms for my sample varies – the Republicans held the majority in the 106th, 108th, and 109th Congresses, the Democrats held it in the 110th, and there were multiple switches in the 107th.[2] Thus, although Republicans were the majority party for most of the time, each senator faced some period in which the Democrats were in control. Not unexpectedly, bill success is more common among Republicans (61 percent of those in the sample had at least one promise-keeping measure pass into law), but Democrats also had substantial success (39 percent of them had a measure pass) and this was not limited to the two congresses in which they held partial or full control. Indeed, eleven of the fifteen "successful" Democratic senators in the sample passed bills in the 106th, 108th, and 109th – congresses in which the Republicans held the majority for the entire period.

The analyses in Table 8.1 are designed to provide a more rigorous assessment of the determinants of promise-keeping bill success. The dependent variable in each model is a dichotomous indicator of whether or not a legislator had one of his or her campaign-themed introductions become law. The independent variables include individual-level characteristics such as party, seniority, and ideological extremity, as well as election year and several features of legislators' appeals and promise-keeping activity, such as the number of themes they raised in the campaign, the number of issues for which they made a specific claim, the legislative salience of these issues, and the number of bills they introduced on their promises. In addition, for the Senate I limit the analyses to those who served a full term, and for the House and the Senate I focus on legislators who introduced at least one measure on their appeals. As always, in the House models, the standard errors are clustered on the legislator.

The results confirm that in both chambers, status as a Republican is a significant predictor of success, even after taking all of the other factors into account. In addition, in the Senate, senior members and those who introduced a lot of promise-keeping measures were more successful. In the House, there is no effect of seniority, but relatively moderate and more active members were more likely to have a bill become law. Interestingly,

[1] In the 107th Congress, Mark Udall's HR 1576 ("A bill to designate the James Peak Wilderness and Protection Area in the Arapaho and Roosevelt National Forests in the State of Colorado, and for other purposes") became law.

[2] This is a function of multiple factors, including the switch of Vermont's Jim Jeffords from Republican to Independent (but caucusing with the Democrats) and the fifty–fifty tie at the beginning of the 107th Congress, broken first by Al Gore and then by Dick Cheney as the presidential administration changed.

TABLE 8.1 *Factors Explaining Legislators' Promise-Keeping Bill Success*

Factor	House	Senate
Democrat	−1.676***	−1.123***
	(.414)	(.417)
Seniority	.028	.066***
	(.021)	(.026)
Ideological Extremity	−1.874**	1.563
	(.800)	(1.687)
# of Campaign Issues	−.169	−.056
	(.125)	(.192)
# of Specific Issues	.231**	.054
	(.091)	(.136)
Issue Salience	.000	.000
	(.000)	(.000)
Promises Intros	.069**	.017**
	(.029)	(.007)
2000 Election	.272	−.536
	(.360)	(.489)
2002 Election	.420	−.674
	(.389)	(.488)
Constant	−1.189	−1.877
	(.497)	(.853)
N	296	71
Pseudo R^2	.26	.31

Note: Cell entries are probit coefficients (with standard errors in parentheses) where the dependent variable is a dummy for whether or not one of a legislator's promise-keeping introductions became law.
***= p < .01; **= p < .05; *= p < .10.

for representatives, the specificity of appeals is significant too; those who offered specific claims about a larger number of their issues had their introductions pass into law at a higher rate. This has its roots in the individual introductions – when I examine the particular bills that were successful, I find that 29 of the 33 were on an issue about which the sponsor had made a specific appeal (and the same holds true for 84 of the 107 for senators). This may be because sponsors pursue these bills more intently after they have been introduced,[3] or it could be that candidates tend to be more specific about more salient issues.

[3] Unless representatives advocate across chambers for these bills, though, this is not likely to be the full explanation. When I use as a dependent variable passage in the House (which, unlike passage into law, does not require the consent of the Senate or the president), there is not a significant relationship between specificity and the probability of passing a bill.

ASSESSMENTS OF INDIRECT POLICY IMPLICATIONS

Of course, whether or not bills pass is largely outside the control of their sponsors, even given their sincerest intentions and best efforts to promote their legislation. However, there are a number of ways short of becoming law that activities can influence policy making. When issues get more attention, when bills are the subject of discussion and debate, and when legislators work formally and informally to pursue their interests, this can contribute to policy change. Although these effects are indirect, together and over time they can add up to a substantial influence (Kingdon 1984).

Aggregate Relationships between Campaign and Legislative Attention

To evaluate these possibilities, I first examine the aggregate relationships between campaign attention and legislative attention. Put simply, do we see more attention to issues in Congress when more legislators focused on them in the previous campaign? We must be careful about making causal claims here, as it is possible, and even likely, that some of the same factors that lead an issue to be raised frequently in a campaign season also make it more salient in the next congress. Nonetheless, by examining how these aggregate agendas move together, we can see how campaigns might contribute to the broader agenda-setting process.

I assess this via an OLS regression analysis, where the dependent variable is legislative attention to each issue in a particular term (i.e., a congress for the House and three congresses for the Senate). In the first set of models in Table 8.2, this is a count of the number of bills introduced on an issue, and in the second set of models, it is the percentage of bills on that issue. The independent variable of interest is the number or percentage of winning candidates who raised the issue in the previous election. Thus, my units of analysis are an issue/term, and there are a total of fifty-one observations for the House and for the Senate (seventeen issue categories[4] * three election years/terms). The appropriate controls include dummy variables for each election year and dummies for each of the issue categories, to take into account differences in the salience of issues. The coefficients on these controls are not particularly informative, so in the interest of space, I do not present them in the table and instead present just the coefficients on campaign attention.

[4] I omit corporate regulation from these analyses since it was only an issue in one election year.

TABLE 8.2 *Campaign Agendas and Legislative Attention*

	Model 1: Counts		Model 2: Percents	
	House	Senate	House	Senate
Campaign Attention	1.433**	5.789*	.043**	.010
	(.570)	(3.111)	(.016)	(.008)
Constant	76.27	343.113	1.603	.932
	(23.67)	(70.159)	(.518)	(.296)
N	51	51	51	51
Adjusted R^2	.98	.99	.98	.99

Note: Cell entries are OLS regression coefficients (with standard errors in parentheses) where the dependent variable is a count of the number of bills devoted to an issue in a term, or the percentage of bills on an issue.
***$p < .01$; **$p < .05$; *$p < .10$.

The results in Model 1 reveal a significant relationship: in both the House and the Senate, the greater the number of candidates who talk about an issue, the more bills that are introduced on that issue in the next term. In the House, every additional candidate who mentions an issue in his or her campaign translates into one to two additional introductions in the next congress, and, in the Senate, every additional campaign means about six more introductions. The size of these effects is not directly comparable, since there are many more House campaigns than Senate campaigns, but we can conclude that there is a campaign and legislative agendas link for both chambers.[5] For the second model, when the campaign and legislative attention variables are measured as proportions rather than raw counts, the relationship between the two remains for the House, but drops to insignificance (though just barely) in the Senate. However, the presence of more robust relationships for the House makes sense within the context of the patterns in Chapters 3 and 4, since those analyses established that there are also stronger links between appeals and activity at the individual level for that chamber.

Thus, although it varies a bit by chamber, there is indeed an aggregate relationship between campaign and legislative attention to issues – the more an issue is featured in campaigns, the more activity we see on it in

[5] It is also important to keep in mind that the "mentions" variable is limited to those candidates in the sample, so the results should be interpreted with caution (since we don't know what issues those candidates not in the sample discussed), particularly for the House. If the issue choices of the sampled candidates are representative of those of the nonsampled, though, these results should be generalizable.

the next congress. Changes like this in agenda status alone can be important in affecting policy. For example, research on agenda setting has shown that sharp increases in attention to an issue are often accompanied by policy change (Baumgartner and Jones 2009). However, it is also true that not all introductions are equal in this sense; measures are more likely to elicit attention and have a lasting effect when they reach the point where someone other than just the sponsor knows of them and is talking about them. One indicator of this, explored in more detail in the next section, is their progress through the legislative process. In particular, do the fates of introductions that originate as promise keeping differ from those of others? Another is their relative importance. To what extent are the measures that representatives and senators introduce on their campaign themes central to legislative debates about these issues?

The Importance of Promise-Keeping Measures

The "importance" of legislation is a notoriously difficult concept to quantify, but legislative scholars have come up with a number of possibilities. One of the most straightforward is whether a measure was included in the *CQ (Congressional Quarterly) Almanac*'s end-of-the-year write-up on each congressional session.[6] The staff at *CQ* breaks out legislative action by issue area and identifies those bills in each area that reflected the most important debates and/or marked changes in policy. Although these procedures introduce some subjectivity to the process and mean that bills in certain issue areas may have a higher probability of appearing on the list than those in others,[7] as Volden and Wiseman (2009) note, they nevertheless provide a good indicator of whether or not a bill was "substantively significant."

The number of measures identified by *CQ* varies a bit from year to year, but the average is about one hundred House bills and sixty Senate bills. Across the congresses that I examine, this sums to a total of 607 House measures and 604 Senate measures, or about 3 to 4 percent of all

[6] Other well-known approaches to measuring importance (e.g., Mayhew 2005) focus on statutes rather than bills and are thus less appropriate for my purposes.

[7] Most obviously, the list includes a large number of measures on moral/social/cultural issues such as abortion, flag burning, the pledge of allegiance, and so on. However, these issues do not tend to occupy a central place in congressional campaigns, and the overall volume of introduced legislation on them is relatively low.

introduced bills. General appropriations bills comprise about 10 to 12 percent of the total,[8] but the rest align with my definition of policy relevance. For the Senate, 257 of these were introduced by members of the sample (during the years in which they were in the sample), and 136 of these (53 percent) focused on their campaign themes. These were introduced by forty-five different senators, so over half sponsored at least one promise-keeping measure deemed to be among the most substantively important pieces of legislation to be considered during their terms. In the House, 116 of the "important" bills were introduced by the sampled legislators and thirty-five of these (about 30 percent) were on their campaign themes. This includes activity by twenty-three different representatives.

Thus, a fairly large number of promise-keeping bills introduced by a wide swath of representatives and senators were among the most crucial measures in setting the agenda and policy about their respective issues. These include bills on privatizing Social Security, on changing the rules guiding the gathering of intelligence by the federal government, on providing a Medicare prescription drug program, on developing a national energy policy, on passing a Patients' Bill of Rights, on promoting aviation security, on routinizing criminal penalties for minors and sex offenders, on repealing the estate tax, and so on. In other words, almost every major policy issue of the time was reflected in bills that originated as promise keeping on the part of their sponsors.

In addition, once again we see that compared to representatives, senators are more likely to be involved in important policy making on their campaign themes. This is not something about which we should judge representatives harshly, as not every legislator has an equal shot at being the sponsor of high-profile legislation. The smaller size of the Senate privileges those members on this dimension, as a higher proportion of them occupy committee chairs and other positions that are important for policy making. Nonetheless, these findings confirm that senators' promise-keeping activities do have an impact, even if their campaign appeals serve as relatively weaker signals about the subsequent volume of their activity on issues. They also suggest that it may be valuable to look beyond just the most important measures and track the legislative progress of all promise-keeping bills.

[8] I code these under the "governmental operations" category since they cannot be classified as being about one issue or another.

How Do Promise-Keeping Measures Fare?

In all, the representatives in the sample introduced 1,420 policy-relevant (i.e., nongovernmental operations) bills and joint resolutions on their campaign themes, and the sampled senators introduced 3,750. These comprise about 37 percent of all policy-relevant measures in the House and 57 percent in the Senate, so a sizable portion of legislative activity in both chambers consists of representatives and senators following through on their campaign issues. About three-quarters of these promise-keeping measures received at least one cosponsor, and of these the average was twenty-seven cosponsors for House bills and five to six cosponsors for Senate bills. In the House, about 7 percent of measures were reported out of committee, and in the Senate about 10 percent were, although this understates the number of measures that progressed, as bills can proceed to votes without being formally reported. Finally, in both the House and Senate, about 7 percent of bills passed the chamber of origin and 2 to 3 percent also passed in the other chamber, were signed by the president, and became law.

Regardless of the measure, then, the fact remains that a low percentage of promise-keeping bills and resolutions make it very far in the legislative process. This is not unexpected, as very few bills of any type progress much beyond the introduction stage. The question of real interest is whether there is a systematic difference in the fates of promise keeping and other measures. How might such differences arise? Although they may not be able to control the ultimate fates of their introductions, primary sponsors of bills and resolutions do have the choice of how actively to promote their legislation. If their greater levels of interest in their campaign themes relative to other issues lead legislators to pursue their promise-keeping activities more aggressively, this could translate into more evidence of efforts at coalition building (i.e., more cosponsors for these measures) and perhaps more progress. If, however, follow-through is mostly for show and sponsors take their promise-keeping measures less seriously (either because the bills are written in a way that makes it less likely that they will progress or because the sponsor largely ignores them), then these bills and resolutions could fare worse than those on other issues.

I evaluate these possibilities in two ways. First, I track the progress of individual bills, comparing to others those that were on an issue that was a campaign theme of their sponsor's. Then I compare *within* individual legislators' activity, to determine whether, on average, their campaign and non–campaign-themed introductions fare differently. For the aggregate

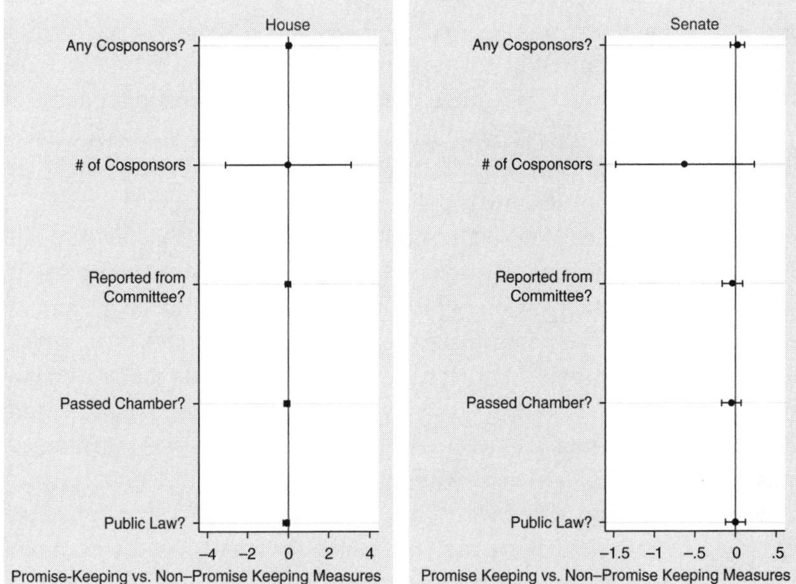

FIGURE 8.2 Are There Differences in the Progress of Promise-Keeping and Non–Promise-Keeping Introductions?

Note: The figure summarizes the results of a series of regression analyses where the units of analysis are introductions and the dependent variables are measures of their progress (whether they received cosponsors, etc.). The independent variable of interest is whether the introduction dealt with one of the sponsor's previous campaign issues. The dots represent the coefficients on this independent variable, and the lines represent the 90 percent confidence intervals.

analyses, summarized in Figure 8.2, the units of analysis are the individual bill, and the dependent variables are whether it got any cosponsors (and if so, how many), whether it was reported out of committee, whether it passed the chamber of origin, and whether it became law. The independent variable in all models is whether or not the introduction dealt with one of the sponsor's campaign issues. To account for the effects of party, I include a control for whether the sponsor was a Democrat, and to control for differences in rates of bill success across issues and across time, I include a full set of dummy variables for all of the issues and all of the congresses. Finally, to make for a stricter comparison, I limit the analyses to policy-relevant bills and joint resolutions. The figure presents the coefficients on whether or not an introduced measure was a campaign theme of the sponsor's.

As shown, there appear to be no systematic differences in the fates of promise-keeping and non–promise-keeping introductions. They attract cosponsors, are reported from committee, pass the chamber, and become law at the same rates. There are more negative coefficients than positive ones,[9] though we should probably not make too much of this, as there are a number of potential complicating factors. For example, the investigation of promise keeping on defense and the environment in Chapter 5 revealed a tendency for repeated identical introductions on campaign issues – if a bill did not pass, the legislator kept introducing it in successive congresses. If this happens less often for lower-priority issues, it could inflate the failure rate of promise-keeping introductions in any given congress, even if persistence eventually paid off. More generally, there may be systematic differences in the distribution of rates of success for issues that are and are not campaign themes. Indeed, several of the issues that were mentioned only rarely in campaigns enjoyed relatively high levels of legislative success, while some issues that were quite salient were less likely to progress (in large part because they are competing against many other introductions on the same topic). To give just one example, in the Senate across this time period, the most successful issue by far was civil rights – 29 percent of introductions on it were reported out of committee and/or passed the chamber and 13 percent became law. In contrast, only about 5 percent of education introductions progressed beyond committee, and only 1 percent of these became law. However, as we saw in Chapter 3, many candidates discussed education, but only a handful discussed civil rights (in the sample, seventy candidates versus nine candidates). The dummy variables for issue categories account for some of these differences, but likely do not capture all of them.

Similar caveats hold for the within-legislators analyses. For these, I focus on rates of cosponsorship and legislative success for representatives' and senators' introductions on campaign and noncampaign issues. The purpose here is to control for individual-level differences in attention that cannot be addressed using the aggregate approach summarized in Figure 8.2. Thus, I conduct a series of paired-samples t-tests comparing the percentage of each legislator's promise-keeping and non–promise-keeping introductions that received cosponsors (and for those that did receive at least one, the count), were reported out of committee, passed

[9] Interestingly, when the independent variable is whether or not the sponsor had made a *specific* appeal on the issue, these coefficients flip to positive for the House (though still insignificant) but remain negative for the Senate.

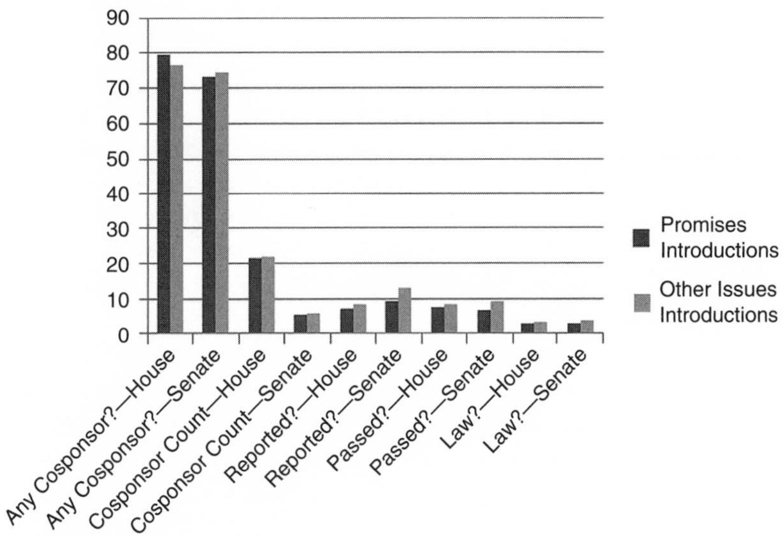

FIGURE 8.3 Comparing Legislators' Promise-Keeping and Other Introductions
Note: The figure presents the percentage of promise-keeping and non–promise-keeping bills that were successful at each stage of the legislative process, and the average number of cosponsors each type of bill received.

in the chamber, and became law. Figure 8.3 illustrates these percentages. In the House, the results reveal no significant difference across any of these categories. In the Senate, promise-keeping and non–promise-keeping introductions are equally likely to receive cosponsorships and attract the same number. However, non–promise-keeping measures progress beyond committee and pass the chamber at slightly higher rates (9.1 percent of promise-keeping measures are reported out of committee compared to 13.1 percent for others, $t = 2.8$, $p < .01$; 6.8 percent of promise-keeping measures pass the chamber compared to 9.4 percent of others, $t = -2.3$, $p < .05$). These differences are likely driven by the variation in the success of different issues, and they disappear when the comparison is the proportion of bills that actually pass into law. Senators' non–promise-keeping measures are no more likely than those on their campaign themes to become law.

What should we conclude from these analyses? It is important to acknowledge that they do not provide evidence that promise-keeping measures are somehow advantaged in the process or that sponsors pursue these introductions more intently. On the other hand, neither is it the case that promise-keeping measures are more symbolic or less important than others, particularly when we consider that routine governmental operations measures (which comprise nearly one-fifth of all introductions) are removed from the comparisons and that the measures of sponsor attentiveness (i.e., the presence and number of cosponsors) are pretty blunt. Legislators' more under-the-radar efforts in committee and among their peers may play an important role in pushing their priority issues, even if their particular introductions on them are not decisive. Of course, as a regular part of the legislative process, bills are combined, substituted, and so on, so focusing on whether a particular introduction passes or not may at least sometimes fail to capture its real impact and legacy. Thus, we should be comfortable concluding that promise keeping has just as much effect on policy as any other legislation and, under certain circumstances, may leave a crucial imprint.

DO APPEALS CONDITION OTHER ACTIVITY?

As a final step, I examine one such mechanism through which such an imprint might occur, and that is how legislators' previous commitments condition their responses to new and unexpected circumstances. Much of my theory of promise keeping focuses on legislators' expectations about the future. In short, they talk about issues in their campaigns knowing that they will act on them in the next congress. What happens when serious and unforeseen events occur, such as the terrorist attacks of September 11, 2001, or Hurricane Katrina in August of 2005? The popular wisdom is that the dramatic nature of these events led all legislators to respond to them. Was this actually the case, or was participation selective? In particular, does knowing whether a legislator had talked about defense or jobs and infrastructure issues[10] in the previous campaign help us to predict whether he or she was among those who responded to 9/11 or Katrina by introducing legislation? If so, this suggests another way in which appeals may matter: by providing information about who will step up when emergencies on an issue arise.

To address this question, I analyzed the content of legislation that was introduced in the days immediately following September 11, 2001, and August 29, 2005 (when Katrina hit New Orleans), up through the end of that particular congress – the 107th for 9/11 and the 109th for Hurricane Katrina. I limit my scope in this way because my intent is to examine how

[10] This is the issue category under which measures on disasters and disaster relief are coded.

legislators who could not have anticipated the event responded. Thus, I do not want to consider behavior on these issues in congresses following the election after these events, since legislators would have had the opportunity to discuss them in that campaign. This means that my analyses for 9/11 target the activity of the 130 representatives in the 2000 election sample and the 57 senators in the 1998 and 2000 election samples. Hurricane Katrina occurred after the House terms I study had ended, so I cannot include representatives. I focus my illustration here on the 27 senators in the 2002 election sample.

The goal of the recoding was to identify all measures dealing specifically with the event of interest. For 9/11, I first reexamined all legislation in the defense category and determined whether it addressed the attacks, terrorism, homeland security, or similar topics. Then I also used these search terms to identify introductions in other issue areas that also focused on the aftermath of the attacks. For example, there were education bills designed to increase funding to New York City schools to provide counseling and other programs to students, jobs and infrastructure bills to include relief efforts under existing domestic disaster relief programs, bills to protect agriculture from bioterrorism, and so on. In all, there are a total of 233 House measures, 66 of which were introduced by members of the sample, and 99 Senate bills, of which 72 were introduced by the sample.

I used a similar procedure for Hurricane Katrina, identifying measures that mention Katrina or Hurricane Rita (which occurred in the same time period) or federal disaster relief efforts. The majority of these fall under the "jobs and infrastructure" category, but there were a handful of bills in agriculture, defense (i.e., protecting vulnerable cities from further attack), education, and health care. In all, this included 121 measures in the 109th Senate, 39 of which were introduced by members of my sample.

Beginning with responses to September 11, my dependent variable is either whether a legislator introduced *any* bill or joint resolution dealing with the event or whether he or she introduced a specifically defense-related measure. For the Senate, I find that 24 of the 57 legislators introduced a measure on 9/11; 20 did so on defense, and 8 did so on another issue (some did both). For the House, a total of 38 of the 130 representatives introduced a measure – 33 on defense and 12 on other issues.[11]

[11] Interestingly, six of the eight senators and nine of the twelve representatives who introduced nondefense bills on 9/11 had the issues that were the subjects of these bills as campaign themes, and the same holds true for five of the six senators who introduced Hurricane Katrina bills that did not deal with jobs and infrastructure. This suggests that

TABLE 8.3 *Who Responded to 9/11 and Hurricane Katrina?*

	House Any 9/11	House Defense 9/11	Senate Any 9/11	Senate Defense 9/11	Senate Any Katrina	Senate Jobs Katrina
Mentioned	.057	.225	1.05***	.753*	.960	.574
Issue	(.352)	(.356)	(.40)	(.403)	(.677)	(.680)
Democrat	.025	.067	.220	.261	1.315*	1.039
	(.245)	(.253)	(.393)	(.391)	(.708)	(.731)
Total Activity	.017	.023*	−.002	−.004	.001	−.004
	(.013)	(.013)	(.004)	(.004)	(.007)	(.007)
From Area?	−.329	−.193	1.220	1.469	–	–
	(.480)	(.483)	(.921)	(.92)		
Constant	−.754	−.998	−.709	−.610	−1.433	−1.074
	(.250)	(.263)	(.478)	(.478)	(.833)	(.802)
N	130	130	50	50	26	26
Pseudo R^2	.01	.02	.12	.09	.15	.08

Note: Cell entries are probit coefficients (with standard errors in parentheses) where the dependent variable is whether a legislator made an introduction dealing with the aftermath of the September 11 terrorist attacks or Hurricane Katrina.
***= p < .01; **p < .05; *p < .10.

My independent variables include whether the legislator had discussed defense in the previous campaign, his or her party, the total amount of activity he or she engaged in during the 107th Congress, and whether he or she represented New York or Pennsylvania, two of the sites of the attacks.[12] The results are presented in Table 8.3.

For the Senate, there are strong relationships; having mentioned defense is a significant predictor of introducing a measure on 9/11, overall or defense-specific. For example, the probability of introducing a 9/11 bill for those who had not talked about defense is 25 percent, but jumps to 61 percent for those who did. Importantly, this holds even after controlling for how much other defense activity a legislator engaged in. For the House, the relationships are positive, but not significant. However, we should keep in mind that very few representatives discussed defense in their 2000 campaigns, so to see a significant result, there would have to be a very large difference in their behavior relative to others.

preexisting priorities affected legislators' responses to these exogenous shocks. In other words, they addressed them, but in a manner consistent with their other priorities.

12 I also examined the effects of committee assignments and constituency characteristics, but these had little effect once the other variables were included.

I conduct similar analyses for the senators in the 2002 election sample who were in office when Hurricane Katrina hit. Here the campaign issue of interest (the independent variable) is jobs and infrastructure. The coefficient on having mentioned this issue is very close to standard levels of statistical significance, and reaches it if I limit the sample to those who ran for reelection. For this group, the probability of introducing a measure on Katrina jumps from 15 to 36 percent for candidates who had not discussed jobs and infrastructure in the preceding campaign compared to those who had.

Thus, those senators who had spoken about defense (in the case of September 11) or jobs and infrastructure (in the case of Hurricane Katrina) in their previous campaigns were more likely to be active when big crises relating to them arose. This is particularly interesting because defense and jobs and infrastructure were not among the issues for which we saw a general promise-keeping effect. Overall, Senate candidates who had discussed them were *not* more active on them. This indicates once again that there are indeed different promise-keeping dynamics in the House and Senate. In the Senate, appeals may be less informative about the day-to-day content of legislators' activities in office but, compared to those of House candidates, are more informative about the bigger issues of passing law and stepping up to address unforeseen situations.

CONCLUSIONS

The policy implications uncovered here underscore the importance of promise keeping in assessments of responsiveness and accountability. The introductions that representatives and senators make on their campaign themes are not solely symbolic and have the potential to leave a lasting trace in lawmaking and public policy. Of course, not all of them actually do so, but to expect as much would be unrealistic given the vagaries and complications of the policy process. Instead, it is appropriate to conceive of legislators' follow-through on their campaign appeals as an integral part of normal congressional business. The themes that winning House and Senate candidates talk about in their campaigns presage the issues that will be the subject of policy making in the years to come. Promise keeping thus leads to responsiveness both at the dyadic and at the aggregate levels, linking all stages of the democratic process, from campaigns to legislative activity to policy outputs.

9

Representation, Responsiveness, and the Electoral Connection

The idea of an electoral connection has long been central both to normative theories of representative government and to empirical work on congressional behavior. However, there has been considerable divergence in opinion about what such a connection between the electoral and legislative arenas does and should entail. On one side lies democratic theorists' contention that campaigns are an implicit contract: that in well-functioning representative systems, candidates use their campaigns to present their plans and priorities to the public and then, to the best of their abilities, pursue these once in office (see, for example, Mansbridge 2003). From this perspective, an electoral connection means that candidates keep their promises and that elections and governing are linked through the behavior of representatives and senators as candidates and as lawmakers.

When scholars of Congress speak of an electoral connection, though, they typically mean something very different. Only rarely have the relationships between campaign appeals, legislative action, and policy outputs been the focus of attention. Instead, studies have built on Mayhew's (1974) argument about the reelection imperative to explore the ways in which legislators' activity in office affects electoral prospects (and vice versa). In this view, a linkage between electoral politics and governing behavior emerges because legislators are reelection-oriented and so act in office in ways that promote their prospects in the next race, or because relative electoral safety or vulnerability affects behavior in Congress. Although there is no inherent reason that a reelection focus need be at odds with providing good representation, the literature has often depicted them in this manner, with legislators using the activities at their disposal to please constituents by engaging in symbolic responsiveness, even in the absence of "real" responsiveness.

My aim in this book has been to unite these perspectives on the links between electoral and legislative politics. In so doing, I have proposed an argument for why following through on campaign appeals, pursuing one's own priorities, representing constituents' interests, and promoting reelection are not incommensurate goals. In short, representatives' and senators' strategies and choices as candidates are driven by many of the same factors that explain their strategies and choices as legislators. When winning legislators act in office on their campaign themes, they do so not just because they are concerned about what will happen to them in the next election if they do not, or because they possess noble sentiments about their roles as elected representatives (though both of these factors contribute, at least at the margins), but because they do not see sharp distinctions between campaigning and governing. Acting on one's priorities in office, talking about those interests and accomplishments in the next race, and then continuing to pursue them in the next term are part of the natural flow of congressional life and should be understood as such. Thus, it should not come as a surprise that legislators often follow through on their campaign appeals in a sincere and meaningful way.

My findings about promise keeping – and, in particular, the agenda-based approach that I advocate for studying it – suggest a conception of legislative representation that diverges in several important ways from the predominant view in the literature. The story that emerges here is that representation is not only about the congruence between legislators' and constituents' issue positions, but also about the relationship between campaigns and governing and the transmission of information between various stages of the political process.

When combined with my earlier findings about winning legislators' uptake of their challengers' campaign issues (Sulkin 2005), this work provides clear evidence that congressional campaigns have a legacy that extends well beyond Election Day. In some cases, they introduce new information into policy making (i.e., when legislators change their agendas in response to their previous challengers' critiques), and, in others they serve to link past priorities to future intentions. Understanding campaigns in this way, as providing signals about subsequent legislative activity and, in some circumstances, even serving as a causal driver of that activity, provides a new context for our theories of candidate and legislator behavior and the representational relationship between legislators and their constituencies. In particular, the study of promise keeping highlights the role of campaigns as a *selection mechanism*, enabling voters to observe a candidate's priorities and elect or reelect him or her knowing what those priorities will be (see Mansbridge 2009).

I develop this argument about representation and selection in more detail later in this final chapter. However, before doing so, it is useful to review some of the most important findings about congressional promise keeping.

THE EXTENT OF FOLLOW-THROUGH

First, and most fundamentally, it bears repeating that legislators do keep their promises. Contrary to the popular wisdom that campaign appeals are meaningless and that candidates regularly lie in their campaigns, saying one thing but then doing another once elected, representatives' and senators' claims often serve as good signals about the issues they will pursue and what they will accomplish in their next terms. Also, as we saw in the case studies of defense and the environment in Chapter 5, the content and direction of their campaign appeals on an issue align with the content and direction of their later activity on it. In other words, there is no evidence that legislators regularly claim to be in favor of particular policies but then work against them. As a result, there is "truth in advertising," such that campaigns provide valuable and useful information to voters about legislators' subsequent behavior.

These links between campaigns and governing are evident not only at the level of individual legislators, but, as we saw in the previous chapter, also yield a measurable effect at the aggregate level. Across the congresses I study, the legislators in my sample introduced 4,828 bills and resolutions on their campaign themes (producing 140 new laws) and cosponsored 44,967. Promise-keeping activity is therefore a central component of the congressional agenda, leaving a tangible and consequential trace in policy outputs.

THE ORIGINS OF FOLLOW-THROUGH

That follow-through occurs at relatively high rates is quite important from a normative perspective. From the point of view of political scientists seeking to understand campaigns and congressional behavior, of equal and perhaps even greater interest is what variation in promise keeping tells us about candidate and legislator strategy. We have seen that the origins of promise keeping lie in issue selection in campaigns. Rather than selecting issues based solely on anticipated constituency reaction, candidates often choose to focus their campaigns on issues for which they have longstanding interest and credible records. When they do so, this sincerity means that their choices serve as good signals about the issues they will pursue in their next terms.

This link (or lack thereof) between candidates' underlying interests and their campaign appeals is the key to understanding how campaign rhetoric is connected to follow-through. Most notably, the results in Chapters 3 and 4 showed that claims candidates make about themselves are much more strongly related to their interests (i.e., as indicated by previous activity, constituency characteristics, and party) than appeals they make about their opponents. Thus, negative campaigns carry less information about winners' priorities than do positive campaigns, which is another reason that high levels of negativity may be a problem. Fenno's lament that negative campaigns produce a situation in which "the winning candidate will have earned the legal right to represent a constituency, but the constituents are left without a clue as to how the incumbent would go about doing it" (1996, 265) seems especially apt.

In contrast, the specificity of candidates' appeals, often thought to be an indicator of sincerity, turns out not to be so. Instead, specificity is largely a reaction to the closeness of a race – candidates are more likely to offer detailed, specific appeals when their contest is tight. As a result, and contrary to the conventional wisdom, specific appeals do not serve as stronger signals about the content of legislators' subsequent agendas. This same conclusion holds for appeals that reference the past or the future, which are also a function of contextual factors, particularly the status of a candidate as an incumbent or challenger.

These results indicate that with the possible exception of critiques about negativity, pundits, reformers, and other observers should often worry less about *how* candidates talk about an issue than *what* issues they talk about. For example, efforts to encourage specificity (e.g., Project Vote Smart's "Political Courage Test," which asks candidates to express their positions on a wide variety of issues) may be valuable in a number of ways, but increasing levels of promise keeping is unlikely to be one of them. In fact, for many voters, such efforts may even dilute the signals about priorities that campaigns provide when candidates make their own choices about what to discuss.[1]

[1] Similarly, much recent work on campaign communication has highlighted the value of campaign websites because they provide information on candidates' views on a wider array of issues than do ads (see, for example, Druckman, Kifer, and Parkin 2009). However, when every candidate talks about every issue, we lose the signal about how much they care about an issue (or, at least, we will have to find new ways of measuring intensity of interest).

DIFFERENCES BETWEEN THE CHAMBERS

This variation in the strength of the links between candidates' issue interests and the content of their campaign appeals also explains differences in patterns of promise keeping in the House and Senate. As the opening chapters demonstrated, appeals serve as a better predictor of winning House candidates' behavior than that of winning Senate candidates. Significant linkages between appeals and activity exist for the vast majority of issues for representatives (for fifteen of the eighteen issues in the scheme, those who talked about the issue in the campaign were more active than those who did not), but the same holds true for only a handful (six of the eighteen) for senators.

Why does this difference emerge? The evidence suggests that it is not because Senate candidates fail to mention their priorities, but because they also talk about other issues that are not as central to their interests. In all likelihood, it is their higher stature and the larger constituencies they represent that compel them to address those issues that are currently prominent on the national scene, even if those issues are not personal priorities for them. House candidates, on the other hand, have agendas that are more tightly focused and are more closely linked to their past records and the nature of their constituencies. The result is more consistent relationships between the content of their campaign and legislative agendas.

However, a weaker appeals–activity link for senators should not be taken to mean that promise keeping is necessarily of higher quality in the House. Although the same factors that explain variation in representatives' promise keeping also explain senators', the former's more focused agendas mean that their appeals serve as stronger signals about their activity, but the latter are better able to deliver on the promises they do make, since they are more likely to be involved in high-impact legislation and are more successful in getting bills passed.

These findings underscore the value of including both the House and Senate in analyses of representation. Had I limited my focus to one of the chambers (or a single stage of the policy process), I would have missed these important dynamics. However, it is common in research on legislative behavior to target either the House or the Senate, but not both.[2] There are many good reasons for doing so, but it introduces complications for

Thus, ads will remain valuable to scholars because they force candidates to make decisions, and these decisions in turn offer insight into their strategies.

[2] In fact, I am guilty of this as well, as my earlier work on promise keeping focused just on the House of Representatives (see Sulkin 2009a, 2009b).

understanding the mechanisms underlying responsiveness. Studying both chambers enables one to determine how variation in institutional incentives and constraints drives behavior, and also offers further insight into how representatives and senators manage their dual roles as campaigners and as policy makers.

THE CAUSES AND CONSEQUENCES OF PROMISE KEEPING

Understanding how follow-through is rooted in the nature of the claims that House and Senate candidates make in their campaigns is a central part of the story about promise keeping. Another important component is how choices about how much responsiveness to engage in and when and where to demonstrate it vary across legislators. Most fundamentally, what explains why some are more attentive to their previous appeals than others?

We have seen that these patterns are systematic, a function of such characteristics as seniority, status in the chamber, and the size and scope of a legislator's agenda. Interestingly, for both representatives and senators there is a consistent positive relationship between previous vote shares and levels of promise keeping, with relatively safe legislators engaging in more follow-through on their appeals than their vulnerable peers. This is, of course, in sharp contrast to the commonly held view that vulnerability is what induces responsiveness and that high reelection rates are problematic because they indicate a lack of accountability. In fact, the opposite appears to be true, suggesting that the causal relationship between electoral safety/vulnerability and behavior in office is more complicated than is often assumed.

Moreover, the analyses in Chapter 7 reveal that promise keeping affects future electoral prospects. There are clear electoral payoffs to following through on one's appeals and electoral costs to failure to do so. Representatives and senators who engage in high levels of promise keeping reduce the opposition they face in the next cycle and, as a result, do better in that election. They are then returned to office motivated to continue the responsive behavior that contributed to their security. That levels of responsiveness are also manifested in legislators' career decisions (i.e., progressively ambitious representatives and senators engage in more and those who plan to retire engage in less) suggests that they are aware of these incentives.

Once again, though, the existence of an electoral payoff should not be interpreted to mean that promise keeping is just a symbolic activity, undertaken to promote reelection, but ultimately insincere. As shown in Chapter 6, representatives and senators demonstrate their responsiveness not just through the comparatively easy activity of cosponsorship, but also on more effort-intensive introductions and, indeed, devote a relatively larger proportion of the latter activity to their campaign themes. It therefore is difficult to argue that addressing these issues is not important to them. In addition, although the raw number of promise-keeping activities decreases in the second year of a term for House members and increases as terms progress for Senate members (as expected given differences in the length of terms and the proximity of the next election), levels of promise keeping as a proportion of their total activity remain constant across their terms. This confirms that it is neither a quickly forgotten nod to the previous campaign nor a last-ditch effort to shore up support. Also, as demonstrated in Chapter 8, legislators' introductions on their campaign themes do make their way into law, these measures are treated no differently by their sponsors and fare no differently in the process, and, at least occasionally, they spark major debates and/or bring about marked shifts in policy. Taken as a whole, then, the policy legacy of promise keeping can be substantial.

AGENDAS AND RESPONSIVENESS

These results all bear on the broader point that there is clear value to extending work on legislative activity, campaign strategy, and representation beyond the idea that candidates' and legislators' issue *positions* should be the primary phenomenon of interest. Considering their issue *priorities* offers substantial theoretical, analytical, and practical leverage.

This agenda-based approach to promise keeping has several distinct advantages. It enables one to examine the subsequent legislative behavior of a broader, more representative group of winning candidates, since they need not stake out specific positions in order to be included in the analysis. Indeed, since candidates often face incentives to be ambiguous, including these sorts of claims results in a more accurate approximation of real-world campaigns. Similarly, expanding measures of congressional behavior to include activities beyond roll call voting provides for a more encompassing view of legislative activity, one that includes multiple stages of the legislative process (rather than focusing on the select group of measures that reach a vote at the very end of the process) and highlights representatives' and senators' entrepreneurial efforts to pursue their interests.

An easy critique of this approach and the findings I have summarized thus far is that agenda-based representation is less meaningful than position-based representation – that what matters to constituents and for policy are legislators' votes. However, the assertion that voters care deeply about the particular solutions that candidates advocate to policy problems simply does not mesh well with what we know about their attentiveness to and understanding of politics. On all but the most salient and/or straightforward policy questions, it is more likely that they are interested in seeing the problem addressed, prefer a candidate who will try to do so, and are open to a range of solutions. Moreover, as we saw in the analyses of defense and the environment in Chapter 5, there is not a clear delineation between priorities and positions. Even vague appeals on an issue often have a valence to them, revealing information about candidates' positions. In other words, candidates do not need to express their views on a variety of policies on the environment for voters to know that they are pro-environment. A claim that "I want to preserve the environment" is just as good a predictor of voting on environmental issues.

On the legislative behavior side, there has been a surge of interest in recent years in activities other than roll call voting, with many studies highlighting the importance of proactive behaviors such as introductions and cosponsorships, both for representation of constituents and for the lawmaking process (Burden 2007; Koger 2003; Rocca and Gordon 2010; Sulkin 2005; Woon 2009). There is also evidence that, not surprisingly, intensity of interest and extremity of positions are connected to one another, such that measures of preference based on agenda activities and those based on voting records are similar (Aleman et al. 2009; Sulkin and Swigger 2008). Thus, the argument that introductions and cosponsorships are just symbolic or epiphenomenal no longer has much traction. Exploring the ways in which legislators signal and pursue their priorities offers new insight into the nature of the electoral connection.

PROMISE KEEPING, SELECTION, AND SANCTIONING

Given the intuitive appeal of promise keeping as a way of measuring representation and the contributions of the findings to our understanding of candidate and legislative behavior, it remains somewhat of a puzzle that it has occupied such a peripheral role in the empirical literature on congressional representation. In the opening chapter, I highlighted a number of reasons for the oversight. Most notably, attention to promise keeping has been hampered by the division of labor in American politics between scholars of electoral politics and those of institutions and policy making. In legislative studies, this has been manifested in the "Two Congresses" divide between those who analyze representatives and senators at home in their districts and those who study legislative behavior and organization in Washington, D.C. The result is that phenomena such as promise keeping that lie at the intersection of these two research agendas tend to fall between the cracks.

Here I would like to propose another reason for the lack of attention, hinted at previously, which is that promise keeping has failed to attract sustained interest from political scientists because the basic assumptions underlying it contradict the view of the relationship between legislators and their constituents that motivates most studies of representation. Specifically, models of legislative responsiveness based on the notion of accountability depict this relationship as a principal–agent problem in which the principals (constituents) and their agents (legislators) have goals that are at odds with one another (see Fearon 1999; Ferejohn 1986; Mansbridge 2009). By this definition, if we observe legislators doing what they want, we must assume that they are acting contrary to what their constituents want. Therefore, quality representation can occur only when constituents exert a particular type of control, using monitoring and sanctions (or the threat of them) to induce their representatives to behave differently than they otherwise would.

If we start with these foundational beliefs, then my argument about promise keeping and its origins just does not seem to fit. The idea that the system works such that legislators and constituents often want the same things (i.e., that voters want winning candidates to do what they said they would, and that winners have incentives to act on the issues about which they made appeals, even in the absence of punishment for a failure to follow through) violates the basic assumptions of the principal–agent relationship that lies at the heart of the sanctions model of representation. A priori, then, this leads to one of two expectations about promise keeping: either that it will be rare, occurring only when fear of electoral retribution forces legislators to act on their appeals; or that if we do observe it at high rates, this means that follow-through is mostly symbolic (i.e., that legislators are appearing to be responsive, but behind the scenes are pursuing other goals). In either case, promise keeping would not seem to be a worthwhile area of inquiry for those interested in studying responsiveness.

Such arguments, though, are all based on the premise that the relationship between legislators and their constituents is necessarily characterized by conflict. As Mansbridge (2009) notes, this depiction of the principal–agent relationship is not the only possible view, and in fact is not even the most normatively desirable or empirically accurate one. In her recent essay on the topic, she builds a case for the reinvigoration of the selection model as the foundation for thinking about legislative representation. Such a model applies in those cases where "a potential agent already has self-motivated exogenous reasons for doing what the principal wants. The principal and agent thus have similar objectives even in the absence of the principal's sanctions" (Mansbridge 2009, 370). Although selection is most often framed as constituents choosing the right "type" of legislator, it also accords well with my conception of promise keeping. From this perspective, selection is not so much about voters selecting a type, but about knowing what their votes are buying them in terms of policy priorities.

Arguments about selection are certainly not new, and in fact were central to the earliest empirical work on legislative representation. For instance, Miller and Stokes identified selection as an important pathway to constituency control, contending that one avenue for strong representational links was "for the district to choose a Representative who so shares its views that in following his own convictions he does his constituents' will" (1963, 50). Along the same lines, in his study of legislators' voting decisions, Kingdon (1973) argued that "the simplest mechanism through which constituents can influence a congressman is to select a person initially for office who agrees with their attitudes .... That the recruitment process affects congressmen's voting is an elemental, easy-to-understand proposition, but its profound importance cannot be emphasized too strongly" (46).

However, this view of selection as a viable mechanism for representation soon fell by the wayside in studies of legislative behavior,[3] not because it failed to have predictive value, but because of a sea change in how congressional scholars thought about legislators and their motivations. As Mansbridge puts it,

> Only a year after Kingdon's book, his "simple," "elemental," "easy to understand" point of "profound importance" began to lose much of its traction in the profession, as a series of works on Congress, beginning with David Mayhew's *Congress: The Electoral Connection* and Morris Fiorina's *Representatives, Roll Calls, and*

[3] However, as Mansbridge (2009) notes, selection (and its counterpart, replacement) has remained at the fore of research on aggregate government responsiveness to public opinion (see, for example, Erikson, MacKuen, and Stimson 2002).

Constituencies, depicted a representative's prime motivation as the desire for reelection, with constituency control working through the sanctions made possible by this desire. (2009, 372)

As discussed earlier, the reelection motivation is not by itself sufficient to lead to the expectation that sanctioning will be necessary to bring the actions of legislators in line with the interests of their constituents, but if we combine it with the claims that legislators are self-interested, and that their interests and those of their constituents often diverge, then we arrive at a scenario in which we might expect little meaningful promise keeping to occur. Although it is only implicit in Mayhew's (1974) argument, the idea that all incumbents prefer to shirk was subsequently made explicit in many formal models of constituency control (e.g., Ferejohn 1986).

Ultimately, of course, whether legislators always want to shirk and, further, whether constituents believe this and act accordingly are empirical questions, and the answer to both is probably no (Bianco 1994, 28). Why, then, have these assumptions become predominant in work on representation? First, there is clearly some truth to them; there are definitely situations in which the preferences of representatives and senators differ from those of their constituents, particularly when we consider the heterogeneity of opinion that often exists within districts or states. Determining whether constituents are able to affect the behavior of their representatives in these cases is clearly important. Second, as others have argued, it may be that the sanctions model of responsiveness is perceived as more interesting, at least from a modeling perspective, than a selection model (see Mansbridge 2009; Pratt and Zeckhauser 1985). Indeed, a story about representation in which candidates tell us what they will do and then do it seems, at least at first glance, to be less intellectually compelling than a situation in which constituents and legislators face inherent tensions and the system must be structured in such a way to induce legislators to respond.

I argue, though, that adhering to an interesting but often unrealistic set of assumptions about legislators and constituents[4] has hampered our ability to understand fully the dynamics of responsiveness. This is not to say that I advocate pushing aside the sanctions model in favor of solely selection-based models. In reality, the two views of representation and the

[4] Fearon (1999) argues that the public's dislike of "office seekers," its general support for term limits (and concomitant lack of concern with last period effects), and the importance that citizens place on consistency all indicate that most voters understand elections as more about selection than sanctioning.

role of elections in promoting them are more interconnected than they might appear. Mansbridge (2009) explains that the motives of legislators and constituents will always be mixed, such that "it helps to think of the selection model as having selection at its core and sanctions at its periphery" (370). We see this clearly with promise keeping. Although legislators have reasons other than a simple fear of sanctions to engage in it, the system is not totally without checks. Representatives and senators who engage in high levels of follow-through do better in the next race, such that the exogenous motives for promise keeping are supplemented by electoral incentives.

Moreover, theories about representation based on selection are not devoid of strategy – for instance, in constructing their agendas, winning legislators must balance the need to follow through on their own themes with the flexibility to address new issues, respond to critiques from challengers, and so on. Also, as we saw with legislators' responses to the 9/11 terrorist attacks, they have the ability to frame their activity in office through the lens of their preexisting priorities. Future research might fruitfully focus on how members of Congress weigh the advantages and disadvantages of various agenda choices.

In short, we gain a more complete view of representation if we think about selection and sanctions as working together. Uniting these perspectives provides space for the coexistence a variety of different conceptions of the relationship between legislators and constituents. In some situations, the interests of the two are in conflict, so healthy representative systems must offer opportunities for citizens to monitor the behavior of elected officials and to reward or punish them accordingly. Much of the time, though, the goals of representative and represented will align, and so elections work to enable voters to choose candidates who will act in their interests, even in the absence of monitoring. Thus, constituents influence policy by selecting representatives who are already inclined to pursue their interests, and also by providing incentives to continue their responsiveness.

CONCLUSIONS

The most important substantive conclusion to be drawn from the analyses here is also the most straightforward. My investigation of promise keeping has underscored that the electoral and legislative arenas are necessarily intertwined, such that the "Two Congresses" divide between legislators' work on Capitol Hill and their activities at home on the campaign trail is largely artificial. The electoral connection therefore means more than just that legislators design their activity in office with an eye toward reelection or that the rules and structure of the institution aid them in their quests. It also means that their priorities manifest themselves in their campaigns and in their legislative agendas, that their experiences as candidates shape and are shaped by their behavior as lawmakers, and that the strength of these links serves as a focal point for evaluating representation and accountability.

Delegating the study of the behavior of candidates to one group of scholars and the study of the behavior of legislators to another group thus has the potential to lead to incomplete views of both pre– and post–Election Day phenomena. Moreover, by uniting electoral and legislative politics, we can extend debates about representation beyond snapshot views of the congruence of positions between citizens and legislators to include the process of responsiveness, as elected officials make appeals during their campaigns and then pursue them (or not) once in office. In so doing, we return to the traditional models of representation that lie at the heart of democratic theory (Mansbridge 2003). The result is a richer conception of the role of campaigns, a more nuanced understanding of the nature and quality of legislative representation, and a more positive assessment of the health and legitimacy of democratic politics in the United States.

References

Abbe, Owen, Jay Goodliffe, Paul Herrnson, and Kelly Patterson. 2003. "Agenda Setting in Congressional Elections: The Impact of Issues and Campaigns on Voting Behavior." *Political Research Quarterly*. 56(4): 419–30.

Adler, E. Scott. 2000. "Constituency Characteristics and the "Guardian" Model of Appropriations Subcommittees, 1959–1998." *American Journal of Political Science*. 44 (1): 104–14.

Adler, E. Scott, and John Lapinski. 1997. "Demand Side Theory and Congressional Committee Composition: A Constituency Characteristics Approach." *American Journal of Political Science*. 41(3): 895–918.

Ahuja, Sunil. 1994. "Electoral Status and Representation in the United States Senate." *American Politics Quarterly*. 22(1): 104–18.

Aldrich, John. 1995. *Why Parties? The Origin and Transformation of Party Politics in America*. Chicago: University of Chicago Press.

Aleman, Eduardo, Ernesto Calvo, Mark Jones, and Noah Kaplan. 2009. "Comparing Cosponsorship and Roll Call Ideal Points." *Legislative Studies Quarterly*. 34(1): 87–116.

Ansolabehere, Stephen, and Shanto Iyengar. 1994. "Riding the Wave and Claiming Ownership over Issues: The Joint Effects of Advertising and News Coverage in Campaigns." *Public Opinion Quarterly*. 58(3): 335–57.

1995. *Going Negative: How Attack Ads Shrink and Polarize the Electorate*. New York: Free Press.

Ansolabehere, Stephen, James M. Snyder, Jr., and Charles Stewart, III. 2001. "Candidate Positioning in U.S. House Elections." *American Journal of Political Science*. 45(1): 136–59.

Arnold, R. Douglas. 1990. *The Logic of Congressional Action*. New Haven: Yale University Press.

2004. *Congress, the Press, and Political Accountability*. Princeton: Princeton University Press.

Atkeson, Lonna, and Randall Partin. 2001. "Candidate Advertisements, Media Coverage, and Citizen Attitudes: The Agendas and Roles of Senators and Governors in a Federal System." *Political Research Quarterly*. **54**(4): 795–813.

Bachrach, Peter, and Morton Baratz. 1962. "Two Faces of Power." *American Political Science Review*. **56**(4): 947–952.

Bailey, Michael. 2001. "Quiet Influence: The Representation of Diffuse Interests on Postwar Trade Policy." *Legislative Studies Quarterly*. **26**(1): 45–80.

Baker, Ross K. 2008. *House and Senate*. 4th edition. New York: W. W. Norton.

Barone, Michael, Richard Cohen, and Grant Ujifusa, eds.2002. *The Almanac of American Politics*. Boston: Gambit.

eds. 2004. *The Almanac of American Politics*. Boston: Gambit.

eds. 2008. *The Almanac of American Politics*. Boston: Gambit.

Barone, Michael and Grant Ujifusa, eds. 2000. *The Almanac of American Politics*. Boston: Gambit.

Bass, Charles F. 2009. "Forests Can Provide Both Heat and Lights: Power Plants, Pellet Makers Can Coexist." *Concord Monitor*, March 6.

Bauer, Raymond, Ithiel de Sola Pool, and Lewis Anthony Dexter. 1963. *American Business and Public Policy*. New York: Atherton Press.

Baumgartner, Frank R., and Bryan D. Jones, eds. 2002. *Policy Dynamics*. Chicago: University of Chicago Press.

2009. *Agendas and Instability in American Politics*. Chicago: University of Chicago Press.

Bender, Bruce, and John R. Lott, Jr. 1996. "Legislator Voting and Shirking: A Critical Review of the Literature." *Public Choice*. **87**(1): 67–100.

Bernhard, William, and Brian R. Sala. 2006. "The Remaking of an American Senate: The 17th Amendment and Ideological Responsiveness." *Journal of Politics*. **68**(2): 345–57.

Bernstein, Robert A. 1988. "Do U.S. Senators Moderate Strategically?" *American Political Science Review*. **82**(1): 237–41.

Bianco, William T. 1994. *Trust: Representatives & Constituents*. Ann Arbor: University of Michigan Press.

Bimber, Bruce, and Richard Davis. 2003. *Campaigning Online: The Internet in U.S. Elections*. New York: Oxford University Press.

Boatright, Robert G. 2004. *Expressive Politics: The Issue Strategies of Congressional Challengers*. Columbus: Ohio State University Press.

Bond, Jon R. 1985. "Dimensions of District Attention over Time." *American Journal of Political Science*. **29**(2): 330–47.

Bovitz, Gregory, and Jamie Carson. 2006. "Position-Taking and Electoral Accountability in the U.S. House of Representatives." *Political Research Quarterly*. **59**(2): 297–312.

Brady, David. 1988. *Critical Elections and Congressional Policy Making*. Stanford: Stanford University Press.

Brasher, Holly. 2003. "Capitalizing on Contention: Issue Agendas in U.S. Senate Campaigns." *Political Communication*. **20**(4): 453–71.

Brooks, Deborah Jordan. 2006. "The Resilient Voter: Moving toward Closure in the Debate over Negative Campaigning and Turnout." *Journal of Politics*. **68**(3): 684–96.

Brooks, Deborah Jordan, and John Geer. 2007. "Beyond Negativity: The Effects of Incivility on the Electorate." *American Journal of Political Science*. 51(1): 1–16.

Budge, Ian, and Richard Hofferbert. 1990. "United-States Party Platforms and Federal Expenditures." *American Political Science Review*. 84(1): 111–31.

Burden, Barry. 2007. *Personal Roots of Representation*. Princeton: Princeton University Press.

Burden, Barry C., and David C. Kimball. 2002. *Why Americans Split Their Tickets: Campaigns, Competition, and Divided Government*. Ann Arbor: University of Michigan Press.

Cain, Bruce, John Ferejohn, and Morris Fiorina. 1987. *The Personal Vote: Constituency Service and Electoral Independence*. Cambridge: Harvard University Press.

Cameron, Charles. 2000. *Veto Bargaining: Presidents and the Politics of Negative Power*. New York: Cambridge University Press.

Canes-Wrone, Brandice, David W. Brady, and John F. Cogan. 2002. "Out of Step, Out of Office: Electoral Accountability and House Members' Voting." *American Political Science Review*. 96(1): 127–40.

Carey, John M. 1998. *Term Limits and Legislative Representation*. New York: Cambridge University Press.

Carson, Jamie, Erik Engstrom, and Jason Roberts. 2007. "Candidate Quality, the Personal Vote, and the Incumbency Advantage in Congress." *American Political Science Review*. 101(2): 289–301.

Cobb, Roger W., and Charles D. Elder. 1983. *Participation in American Politics: The Dynamics of Agenda-Building*. Boston: Allyn and Bacon.

Conley, Patricia H. 2001. *Presidential Mandates: How Elections Shape the National Agenda*. Chicago: University of Chicago Press.

Craig, Stephen C., Richard G. Niemi, and Glenn E. Silver. 1990. "Political Efficacy and Trust: A Report on the NES Pilot Study Items." *Political Behavior*. 12(3): 289–314.

Dahl, Robert A. 1989. *Democracy and Its Critics*. New Haven: Yale University Press.

Downs, Anthony. 1957. *An Economic Theory of Democracy*. New York: Harper.

1972. "Up and Down with Ecology: The Issue Attention Cycle. *Public Interest*. 28(2): 38–50.

Druckman, James N., Martin Kifer, and Michael Parkin. 2007. "The Technological Development of Congressional Candidate Websites: How and Why Candidates Use Web Innovations." *Social Science Computer Review*. 25(4): 425–42.

2009. "Campaign Communications in U.S. Congressional Elections." *American Political Science Review*. 103(3): 343–66.

Environmental Protection Agency. 2002. "Fact Sheet: New Source Review (NSR) Report and Improvements." June 13. http://www.epa.gov/nsr/facts.html.

2009. "Clear Skies." http://www.epa.gov/clearskies/.

Erikson, Robert S. 1971. "The Electoral Impact of Congressional Roll Call Voting." *American Political Science Review*. 65(4): 1018–32.

Erikson, Robert S., Michael B. MacKuen, and James A. Stimson. 2002. *The Macro Polity*. Cambridge: Cambridge University Press.

Erikson, Robert S., and Gerald C. Wright. 2000. "Representation of Constituency Ideology in Congress." In *Continuity and Change in Congressional Elections*, eds. David Brady and John Cogan. Stanford: Stanford University Press.

Fearon, James. 1999. "Electoral Accountability and the Control of Politicians: Selecting Good Types versus Sanctioning Poor Performance." In *Democracy, Accountability, and Representation*, eds. Adam Przeworski, Susan Stokes, and Bernard Manin. New York: Cambridge University Press.

Fenno, Richard F. 1973. *Congressmen in Committees*. Boston: Little, Brown.

1978. *Home Style*. Boston: Little, Brown.

1989. *The Making of a Senator: Dan Quayle*. Washington, DC: CQ Press.

1996. *Senators on the Campaign Trail: The Politics of Representation*. Norman: University of Oklahoma Press.

2007. *Congressional Travels: Places, Connections, and Authenticity*. New York: Pearson Longman.

Ferejohn, John. 1986. "Incumbent Performance and Electoral Control." *Public Choice*. 50(1): 5–25.

Fiorina, Morris P. 1974. *Representatives, Roll Calls, and Constituencies*. Boston: DC Heath.

Fishel, Jeff. 1985. *Presidents and Promises: From Campaign Pledge to Presidential Performance*. Washington: Congressional Quarterly Press.

Fowler, Linda L., Scott R. Douglass, and Wesley D. Clark, Jr. 1980. "The Electoral Effects of House Committee Assignments." *Journal of Politics*. **42**(1): 307–19.

Francis, Wayne L., and Lawrence W. Kenny. 1996. "Position Shifting in Pursuit of Higher Office." *American Journal of Political Science*. 40(3): 768–86.

Franklin, Charles H. 1991. "Eschewing Obfuscation? Campaigns and the Perception of U.S. Senate Incumbents." *American Political Science Review*. 85(4): 1193–1214.

Frisch, Scott, and Sean Kelly. 2006. *Committee Assignment Politics in the U.S. House of Representatives*. Norman: University of Oklahoma Press.

Geer, John G. 2006. *In Defense of Negativity: Attack Ads in Presidential Campaigns*. Chicago: University of Chicago Press.

Goldstein, Kenneth. 2000. "Political Advertising in 1998." Final release. Madison: Department of Political Science at University of Wisconsin–Madison and Brennan Center for Justice at New York University.

Goldstein, Kenneth, Michael Franz, and Travis Ridout. 2002. "Political Advertising in 2000." Final release. Madison: Department of Political Science at University of Wisconsin–Madison and the Brennan Center for Justice at New York University.

Goldstein, Ken, and Paul Freedman. 2002. "Campaign Advertising and Voter Turnout: New Evidence for a Stimulation Effect." *Journal of Politics*. **64**(3): 721–740.

Goldstein, Kenneth, and Joel Rivlin. 2005. "Political Advertising in 2002." Final release. Madison: Wisconsin Advertising Project, Department of Political Science at University of Wisconsin–Madison.

Grofman, Bernard, Robert Griffin, and Gregory Berry. 1995. "House Members Who Become Senators: Learning from a 'Natural Experiment' in Representation." *Legislative Studies Quarterly*. 20(4):513–29.

Groseclose, Timothy, and Keith Krehbiel. 1994. "Golden Parachutes, Rubber Checks, and Strategic Retirements from the 102nd House." *American Journal of Political Science*. 38(1): 75–99.

Grossback, Lawrence, David Peterson, and James Stimson. 2006. *Mandate Politics*. New York: Cambridge University Press.

Hall, Richard L. 1996. *Participation in Congress*. New Haven: Yale University Press.

Hall, Richard, and Robert Van Houweling. 1995. "Avarice and Ambition in Congress: Representatives' Decisions to Run or Retire from the U.S. House." *American Political Science Review*. 89(1): 121–36.

Hammond, Thomas, and Brian Humes. 1993. "The Spatial Model and Elections." In *Information, Participation, and Choice*, ed. Bernard Grofman. Ann Arbor: University of Michigan Press.

Harrington, Joseph. 1993. "The Impact of Reelection Pressures on the Fulfillment of Campaign Promises." *Games and Economic Behavior*. 5(1): 71–97.

Harward, Brian M., and Kenneth W. Moffett. 2010. "The Calculus of Cosponsorship in the U.S. Senate." *Legislative Studies Quarterly*. 35(1): 117–43.

Hayes, Matthew, Matthew Hibbing and Tracy Sulkin. 2010. "Redistricting, Responsiveness, and Issue Attention." *Legislative Studies Quarterly*. 35(1): 91–115.

Herrick, Rebekah, Michael K. Moore and John R. Hibbing. 1994. "Unfastening the Electoral Connection: The Behavior of U.S. Representatives When Reelection Is No Longer a Factor." *Journal of Politics*. 56(1): 214–27.

Herrnson, Paul. 2008. *Congressional Elections: Campaigning at Home and in Washington*. 5th edition. Washington: CQ Press.

Hershey, Marjorie Randon. 1984. *Running for Office: The Political Education of Campaigners*. Chatham, NJ: Chatham House Publishers.

Hibbing, John R. 1986. "Ambition in the House: Behavioral Consequences of Higher Office Goals among U.S. Representatives." *American Journal of Political Science*. 30(3): 651–65.

Hibbing, John R., and Elizabeth Theiss-Morse. 1995. *Congress as Public Enemy: Public Attitudes toward American Political Institutions*. New York: Cambridge University Press.

Holian, David. 2004. "He's Stealing My Issues!: Clinton's Crime Rhetoric and the Dynamics of Issue Ownership." *Political Behavior*. 26(2): 95–124.

Hurley, Patricia A. 2001. "David Mayhew's Congress: The Electoral Connection after 25 Years." *PS: Political Science and Politics*. 34(2): 259–61.

Jacobson, Gary C. 1978. "The Effects of Campaign Spending in Congressional Elections." *American Political Science Review*. 72(2): 469–91.

1990. *The Electoral Origins of Divided Government: Competition in U.S. House Elections, 1946–1988*. Boulder: Westview Press.

1993. "Deficit-Cutting Politics and Congressional Elections." *Political Science Quarterly*. 108(3): 375–402.

2001. *The Politics of Congressional Elections*. 5th edition. New York: Longman.

2004. *The Politics of Congressional Elections*. 6th edition. New York: Longman.
Jacobson, Gary, and Samuel Kernell. 1983. *Strategy and Choice in Congressional Elections*. 2nd edition. New Haven: Yale University Press.
Jamieson, Kathleen Hall. 1992. *Dirty Politics: Deception, Distraction, and Democracy*. New York: Oxford University Press.
2000. *Everything You Think You Know about Politics … and Why You're Wrong*. New York: Basic.
Janofsky, Michael. 2005. "Clear Air Change Is Built into Bill." *New York Times*, April 16.
Johannes, John R. 1984. *To Serve the People: Congress and Constituency Service*. Lincoln: University of Nebraska Press.
Johannes, John R., and John McAdams. 1981. "The Congressional Incumbency Effect: Is It Casework Policy Compatible, or Something Else?" *American Journal of Political Science*. 25(3): 512–42.
Jones, Bryan D. 1994. *Reconceiving Decision-Making in Democratic Politics*. Chicago: University of Chicago Press.
Jones, Bryan D., and Frank R. Baumgartner. 2005. *The Politics of Attention: How Government Prioritizes Problems*. Chicago: University of Chicago Press.
Jones, Bryan D., Heather Larsen-Price, and John Wilkerson. 2009. "Representation and American Governing Institutions." *Journal of Politics*. 71(1): 277–90.
Kahn, Kim Fridkin, and Patrick Kenney. 1999. *The Spectacle of U.S. Senate Campaigns*. Princeton: Princeton University Press.
Kamarck, E. C. 1999. "Campaigning on the Internet in the Elections of 1998." In *Democracy.com?: Governance in a Networked World*, eds. E. C. Kamarck and J. S. Nye. Hollis, NH: Hollis.
Kaplan, Noah, David Park, and Travis Ridout. 2006. "Dialogue in American Political Campaigns? An Examination of Issue Convergence in Candidate Television Advertising." *American Journal of Political Science*. 50(3): 724–36.
Kaufmann, Karen. 2004. "Disaggregating and Reexamining Issue Ownership and Vote Choice." *Polity*. 36(2): 283–99.
Kelley, Stanley. 1960. *Political Campaigning: Problems of Creating an Informed Electorate*. Washington: Brookings Institution Press.
Kessler, Daniel, and Keith Krehbiel. 1996. "Dynamics of Cosponsorship." *American Political Science Review*. 90(3): 555–66.
King, Gary, and Michael J. Laver. 1993. "On Party Platforms and Government Spending." *American Political Science Review*. 87(3): 744–50.
King, Gary, Michael Tomz, and Jason Wittenberg. 2000. "Making the Most of Statistical Analyses: Improving Interpretation and Presentation." *American Journal of Political Science*. 44(2): 347–61.
Kingdon, John W. 1968. *Candidates for Office: Beliefs and Strategies*. New York: Random House.
1973. *Congressmen's Voting Decisions*. New York: Harper & Row.
1984. *Agendas, Alternatives, and Public Policies*. Boston: Little, Brown.
1989. *Congressmen's Voting Decisions*. 3rd edition. New York: Harper & Row.
Klingemann, Hans-Dieter, Richard I. Hofferbert, and Ian Budge. 1994. *Parties, Policies, and Democracies*. Boulder: Westview Press.

Koger, Gregory. 2003. "Position-Taking and Cosponsorship in the U.S. House." *Legislative Studies Quarterly*. 28(2): 225–46.

Krasno, Jonathan S. 1994. *Challengers, Competition, and Reelection: Comparing Senate and House Elections*. New Haven: Yale University Press.

Krehbiel, Keith. 1995. "Cosponsors and Wafflers from A to Z." *American Journal of Political Science*. 39(4): 906–23.

Krukones, Michael. 1984. *Promises and Performance: Presidential Campaigns as Policy Predictors*. New York: University Press of America.

Kuklinski, James H. 1977. "District Competitiveness and Legislative Roll-Call Behavior: A Reassessment of the Marginality Hypothesis." *American Journal of Political Science*. 21(3): 627–38.

Ladd, E. C. 1990. "Public Opinion and the 'Congress Problem.'" *Public Interest*. 90(100): 57–67.

Lau, Richard R., and Gerry Pomper. 2004. *Negative Campaigning: An Analysis of U.S. Senate Elections*. Lanham, MD: Rowman Littlefield.

League of Conservation Voters. 2004. "National Environmental Scorecard." February. http://www.lcv.org/images/client/pdfs/2003lcvsc_final.pdf.

Lott, John R. 1987. "Political Cheating." *Public Choice*. 52(2): 169–86.

Mansbridge, Jane. 2003. "Rethinking Representation." *American Political Science Review*. 97(4): 515–28.

2009. "A 'Selection Model' of Political Representation." *Journal of Political Philosophy*. 17(4): 369–98.

Matthews, Donald R., and James A. Stimson. 1975. *Yeas and Nays: Normal Decision-Making in the U.S. House of Representatives*. New York: Wiley.

Mayhew, David R. 1974. *Congress: The Electoral Connection*. New Haven: Yale University Press.

2005. *Divided We Govern: Party Control, Lawmaking, and Investigations, 1946–2002*. New Haven: Yale University Press.

McLeod, Scott. 2001. "Taylor to Seek TVA Reduction Base on Data in GAO Report." *Smoky Mountain News*, May 30.

Miller, Warren E., and Donald E. Stokes. 1963. "Constituency Influence in Congress." *American Political Science Review*. 57(1): 45–56.

Moore, Michael K., and John R. Hibbing. 1992. "Is Serving in Congress Fun Again? Voluntary Retirements from the House since the 1970s." *American Journal of Political Science*. 36(3): 824–28.

Mund, Nat. 2004. "Bush Administration Sticks to Pro-Polluter Agenda Despite Decision to Reopen New Source Review." http://www.sierraclub.org/press room/releases/pr2004–06–30a.asp.

Murakami, Michael. 2009. "Minority Status, Ideology, or Opportunity: Explaining the Greater Retirement of House Republicans." *Legislative Studies Quarterly*. 34(2): 219–44.

Oleszek, Walter J. 2004. *Congressional Procedures and the Policy Process*. 6th edition. Washington: CQ Press.

Page, Benjamin. 1976. "The Theory of Political Ambiguity." *American Political Science Review*. 70(3): 742–52.

Parker, Glenn R. 1980. "Sources of Change in Congressional District Attentiveness." *American Journal of Political Science*. 24(1): 115–24.

1992. *Institutional Change, Discretion, and the Making of Modern Congress*. Ann Arbor: University of Michigan Press.

Petrocik, John. 1996. "Issue Ownership in Presidential Elections, with a 1980 Case Study." *American Journal of Political Science*. 40(3): 825–50.

Polsby, Nelson W., and Eric Schickler. 2002. "Landmarks in the Study of Congress since 1945." *Annual Review of Political Science*. 5: 333–67.

Pomper, Gerald. 1968. *Elections in America: Control and Influence in Democratic Politics*. New York: Dodd, Mead.

Pratt, John, and Richard Zeckhauser, eds. 1985. *Principals and Agents: The Structure of Business*. Boston: Harvard Business School Press.

Price, David. 1989. "The House of Representatives: A Report from the Field." In *Congress Reconsidered*. 4th edition, eds. Lawrence Dodd and Bruce Oppenheimer. Washington: Congressional Quarterly Press.

Ragsdale, Lyn, and Timothy E. Cook. 1987. "Representatives' Actions and Challengers' Reactions: Limits to Candidate Connections in the House." *American Journal of Political Science*. 31(1): 45–81.

Rainie, Lee, and John Horrigan. 2007. "Election 2006 Online." January 17. http://www.pewinternet.org/Reports/2007/Election-2006-Online.aspx?r=1.

Rauber, Paul. 2001. "Lay of the Land: Old King Coal." *Sierra Magazine*, July/August. http://sierraclub.org/sierra/200107/lol3.asp.

Riker, William. 1986. *The Art of Political Manipulation*. New Haven: Yale University Press.

1996. *The Strategy of Rhetoric: Campaigning for the American Constitution*. New Haven: Yale University Press.

Ringquist, Evan, and Carl Dasse. 2004. "Lies, Damned Lies, and Campaign Promises: Environmental Legislation in the 105th Congress." *Social Science Quarterly*. 85(2): 400–19.

Rocca, Michael S., and Stacy Gordon. 2010. "The Position Taking Value of Bill Sponsorship in Congress." *Political Research Quarterly*. 63(2): 387–97.

Rothenberg, Lawrence S., and Mitchell S. Sanders. 2000. "Severing the Electoral Connection: Shirking in the Contemporary Congress." *American Journal of Political Science*. 44(2): 316–25.

Schattschneider, E. E. 1942. *Party Government*. New York: Holt.

1960. *The Semisovereign People*. New York: Holt, Rinehart and Winston.

Schedler, Andreas. 1998. "The Normative Force of Electoral Promises." *Journal of Theoretical Politics*. 10(2): 191–214.

Schiller, Wendy J. 1995. "Senators as Political Entrepreneurs: Using Bill Sponsorship to Shape Legislative Agendas." *American Journal of Political Science*. 39(1): 186–203.

2000. *Partners and Rivals: Representation in U.S. Senate Delegations*. Princeton: Princeton University Press.

Schlesinger, Joseph. 1966. *Ambition and Politics: Political Careers in the United States*. Chicago: Rand-McNally.

Sellers, Patrick J. 1998. "Strategy and Background in Congressional Campaigns." *American Political Science Review*. 92(1): 159–71.

Semiatin, Richard. 2005. *Campaigns in the 21st Century: The Changing Mosaic of American Politics*. Boston: McGraw-Hill.

Shapiro, Catherine R., David W. Brady, Richard Brody, and John A. Ferejohn. 1990. "Linking Constituency Opinion and Senate Voting Scores: A Hybrid Explanation." *Legislative Studies Quarterly*. 15: 599–622.

Shepsle, Kenneth. 1972. "The Strategy of Ambiguity: Uncertainty and Electoral Competition." *American Political Science Review*. 66(2): 555–68.

Shepsle, Kenneth A., Robert P. Van Houweling, Samuel J. Abrams, and Peter C. Hanson. 2009. "The Senate Electoral Cycle and Bicameral Appropriations Politics." *American Journal of Political Science*. 53(2): 343–59.

Sides, John. 2006. "The Origins of Campaign Agendas." *British Journal of Political Science*. 36(3): 407–36.

2007. "The Consequences of Campaign Agendas." *American Politics Research*. 35(4): 465–88.

Sigelman, Lee, and Emmett Buell. 2003. "You Take the High Road and I'll Take the Low Road? The Interplay of Attack Strategies and Tactics in Presidential Campaigns." *Journal of Politics*. 65(2): 518–31.

2004. "Avoidance or Engagement? Issue Convergence in U.S. Presidential Campaigns, 1960–2000." *American Journal of Political Science*. 48(4): 650–61.

Simon, Adam F. 2002. *The Winning Message: Candidate Behavior, Campaign Discourse, and Democracy*. Cambridge: Cambridge University Press.

Sinclair, Barbara. 1977. "Party Realignment and the Transformation of the Political Agenda: The House of Representatives, 1925–39." *American Political Science Review*. 71(3): 940–53.

1989. *The Transformation of the U.S. Senate*. Baltimore: Johns Hopkins University Press.

2006. *Party Wars: Polarization and the Politics of National Policy Making*. Norman: University of Oklahoma Press.

Smith, Aaron. 2009. "The Internet's Role in Campaign 2008." April 15. http://www.pewinternet.org/Reports/2009/6–The-Internets-Role-in-Campaign-2008.aspx?r=1.

Spiliotes, Constantine, and Lynn Vavreck. 2002. "Campaign Advertising: Partisan Convergence or Divergence?" *Journal of Politics*. 64(1): 249–61.

Squire, Peverill. 1989. "Challengers in U.S. Senate Elections." *Legislative Studies Quarterly*. 14(4): 531–547.

1995. "Field Essay: Candidates, Money, and Voters – Assessing the State of Congressional Election Research." *Political Research Quarterly*. 48(4): 891–917.

State Environmental Resource Center. 2003. "Clean Power." July 24. http://www.serconline.org/clean/background.html.

Stokes, Donald. 1992. "Valence Politics." In *Electoral Politics*, ed. Dennis Kavanagh. New York: Oxford University Press.

Sulkin, Tracy. 2005. *Issue Politics in Congress*. New York: Cambridge University Press.

2009a. "Promises Made and Promises Kept" in *Congress Reconsidered*, eds. Lawrence Dodd and Bruce Oppenheimer. 9th edition. Washington, DC: CQ Press.

2009b. "Campaign Appeals and Legislative Action." *Journal of Politics*. 71(3): 1093–1108.

Sulkin, Tracy, Cortney Moriarty, and Veronica Hefner. 2007. "Congressional Candidates' Issue Agendas On- and Off-Line." *Harvard International Journal of Press/Politics*. **12**(2): 63–79.

Sulkin, Tracy, and Nathaniel Swigger. 2008. "Is There Truth in Advertising? Campaign Ad Images as Signals about Legislative Behavior." *Journal of Politics*. 70(1): 232–44.

Sullivan, John, and Robert E. O'Connor. 1972. "Electoral Choice and Popular Control of Public Policy: The Case of the 1966 House Elections." *American Political Science Review*. **66**(4): 1256–68.

Tomz, Michael, and Robert Van Houweling. 2008. "Candidate Positioning and Voter Choice." *American Political Science Review*. **102**(3): 303–18.

2009. "The Electoral Implications of Candidate Ambiguity." *American Political Science Review*. **103**(1): 83–98.

Tomz, Michael, Jason Wittenberg, and Gary King. 2003. CLARIFY: Software for Interpreting and Presenting Statistical Results. Version 2.1. Stanford University, University of Wisconsin, and Harvard University. January 5. Available at http://gking.harvard.edu/.

Vavreck, Lynn. 2001. "The Reasoning Voter Meets the Strategic Candidate: Signals and Specificity in Campaign Advertising, 1998." *American Politics Research*. **29**(5): 507–29.

Volden, Craig, and Alan Wiseman. 2009. "Legislative Effectiveness in Congress." Working Paper. Ohio State University.

Wattenberg, Martin P., and Craig Leonard Brians. 1999. "Negative Campaign Advertising: Demobilizer or Mobilizer?" *American Political Science Review*. **93**(4): 891–9.

Wawro, Gregory. 2000. *Legislative Entrepreneurship in the U.S. House of Representatives*. Ann Arbor: University of Michigan Press.

Westlye, Mark C. 1991. *Senate Elections and Campaign Intensity*. Baltimore: Johns Hopkins University Press.

Willett, David. 2003. "Bush Touting Plan to Weaken Clean Air Act: Sierra Club Fact Sheet on So-Called 'Clear Skies.'" September 13. http://www.sierraclub.org/pressroom/releases/pr2003–09–16.asp.

Wilson, Rick K., and Cheryl D. Young. 1997. "Cosponsorship in the U.S. Congress." *Legislative Studies Quarterly*. **22**(1): 25–43.

Wooldridge, Jeffrey M. 2002. *Econometric Analysis of Cross Section and Panel Data*. Cambridge: MIT Press.

Woon, Jonathan. 2009. "Issue Attention and Legislative Proposals in the U.S. Senate." *Legislative Studies Quarterly*. **34**(1): 29–54.

Wright, Gerald C., and Michael B. Berkman. 1986. "Candidates and Policy in United States Senate Elections." *American Political Science Review*. 80(2): 567–88.

Zupan, Mark A. 1990. "The Last Period Problem in Politics: Do Congressional Representatives Not Subject to a Reelection Constraint Alter Their Voting Behavior?" *Public Choice*. **65**(2): 167–80.

Index